Roger Casement

Also by William Bryant

Fiction

Ross: T. E. Lawrence Discovers America

Iquitos 1910: Roger Casement and Alfred Russel Wallace on the Amazon

Non-Fiction

Dark Desert Hot River: The Middle East in Time of War

The Al-Batin Diaries: A Season in the Work Camps of Saudi Arabia

Biography

Naturalist in the River: The Life and Early Writings of Alfred Russel Wallace

Roger Casement

A Biography

William Bryant

iUniverse, Inc.
New York Lincoln Shanghai

Roger Casement
A Biography

iUniverse books may be ordered through booksellers or by contacting:

iUniverse
2021 Pine Lake Road, Suite 100
Lincoln, NE 68512
www.iuniverse.com
1-800-Authors (1-800-288-4677)

ISBN: 978-0-595-44795-4 (pbk)
ISBN: 978-0-595-89114-6 (ebk)

Printed in the United States of America

For Barney and Astrid

With gratitude and love

Contents

I Feel Like a Boy 1

The Legacy of the Congo 13

Enter Leopold. 22

Consul Casement 36

The 1903 Diaries. 44

The Congo Report 70

Leopold Again 89

Red Rubber in the Amazon 93

The 1910–11 Diaries. 112

The Putumayo Report. 152

The Cash Ledger 1911 173

Headlong into Chaos 198

America's Long Hot Summer. 210

The Berlin Panopticon 220

Journey into Night 249

Minimal Losses. 268

The Blackness: Diaries and Death 279

Selected Bibliography 299

I Feel Like a Boy ...

1

"I feel just as if they were going to kill a boy. For I feel like a boy—and my hands are so free from blood and my heart always so compassionate and pitiful that I cannot comprehend how anyone wants to hang me...."

Roger David Casement wrote these words—imbedded in a rambling final passage on Ireland—in his cell at Pentonville Prison in London, 2 August 1916. The next morning he was hanged.

The jury returned its verdict: "Death due to execution."

Casement's body was left to hang for an hour before being taken down and disposed of. Outside the prison, the small crowd of the curious and viciously patriotic seemed satisfied—to judge by the weak cheers—that the traitor had died, and slowly filtered away into the grim summer air. The coroner, Mr. Walter Schroder, inquired of the dead man's counsel, Gavan Duffy, what Casement's last address had been in England—as if this were a mystery: Scotland Yard had ransacked Casement's lodgings and taken away important documents some time before. Gavan Duffy asked the coroner about the arrangements to be made for burial and was answered tersely that the order for burial would be duly issued and handed to the Governor for action. "As to any matter in reference to the burial of the body beyond that, any application must be made to the authorities." Duffy replied that he had applied for permission from the Home Office for permission to have the body. "I consider it a monstrous act of indecency to refuse it," he protested. The coroner replied that he could not express an opinion on that.

The request by Casement's relatives for burial outside the prison was refused. That same day the body was buried in the yard of Pentonville Prison.

The brutality of the treason trial and the mockery of British "justice" had not been ignored by the international press, who had been leaked snippets of Casement's diaries. Even the *Times* commented dryly on 4 August: "… if there was ever any virtue in the pomp and circumstance of a great state trial, it can only be weakened by inspired innuendoes which, whatever their substance, are now irrelevant, improper, and un-English." The newspaper referred to the "Black Diaries"—containing explicit homosexual passages—which had been shrewdly circulated to journalists and several key figures in government, including King George V, during the progress of the trial. Even John Quinn the distinguished American lawyer and supporter of Irish independence had received photos of some pages of the diaries. On 9 September 1916 he wrote to Gavan Duffy (he also wrote to the British Ambassador and the British Naval Attaché in Washington) stating that it was a "dirty piece of business to circulate such reports; that even if the statements were true, [Casement's] private life had nothing to do with his public acts. If this stuff on semi-official Scotland Yard business continues," he added, he might be tempted to open up again and re-tell the story of the Pigott forgeries. (In 1887 the *Times* had published what purported to be a facsimile of a letter of Charles Parnell, the great Irish politician, implicating him in the Phoenix Park murders. The British government turned out to be deeply implicated in this absurd tangle of libel, and eventually the forger, a Richard Pigott, was brought to an official hearing and subsequently confessed. The hearing was a mockery, and Parnell's counsel brilliant. Pigott would later, on being apprehended in Madrid, blow his brains out.) The British authorities had had Casement's diary for months and had only waited till he was in their hands to show it. It would have been fairer, Quinn added, to reveal them when Casement was in Germany, recruiting an Irish Brigade to fight for Irish Independence.

Casement's beloved cousin Gertrude ("Gee") Bannister requested the return of all his papers. On 23 August she was informed that "The prisoner's diaries and certain other papers which came into the hands of the Police in connection with the criminal charge must be retained by them."

Not all the "copies" of the diary pages had been returned; there was also a complete typescript out there, waiting for publication.

That was certainly not the end of the Black Diaries. It was not the end of Roger Casement's martyrdom.

2

According to Burke's *Irish Landed Gentry*, the Casements were an old Manx family that had come from France (the original spelling of the name was Caissement). During the early eighteenth century, like so many other Protestant families, the direct line of Casements migrated to Ulster and settled on an estate in County Antrim called Margherintemple. In *The Ghost of Roger Casement* W. B. Yeats writes:

> I poked about a village church
> And found his family tomb
> And copied out what I could read
> In that religious gloom
> Found many a famous man there;
> But fame and virtue rot …

Casement's father, Roger senior, was neither famous nor rich, but he had had an "interesting" career. Born in Belfast in 1819, the son of a prosperous shipbuilder, he made the Grand Tour before turning twenty. In September of 1840 he purchased a Coronetsy in an Indian regiment for £840. He sailed on the S/S *John Bull* on 16 November of that year and was posted to the Third King's Own Light Dragoon Guards which saw action against the Afghans in Peshawar in 1842 and against the Sikhs in 1848. He was promoted to Lieutenant in 1843 but by August 1848 was fed up with the military and sold his commission for £350. Not long afterward he rushed to join the Hungarian patriots in their war of independence. Before he could get there, however, Kossuth's rebellion was crushed at Vilagos and part of his revolutionary army managed to reach Turkey. Casement reached Widdin on the Danube. Here the Hungarians were interned by the Turks who were carrying out negotiations to send them back to certain death. Casement determined to obtain English support for the Hungarian patriots. He left for London, carrying with him a letter from Kossuth requesting English support. Reaching London, Casement was received by a sympathetic Palmerston. Brought to the Prime Minister's dinner table, he presented the letter and explained the grave emergency. Immediate English intervention was responsible for saving Kossuth and his men. Later Kossuth lived in exile for many years in England. He was a popular figure there and also in America where, in his biography, he describes traveling to Niagara Falls: "... our train stopped at a station to let the train from the opposite direction pass. At the wish of the assembled multitude, I stepped to the carriage window. From the window of the passing train a man's arm was stretched out and handed me a card. I took it. It bore the name 'Mr. Roger Casement', and underneath, in pencil, the words: 'I handed to Palmerston the letter from Widdin.'" This story was told and retold in the family circle. Roger junior even wrote a long article on the theme for the *United Irishman*. He also kept a copy of Kossuth's biography on his bookshelf. This book may have been the anonymous memoir of the Hungarian put together by Susan Horner—who almost married Charles Darwin. The hero of this vignette, Casement's father, seems to have come to a mysterious end.

Roger Casement senior's movements were restless. In the 1850s he was in Paris, where he met and married Anne Jephson, a Catholic girl from County Wicklow. They returned to Ireland, coming to rest in County Antrim in 1856. They had one daughter, Agnes Jane ("Nina") and three sons, Tom, Charles and Roger (born 1 September 1864 at Lawson Terrace, Sandycove, County Dublin). After 1873, when his wife died in childbirth, Roger Casement senior packed the children off to Margherintemple to be raised by uncle John Casement and the family. In fact, it appears that he abandoned his children to take up a career in spiritualism—holding seances in a hotel in Ballymena (an essay by him on spiritual topics, describing his Indian experiences, is supposedly still extant). He seems to have died in Ballymena at the Adair Arms Hotel, only twenty-seven miles from Margherintemple, a curious fate and a disreputable one, considering his solid family background.

The Victorian Age brought a dark blossoming of mysticism, of spiritualists and supernatural phenomena, just as it had brought commercial expansion, industrialism, colonialism and sexual prudery.

The middle and working classes of Victorian England were growing, assimilating the "rules" of good society. Morality and ethics became momentous matters, and increasingly discretion was necessary in all things, both sensual and political. What was immoral might be pleasurable, but one had to disavow that pleasure. What was unethical but advantageous economically had to be explained away. The Queen was typical of the times, stubborn, narrow in outlook, fat and fond of money. She was niece of Leopold I, the charming constitutional monarch of Belgium whose son would be the absolute ruler of the Congo and whose atrocities would move the younger Casement to protest. She was grandma to the Empress of Russia, and to the German Kaiser, whose nation would be responsible, in a very real sense, for the failure of the Easter Uprising in Dublin and for Roger Casement's death by hanging. Victoria reigned for sixty-four years, until her death in 1901, over the greatest empire ever known, and morally one of the most despotic.

As wards of chancery the Casement orphans' new guardian was their uncle John Casement, a Director of the Elder Dempster Shipping Company, described as a "staunch" Ulsterman: a member of the established Protestant moneyed class. Roger was sent to Diocesan school at Ballymena and he afterwards marveled that he learned nothing at all there of Irish history or culture. He and his brothers were not prepared for university, but for business.

On the mother's side of the family, Anne Casement's sister Grace had married Edward Bannister, who also worked for the Elder Dempster Shipping Company, based in Liverpool. Edward was in charge of the West African interests of the company. There was some passing around of the children from household to household. The children often stayed with the Bannisters in Liverpool during school vacations. Roger's favorite cousin, Gertrude ("Gee") Bannister, nine years junior, was very close to him. "He was always fond of painting and of inventing stories," she recalled later. He would spin fairy tales, dress up in weird improvised African costumes and was a lot of fun. He was nicknamed "Roddie." Roddie was a great reader and had a rich baritone voice.

Typically, the Casement brood would later emigrate: Charlie to Australia, Tom to South Africa and Nina (eight years older than Roger—he called her "old Nina" in his diaries) to America where, after Casement's execution, she would surface briefly during a public lecture by Alfred Noyes to defend her brother's reputation.

We know little of Roger Casement's background. Much can be guessed: his early diaries might have given clues to his character, but these diaries were fed to the fire. In 1880 he took up residence in the Bannister household. By now he was over six feet tall, had gray deep-set eyes and a thin face. His hair was black and curly. He had good teeth and clear skin. Although he could be boisterous at home and full of fun he was described as quiet, withdrawn and unobtrusive. His "academic" career was practically nonexistent. Although he opted for the Civil Service when he reached the age of seventeen, it soon became evident that he was bored and impatient at studying for the examinations. His uncle Edward arranged for him to be taken on as clerk in the offices of the Elder Dempster line in Liverpool, which had special shipping rights in the West African trade. (The head of the firm, Alfred Jones, was an old family friend of the Bannisters.)

As junior clerk Roger continued to be bored and restless with office drudg-ery. Like so many young men of the time, he was excited by the feats of Speke, Burton, Livingstone, Stanley, Grenfell and intrigued by the dangers and exot-icism of Africa. He wanted to travel, to explore the world, not huddle over a desk. He haunted the docks. Finally, in 1883, he was sent overseas as purser on a company ship, the *S/S Bonny*, trading with West Africa. During that year he made three round trips to Africa. By then his uncle Edward was stationed there. (Curiously, Edward Bannister would precede Roger in two West Afri-can appointments as vice-consul; he also anticipated some of his nephew's later findings of atrocities in the Congo.) Roger fell in love with Africa. He would later write that Africa had been the best time of his life.

Almost at once, in 1884, he left Elder Dempster to take a position with the African International Association under the chairmanship of Leopold II of Belgium.

In a letter of 17 June 1904 to E. D. Morel, the celebrated reformer, he wrote a sketch of his early experience: "As you know, in 1884, when I was 20, I went out to the Congo in the service of the Association itself.... In 1886 I joined ... the Sanford exploring expedition in which was Major Parminter (now dead) and various Englishmen, among them Herbert Ward who had been, like me, in the Association with many good Englishmen. I left the San-ford expedition to go elephant shooting in 1888, and for some months I com-manded the Congo Railway Company's advance expedition in its survey—finally coming home, a complete free-lance, in 1889, when only twenty-five years of age.... Now all that service in Congoland honorably reflected only credit on me. I had no enmities only friendships.... Coming home in 1889, I found myself, still a very young man, with all the love of Africa upon me, but with no wish to continue in what was clearly becoming a Belgian enterprise.... I went out in 1900, however, at the request of Major Parminter and I organized the transport on the Lower Congo for the Belgian authorities. I was in no sense a trader neither bought nor sold produce at any time."

There are some amusing details here. Roger had no knowledge of "elephant shooting" or even how to handle a pistol. He also worked for groups primarily interested in "trade" and in opening up the African continent to international commerce. The Sanford Expedition was given the only trading concession on the Upper Congo. "General" Sanford had been the American Minister to Bel-gium in 1861 and was delegate to the Brussels Conference of 1876 which cre-ated the African International Association, of which he was a member of the executive committee. In 1884 he was instrumental in getting US recognition of the Congo Free State. Casement, along with Edward Glave, signed on for the 1886 expedition, claiming that he joined it with the understanding that the work would be for the benefit of the indigenous population. His main work was in solving communications problems. Ultimately his interest was in probing the dark continent, but in no sense was this "exploration" of new territory. Most of the biographies mention Casement's trip with Sanford to America, touring and giving lectures on Africa. Casement himself does not mention this anywhere. The fact seems to be that Casement left the Sanford Expedition when it was convenient for him to do so.

3

Ambiguities run deep in the Irish. Ireland has a history of deadly surprises, many of them orchestrated by the British. In 1846 the population was around nine million and thousands were starving, yet in spite of the terrible famine Ireland was still exporting a hundred million pounds worth of food to England. (The number of deaths in 1845–47 alone was 1,240,000. By 1910 the population would be reduced to half that of 1845 due to high mortality rates and emigration.) Irish poverty would be the worst in Europe, the living conditions of the Irish poor abominable. In spite of all this, Ireland remained one of the favorite playgrounds of English tourists, a country where, in the early 20th century, rich English lads raced their powerful new cars without fear of the police (the Royal Irish Automobile Club was founded in 1901).

The Puritanism of Protestantism was severe in Ulster, as was that of the Catholic church. The austere sexual code led to frustration, and a desire to escape. The celibacy rate in Ireland was high around the turn of the century—with only about 38 percent of males over fifteen years of age married. The conflicts of religion, social status and occupation were obviously profound. The "working class" boys were debased, as they were in Britain. Roger Casement had excellent pickings in the "lower" orders, where boys fairly openly committed sodomy in defiance of the rules of the church. Casement arrogantly defied the social conventions of his class, but he was not the only one, and Victoria was a bitch. Economics was the rule. As his cash ledger for 1911 clearly records, he generally paid his Irish tricks a little less than usual.

"Class" was important, too, in middle class Ireland as well as Britain. Casement was penniless and had to earn his living yet he belonged to two distinguished families, even though he had little contact with (and less information

about) his mother's side. Early on he made numerous investigations, especially
of the Mounteney Jephsons, in an attempt to determine his antecedents. In
1887, when traveling for the Sanford expedition he had a surprise meeting in
the jungle with a member of his mother's family, A.J. Mounteney Jephson
who later wrote: "Casement of the Sanford Expedition came up and camped
by me. We bathed and he gave me a very good dinner—he is traveling most
comfortably and has a large tent and plenty of servants. It was delightful sitting down to a *real* dinner at a *real* table with a table cloth and dinner napkins
and plenty to eat with Burgundy to drink and cocoa and cigarettes after dinner—and this in the middle of the wilds—it will be a long time before I pass
such an evening again." Later Mounteney Jephson, lost and feverish, would be
"rescued" by Casement, who happened to be in the vicinity with his fancy caravan.

Exploration of the African jungle enthralled Casement—as it enthralled
other less fortunate Irishmen. It was "exploration" of a fabulous kind, far from
the work of naturalists and collectors. Casement was no naturalist, nor was he
interested, except occasionally, in natural history. His training and pastimes
did not fit him for scientific reporting (only late in his career did David Livingstone himself, the most celebrated explorer of the times, begin to enter
exact measurements and factual data in his diaries). He was, however, sympathetic toward the "natives" and described their situation in letters. Others in
the field were similarly affected by the suffering of the natives. His friends at
that time were African hands: Edward Glave, W. G. Parminter, Alfred Parminter, Frederick Puleston and Herbert Ward. Casement was a charmer with
the Irish gift of gab. His "creativity" poured out through conversation and long
letters, though he was a secret poet as well as diarist.

Casement's affluent travel in the jungle—excellent dinners, Burgundy, servants, commodious tents—came to an abrupt halt at the end of 1887 when the
Sanford Survey wound up its work. Casement resigned from the Survey. He
was increasingly disappointed in the results of the studies designed to ascertain
the viability of commercial development. While in charge of the station on the
Equator in the Upper Congo, he recognized the futility inherent in western-
style "development." None of the Europeans could see this. "The difficulty
here is not that the country is not fertile," he wrote, "but that the people do
not work." Better organization was needed; and the natives would have to be
educated.

Casement was left afloat now. He did not intend to be employed again by
King Leopold's faltering State. By luck he was offered a temporary job by the

Reverend W. Holman Bently, an English missionary, to handle his station's transport, building, planting, accounts and correspondence. His salary was £10 per month. He left at the end of the rainy season, having given the Reverend satisfaction ("Roger Casement was a gentleman and I have the assurance that there had been nothing in his manner of life which would cast reflection on us.") On departure his final gesture was to donate a generous £3.10/- to the mission.

Casement may have had deep feelings of distrust, but he returned after a few months of leave to work for the Belgians again in 1890 as manager on the railway construction project from Matadi to Stanley Pool. He traveled to Brussels to sign his contract—Joseph Conrad also would soon sign on in the gray capital of the dreadful King—and went out to take over his post, an excellent one for a young man of twenty-six. The Congo was one of the last wild frontiers but it was deadly and the mortality rate horrendous. He finished a year contract and returned home having performed his duties with enthusiasm. His superiors called him "*un agent exceptionnel.*" He had survived the tour of duty, though certainly not without recurrent fever and serious gastrointestinal complaints—the region, as he himself admitted, was probably the most unhealthy in the world. He admitted frankly that the railway could not have been constructed if the Congo Government had not actively intervened in the work—which is to say, if it had not rounded up the slave laborers. The death rate of both whites and Blacks in the project was as usual phenomenal. Casement was left with serious reservations about Belgium and its role in Africa. His tour had been successful; he had not suffered the same humiliations as Conrad, nor had he gone through a personal crisis such as Conrad's. But his health, both mental and physical, was permanently impaired.

4

Conrad was a few years older than Casement. He was born in 1857 in Berdyczow, Poland (now the Ukraine). His full name was Josef Teodor Konrad Korzseniowski, which he later shortened to Conrad to avoid the horrendous mispronunciation of English speakers. His father, Apollo, a writer and revolutionary, moved his family in 1861 to Warsaw to be at the center of the Polish independence movement. Some time before the doomed insurrection of 1863, however, Apollo was arrested and exiled with his sick wife and four-year-old child to Vologda in northeast Russia. His wife died soon after this; then he himself, after long bouts of deep depression. Josef, now eleven, was sent to live with his uncle Tadeusz Bobrowski, conservative and rich, who sent him at sixteen to study as ship's officer in France. In Marseilles, at twenty, during one of his many fits of despair (this one brought on by disastrous gambling losses) he tried to commit suicide by shooting himself through the chest. The bullet went clean through, missing the heart and doing minimal damage. He recovered, went to England to try his luck on British ships, and became the first Pole to become a Master in the British Merchant Service. On shipboard he mastered the English language.

Conrad, like Roger Casement, had always dreamed of Africa. In *A Personal Record* he describes how as a child he saw a map with a blank spot marking the Stanley Falls region and said, "When I grow up I shall go there." Later he would be impressed by Stanley's expeditions in the Congo, funded by King Leopold II. He seized on the idea of working in the new Congo Free State and managed, with the help of his aunt, Margherite Podarowska, a minor novelist, to get a job with the Societé Anonyme Belge pour le Commerce du Haut-Congo as captain of a river steamboat. His assignment would be to take an exploring expedition led by Alexandre Delcommune (brother of the manager of the Kinshasa station) to Katanga. However in Kinshasa there was an immediate confrontation with the manager. Camille Delcommune was insanely angry that Conrad had taken thirty-five days to make the trek from Matadi instead of the usual twenty. Added to this, Conrad found his boat bunged up and inoperable. After two days, however, he started upriver on another steamer, the *Roi des Belges*, in order to learn river navigation from an experienced captain. The voyage was not a triumph. They picked up a company agent by the name of Klein, who promptly succumbed, and when they arrived back at Kinshasa Camille Delcommune informed Conrad that in view of his incompetency he would not be given charge of the exploring party's vessel or even an ordinary steamboat. Soon after this, Conrad became severely ill and terminally depressed—convinced he was a failure and shocked into what he called "moral and emotional maturity."

After more than a decade, Conrad's memories of those times were both romantic and inexact. He had first met Casement at Matadi on 13 June 1890 and regarded the meeting as "a positive piece of luck." In his diary of this date he records: "Made the acquaintance of Mr. Roger Casement, which should consider a great pleasure under any circumstances.... Thinks, speaks well, most intelligent and very sympathetic. The two shared a hut for two weeks. They became friendly. "He knew the coast languages well," Conrad wrote to John Quinn later. "I went with him several times on short expeditions to hold 'palavers' with neighbouring village-chiefs. The object of them was procuring porters for the company's caravans." The horrors described by Conrad's own "Congo Diary" are similar to those described by Casement. Death, mosquitoes, insomnia, heat and bone-stabbing cold. On returning from the dead to London in February 1891 he began a long convalescence; his health had been permanently undermined. The experience further colored his writing; from then on he viewed the world with deep pessimism.

In 1903 he received two letters from Casement requesting help in disseminating Casement's findings in the Congo and to support the setting up of the Congo Relief Association announced for 23 March 1904. Conrad forwarded the letters to his friend, R. B. Cunninghame Graham. He wrote on 26 December 1903, prefacing his remarks with reference to Cunninghame Graham's recent book on Hernando de Soto and the conquistadors.

"Their achievement is monstrous enough in all conscience but not as a great human force let loose, but rather like that of a gigantic and obscene beast. Leopold is their Pizarro, Thys"—the acting manager of the Société Anonyme Belge du Haut-Congo who had interviewed Conrad for his African post—"their Cortez and their 'lances' are recruited amongst the soutenirs, sous-offs, maqereaux, fruit-secs of all sorts on the pavement of Brussels and Antwerp. I send you two letters I had from a man called Casement, premising that I knew him first in the Congo just 12 years ago. Perhaps you've heard or seen in print his name. He's a Protestant Irishman, pious too. But so was Pizarro. For the rest I can assure you that he is a limpid personality. There is a touch of the Conquistador in him too; for I've seen him start off into an unspeakable wilderness swinging a crookhandled stick for all weapons, with two bull-dogs: Paddy (white) and Biddy (brindle) at his heels and a Loanda boy carrying a bundle for all company. A few months afterwards it so happened that I saw him come out again, a little leaner and a little browner, with his stick, dogs, and Loanda boy, and quietly serene as though he had been for a stroll in a park. Then we lost sight of each other. He was I believe Bsh Consul in Beira, and lately seems to have been sent to the Congo again, on some sort of mission by the Br Gov^t. I have always thought that some particle of Las Casas' soul had found refuge in his indefatigable body. The letters will tell you the rest. I would help him but it is not in me. I am only a wretched novelist inventing wretched stories and not even up to that miserable game…. He could tell you things! Things I've tried to forget; things I never did know. He has had as many years of Africa as I had months—almost——" (Actually the country around Matadi was not "unspeakable" but a grassy plain covered with scrub; nor did his duties allow extensive travel for months in the jungle.)

Although he tried to avoid any involvement in the Congo movement, Conrad did invite Casement and Cunninghame Graham to Hythe on 1 January, during which they discussed Africa. (This meeting is mentioned in the surviving 1903 Black Diaries.)

Withdrawn and self-protective, Conrad later refused to add his name to those who later pleaded for Casement's reprieve, doubtless disgusted by the homosexual revelations; but Cunninghame Graham was not this sort. On 27 November 1928 he wrote to H. W. Nevinson about Casement: "He was presumably a brave man, and did splendid work both in the Congo and on the Putumayo. The abnormality of his private life, which I hear from Conrad, from Englishmen who had known him in Paranagua and Rio de Janeiro, did not weigh with me in the least.... it is not a disease that is catching.... He died like a brave man, and for that I respect him, as I respect the consistent courage that he showed throughout his life."

Conrad had changed by 1916. He no longer considered himself a "friend" of Casement. He was, in fact, reported to "despise" him, admitting to J. H. Retinger that he had once shared a hut in the Congo with Casement but had ended by "utterly disliking the man." In refusing to sign appeals for pardon, he explained to John Quinn that Casement had been nothing but a labor procurer in Africa. He had gotten what he deserved. By that time Conrad was comfortably situated in the British Intellectual Establishment. He resisted signing a petition to save the life of a "moral degenerate."

Other members of the establishment did not feel so intimidated.

The Legacy of the Congo

When Casement went to the Congo the heart of Africa was sinisterly dark. The golden days of exploration were finished but the golden days of the British Empire glittered with promise for entrepreneurs. A different kind of slavery was now in place. Flogging, mutilation, massacre of the natives were the rule of the day: King Leopold's Congo was the final unspeakable end of a fascinating period of exploration and discovery stretching over four centuries.

The history of the Europeans in the Congo had begun auspiciously with the Portuguese. In 1482 Diego Cam and his men met the Bakongo at the mouth of the Congo river. There was no massacre, only curiosity: the Bakongo were considered by the Portuguese as handsome and relatively civilized in comparison with other Africans. They were amenable to barter. They treated the white men as gods, perhaps because albinos were highly esteemed in the Bakongo culture. The Portuguese had no color prejudice, assimilating easily with the locals. Diego Cam took four hostages with him back to Portugal, as surety for the Portuguese dispatched on a mission to Mbanza Kongo, the capital of the kingdom. These African hostages were treated as honored guests in Lisbon; they were even taught to speak and write Portuguese. When they returned they described the marvels of European civilization, which encouraged the King of the Congo to send out an ambassador, Nsaka, and a group of nobles, requesting that they learn to read, write and speak Portuguese and also that they become Christian. From 1485–90 the group remained in Lisbon, where Nsaka was baptized and took the Christian name João da Silva. The others were educated by the Canons of St. John the Evangelist and adopted by Portuguese godparents. It was a time of warm and loving relations. Unfortunately, there was also a dark side to development. Many of the Portuguese in the Congo were common criminals, others were out for loot. Even priests were not beyond criticism: they lusted after power and caused scandal in the country by their manner of living and their ambition. The Portuguese slave trade began, causing social and economic havoc.

The Capuchin monks arrived in the Congo in the seventeenth century. They burned pagan idols and herded the population into church, maintaining the "superiority" of the Christian faith to native superstitions. (The French, on the other hand, in the northern part of the Congo river from 1766–76, acquired the local language—Kikongo—and did not impose Christianity on the natives; but the French did not stay.) Soon Portuguese influence, and commercial interests, switched to a more "profitable" Angola. They abandoned the Congo to the natives, who simply left the Christian churches to rot, abandoned their European clothes for nakedness, and used the crucifixes as fetishes. By then the Portuguese Slave traders were making fortunes. By the seventeenth century the Kingdom of the Congo was exporting 15,000 slaves a year to South America. During four centuries the Congo would supply over thirteen million slaves; the slave trade destroyed the prestige of the King of the Congo and led to the kingdom's disintegration. King Leopold's Congo would continue the decline in a dizzying fashion, recorded in detail in Casement's official reports.

One of the major reasons for Britain's entry into the Congo was ostensibly to crush the slave trade at the source. This laudable goal was also in harmony with the spirit of scientific curiosity, linked with zeal for material progress and profit. The pursuit for raw materials and markets for the products of the Industrial Revolution, aided by steam power and advancing technology, made Africa a prime target for British commercial interests. By that time the Dutch, French, Spanish and Portuguese had established factories at Banana and Boma—places that would become hauntingly familiar to Casement.

During the mid nineteenth century the missionary movement was built on the great Christian desire to convert the heathen in Africa. David Livingstone was one of those miracles of dubious British character, the missionary reformer with a taste for exploration. His achievements were also part of the background to Casement's life in Africa.

Livingstone's beginnings were not auspicious. His grandfather Neil was a dispossessed tenant farmer on the island of Ulva; evicted in 1792 he migrated to Glasgow to work in the cotton mill at Blantyre. Livingstone and his two brothers were put to work in the mills as children. He was ten when he began. The work was from six in the morning till eight at night, with a half hour for breakfast and an hour for lunch, six days a week. David was a "piecer"—finding broken threads, scrambling over the looms. The factory was heated to 80 or 90 degrees Fahrenheit and most of the children worked naked in the stifling building. Widespread immorality was the consequence of such degraded conditions.

Livingstone was ambitious and determined to better himself. After work he studied for two hours at the company school. He learned to read and write there, and astounded his schoolmaster by tackling Latin in his second year. He bought textbooks with the few shillings he managed to save from his wages. His character was described as "determined, unsociable, serious and remote." He would not change much over time.

The Livingstones were a religious family, somewhat, but not much, "above" the average. Father Neil was totally abstemious and all books except religious tracts he considered "trash."

Ordained as a missionary after medical training, Livingstone set sail almost immediately on the *George* which almost foundered on the way out to Africa. They wallowed for repairs into Rio de Janeiro, where Casement would be stationed in 1910. It was a wild place, and none too safe. Livingstone nearly caused a riot by distributing temperance tracts in the waterfront bars. After a three-month voyage he was in South Africa, another territory that Casement would know well.

Most African settlements at that time were coastal. There were only a few remote missionary stations in the interior, where Livingstone had been originally assigned. After a stupefying two-month journey by wagon he reached the settlement at Kuruman in Bechuanaland. The community was a nightmare of argument, gossip and backbiting.

He soon grew to abhor the new station and to detest his associates. From the beginning he was more interested in primitive people and in exploring than in conversion; Casement would share the same sentiments, if not the same tastes.

Between 1853 and 1856 Livingstone made important explorations in the Barotse valley in search of a malaria-free trading post; a thousand miles to the Atlantic port of Loanda He made the first crossing of the continent by a European, a stupendous achievement of will and fortitude. After this he sailed for England, arriving 9 December 1856. By this time he had become famous in Britain, a national hero.

Livingstone, unlike Casement, was a fanatical prude in the style of the Great Queen. Casement was fanatically promiscuous, Livingstone was basically uninterested in sex (describing Mananko, the twenty-one year old daughter of the chief of the Balonda as in a state of "frightful nudity" with only a thin strip of leather covering her genitals). All offers of native girls were refused by Livingstone out of hand; one does not read of the offer of young boys. He considered the Portuguese corrupt in their intercourse with native peoples. Fame was of more interest to him than sex. Casement was interested in both.

For the young Casement the story of African exploration and adventure had been fascinating. It was a story of achievement in the worst of conditions, but it was also a story of dangerous diseases, slave trading, sudden death and lunacy. Even the best equipped expeditions, manned by the healthiest men, ended broken. Consular officials (as Casement would soon be) often traveled extensively in the interior and inevitably came down with "fever" and other disgusting ailments. They often died young or were sent home broken in health.

<h2 style="text-align:center">2</h2>

Henry Morton Stanley was another curious hero, well known to Casement through his numerous books, who had made his name in Africa. The bastard son of Betsy Parry, a nineteen-year-old Welsh housemaid, Stanley's father was the town drunk. He was early sent to St. Asaph Union Workhouse where he was brought up. St. Asaph's accepted children and prostitutes; the latter often taught the young girl inmates their professional tricks. An official report on the institution in 1847 mentions the rampant sexuality that was common in workhouse life. Adult males "took part in every possible vice." Children—the older with the younger—snuggled two to a bed, "so that from the very start ... [they] were beginning to practice and understand things they should not." Drunkenness and promiscuity were prevalent.

Little Rowlands was the favorite of the teacher, James Francis (who would be admitted to Denbigh Lunatic Asylum in 1866). Francis left his darling boy "in charge" when he was away, and Little Rowlands (as Stanley had been baptized) turned out to be a strict authoritarian. At fifteen, the same age that Casement was out on his own, Stanley left St. Asaph's, having learned English grammar, acceptable spelling, good penmanship and, certainly, other useful things. Soon he was working as a delivery boy at a wholesale butcher's close to the docks in Liverpool, where David Hardinge, master of a Yankee merchant ship, the *Windermere*, headed for New Orleans, caught sight of him. He offered the sixteen-year-old a job as cabin boy at $5 a month plus seaman's clothes. On the voyage that lasted seven weeks he was clouted, yelled at, abused and threatened: he does not report being abused sexually, but experienced sailors routinely sodomized young crew members. Sodomy was the rule of the sea.

It was normally expected that cabin boys on reaching New Orleans would desert the ship. Rowlands, with another cabin boy, immediately did so. The city was wide open. In his memoirs, Stanley speaks of visiting his first whorehouse there—and at being shocked by the depravity into what would be "a chaste manhood." He was, and would remain for the rest of his life, incredibly shy with the opposite sex. "I can't talk to a woman," he wrote.

In New Orleans the young Rowlands landed a job as junior clerk with Speake and McCreary, a cotton brokerage, helped by a prosperous merchant Henry Hope Stanley, an Englishman who had immigrated to the US in 1815 from Cheshire. Twice married, Stanley had no children but had adopted two daughters. The famous explorer later wrote that Mr. Stanley also adopted *him* and that he lived with the family. These are fabrications. Records show that "J. Rollings" lived in a boardinghouse on Thomas Street, not with the Stanleys. What Mr. Stanley *did* do was dispatch Rowlands to Cypress Bend, Arkansas to work for a trader, a Mr. Altschul. At Cypress Bend he caught "fever" and recovered—which probably accounts for his resistance to the *anopheles* later in Africa—and changed his name to Henry Stanley (he obviously did not know Mr. Stanley's middle name). He also became a sharpshooter, a skill that would be invaluable in the American Civil War, where he fought first as Private Henry Stanley of the Dixie Greasy, and in his expeditions in the West and in Africa. He went through the battle of Shiloh and was sent to Chicago as a prisoner of war. He gained his release by joining the Union Army but was discharged after a couple of weeks because of severe dysentery. In 1863 Stanley was back in America working as a clerk in Brooklyn for Thomas Irwin Hughes, a notary public (Stanley later claimed he was a judge). He hated the job of clerk, as Casement would, and was restless. In July he signed on for a three year stint in the federal navy and observed the shelling of Fort Fisher, North Carolina, the Confederacy's last Atlantic coast stronghold. On board ship he became intimate with a fifteen-year-old sailor, Lewis Noe. The two friends jumped ship and headed for New York. Stanley had conceived the scheme to travel around the world, starting out in Turkey, trekking through

Anatolia to the Caucasus, then on to India and China, reporting on the trip for American newspapers. On 10 July 1866 the friends sailed from Boston for Smyrna on the *E. H. Yarrington*.

In Turkey things went disastrously wrong. Stanley tells the story, but as usual one cannot be sure what is fact. He claimed that near the mountain village of Chi-Hissar the Americans were accosted by a gang of "ruffians" whose leader made sexual advances to the attractive young Lewis. Enraged, Stanley struck the man. The Turks then overpowered him, tied him up and dragged him off to be beaten. Six years later, when Stanley had become famous, Noe himself would describe the events differently. He declared that Stanley had tried to murder a Turk in order to steal his horses, that the Turk had escaped and brought back his clansmen who took the Americans prisoner. "The first night of our imprisonment I was taken out by three of the Turks and treated in a shocking manner," he said. (The entry in Stanley's diary actually reads: *Louis,* [sic] *a boy of 17, was* _____.) The group of Turks had taken the young Noe off and sodomized him, the accepted treatment for such a prisoner. T. E. Lawrence would be scarred psychologically for life by such an experience; for Noe, more pragmatic than either Stanley or Lawrence, it was simply one more unpleasant experience in his accidental existence. For Casement it would have been a frolic.

3

After returning to the US from this complicated and abortive trip, Stanley wrangled a job with James Gordon Bennett, Jr., publisher of the *New York Herald*. Bennett, an impulsive eccentric and drunk, sent Stanley off to Abyssinia where the mad King Theodore was keeping a group of British hostage. This turned out to be Stanley's first coup as a reporter.

By twenty-seven Stanley, like Roger Casement at the same age, had fashioned a personality for himself out of fabrications and secrets. He now joined the regular staff of the *Herald*. He was soon to go out to Africa on assignment.

The famous Dr. Livingstone was "lost" in Africa in 1869. The years between his missionary fiasco on the Zambezi and his final disappearance into the depths of the African jungle had been eventful and disastrous. On 23 October, after three months of gruesome travel he and his small caravan finally reached Ujiji. The stores he expected to be waiting for him there had, as might have been expected, been looted. This was the end. He was now destitute.

Then, a couple of days later, he learned that another white man was in the vicinity.

The winter of 1868 had also been eventful and emotionally disastrous for the young reporter. Stanley, bristling with ambition but plagued with incongruous desires (he asked God to make him nobler, purer; he had "vile thoughts") had had his first brief encounter not only with the Livingstone myth but also with frustrated and forbidden love.

His first stop on the way out to Africa was Paris. Here he met an American family traveling with their young son. Stanley became infatuated with the boy. Edwin was a precocious thirteen-year-old with excellent French, who knew the city well. With this little charmer Stanley was soon touring around Versailles, Vincennes, St. Cloud. Edwin and he would meet at the Hotel du Louvre, where Stanley was staying. The relationship revived the well-traveled yet emotionally puerile Stanley. He wrote the extraordinary Edwin numerous letters. Later, he rashly sent the boy an invitation to accompany him on his travels. His parents, however, gave this invitation a horrified *No.*

Stanley headed into mainland Africa from Zanzibar, the capital of the sultans of Oman and Muscat. The settlement was the headquarters for the Arab slave trade. Stanley reached there at the beginning of 1871. He was not anti-slavery at this time, nor did he have settled ideas about Blacks. Even Burton had had ambivalent feelings about the natives: "One of those childish races ... never rising to man's estate," he had written, "befuddled, ignorant hopeless people." Trading was now mostly with Europe, although in 1859 more than half the sixty-five foreign ships calling at the port of Zanzibar were American. The Civil War has ruined the market. By 1869 only three American ships out of fifty-three were American and the US dollar had been supplanted by the Maria Theresa. The British were now the main trading partners. There were many charms in Zanzibar, many of them in the form of Blacks who were outlandishly endowed. Burton himself mentioned the size of Zanzibari members, one of which was "at least six inches long when *sleeping.*" Casement also had an eye out for such details, amply described in his diaries.

By 4 February 1871 Stanley had put together a vast expeditionary force, one of the best supplied, the most lavish, ever organized in Zanzibar. After months of chaotic and perilous travel, and about a week's march from Lake Tanganyika, Stanley received news of a European who was at Ujiji, an old man with white hair. He drove on, certain that it was Livingstone.

On 3 November, he reached the little port, the stars and stripes flying, the men firing into the air to announce their arrival. A few minutes later Livingstone himself hobbled down to greet the caravan. Stanley, afraid to betray his emotions, kept his poise as he walked through the crowd to where Livingstone stood.

Absurdly, Stanley raised his hat. Even more absurdly he said:

"Dr. Livingstone, I presume?"

He presumed correctly.

4

Livingstone did not survive much longer. Roger Casement was almost ten years old when, on the morning of 15 April 1874, Livingstone's body reached Southampton, causing national mourning. Only a decade later Casement himself would be in Africa, but in far different circumstances from Livingstone's or Stanley's. By then there would be steamers on the Congo, well established stations doing a heavy trade in ivory. History at times moved briskly—at other times it hardly moved at all. The Empire bloomed in the compost of trade, while at home the "lower" classes enjoyed a prehistoric level of existence. In Casement's Ireland it was worse.

The Home Rule question—the "Irish Problem"—was bitter and ceaseless, involving not only the Irish and the English but the Americans as well, where millions of Irish had immigrated to escape famine and poverty. The problem would not go away. Henry James and other Americans of Irish and Scotch-Irish descent felt the pull of allegiance to the Irish cause. Alice James expressed herself committed to Irish independence. Henry, however, was not so excitable; he withdrew from politically charged discussions. Even social contact with Gladstone at one of Lord Rosebery's country homes failed to convert him. The Irish Question would not vanish. "If I had nothing else to do I think I should run over to Ireland," he told Perry in 1886, when there were only "two topics of conversation in London—Ireland & the weather"—"which may seem strange to you on the part of one satiated in youth with Celtic genius. The reason is that I shld. like to see a country in a state of revolution." He believed that an Irish parliament for Irish affairs was in the irresistible march of things. It was self-destructive for England to attempt to maintain Irish subordination; Home Rule would "injure England less.... [Ireland] seems to me an example of a country more emancipated from every bond, not only of despotism but of ordinary law, than any so-called civilized country was before—a country reveling in odious forms of irresponsibility & license. And, surely," he added (in a letter to Grace Norton), "how can one speak of the Irish as a 'great people'? I see no greatness, nor any kind of superiority in them, & they seem to me an inferior & 3rd rate race ... while their vices are peculiarly cowardly & ferocious." He feared to seem brutal and "Anglicized" but that was the way he felt. In 1890, the question was still rankling (Gladstone's Home Rule Bill had failed in 1886). He wryly noted that he had planned to take a short vacation in Ireland, but that it was perhaps "perverse" since "taking refuge from Ireland just now would seem the more natural course." In London there was "nothing but Ireland, & the animosities & separations it engenders—accursed isle! Literature, art, conversation, society—everything lies dead beneath its black shadow."

Great economic interests were at stake in the question. Irish wealth was mostly in the hands of the British. The Irish were a source of manual laborers and servants. They were, as many said—or implied—simply another kind of slave: that was what Roger Casement believed. He had grown up in an environment of national turmoil; he lived through it, and took part in it—even while employed by the British Foreign Office. During this time, however, his major support of the Irish was an insistence, over a period of twelve years dealings with W. J. Allison and Company, outfitters, that the supplies he order be, whenever possible, of Irish manufacture. He was in spite of his Irishness, still a part of the British Establishment.

Enter Leopold

1

The story of Livingstone and Stanley is part of the mythology of the time. Roger Casement while growing up in Ulster was certainly aware of the exciting events that were taking place in Africa. Boys all over the world were learning of the feats of exploration in the Dark Continent. Joseph Conrad had read of them and was eager to go out. In America, Stanley's feats were reported and his dispatches avidly awaited: they sold millions of copies of the *Herald*. In Europe, newspapers were also reporting the events in Africa. King Leopold II of Belgium was intrigued. Son of Leopold I, the astute uncle of Queen Elizabeth who, after forty years of "exile" in England had turned down the throne of Greece and accepted that of King of the Belgians, Leopold II was—unlike his father—ambitious, devious, undependable and power hungry. He was entranced by Stanley's articles, especially one that had praised the Congo as "the great highway of commerce to broad Africa." King Leopold dreamed of a Congo colony—in fact, he had been pursuing the idea of a colony—any colony—since his early manhood (*Il faut à la Belgique une Colonie*, he had ordered inscribed on a slice of marble salvaged from the Acropolis) and eagerly pursued possibilities after his succession in 1865.

"Surrounded by the sea, Holland, Prussia and France, our frontiers can never be extended in Europe. The sea bathes our coast, the universe lies in front of us, steam and electricity have made distances disappear, all the unappropriated lands on the surface of the globe may become the field of our operations and of our successes.... Since history teaches that colonies are useful, that they play a great part in that which makes up the power and prosperity of states, let us strive to get one in our turn." He had shopped around, inquiring if he might buy the Argentine province of Entre Ríos. He considered buying the tiny island of Martín-García at the confluence of the Uruguay and the Paraná. He tried to purchase Borneo from the Dutch. He even tried to "rent" the Philippines from Spain. Finally, he focused on Africa—encouraged by the dark vacuum that lay at the heart of the continent.

Leopold began to formulate his plans. First he organized the International Geographical Congress in Brussels in 1876. Then he formed the Association Internationale Africaine, with himself as chairman. He fixed his sights on the Congo River Basin, where it seemed ever more urgent to forestall the French. An expedition headed by Pierre Savorgnan de Brazza was on its way to the Congo in August 1875. Brazza followed the Ogawe to its source and continued on, having heard of a "big water" further east. Early in 1878 he would reach the land of the Batekes who took him to the Alima, a tributary of the Congo. Coming under attack, he gave up his quest. If he had continued down the Alima he would have come out at the Congo, 200 miles above Stanley Pool itself. Stanley was unaware of the competition, but not so Leopold.

On learning that Stanley was on his way back to England, Leopold sent a delegation to Marseilles to meet him and invite him to Brussels for talks. The men who accosted Stanley at the railway station in Marseilles were Baron Jules Greindl and General Henry B. Sanford, an American with whom Roger Casement would later be associated in the Congo. Stanley, however, begged off. He was rushing to get back home to his deserved acclaim.

Stanley decided, not long after, to accept King Leopold's invitation. He reached Brussels in June 1878. During their interview, the king spoke of an exploratory mission, nothing to provoke Britain, of course. Stanley would simply go out to Africa to investigate the feasibility of setting up stations for the benefit of the Congo and its peoples and for Europe. Stanley, for his part, urged the king to sponsor a company to build a railway between the Lower Congo and Stanley Pool. Talks went on in Paris in August.

In November Stanley was called to Brussels where he learned from Leopold that a group of Belgian, Dutch and British entrepreneurs in the "commercial and monetary world" had decided to organize a Comité d'Études du Haut-Congo, providing a fund of $100.000 to send out an expedition to the Congo. (In 1879, after the Dutch backers went bankrupt, Leopold would buy out the other investors, replacing the Comité with the Association Internationale du Congo.) Stanley was offered a five-year contract at $5000 a year as head of the expedition. He accepted.

Stanley's mission for Leopold was to be confidential. The king did not desire the competition, such as it was, to learn of his plot. Stanley traveled incognito, as M. Henri. A freighter with building materials and four river steamboats, on his orders, were secretly prepared to sail from Antwerp and would rendezvous with him at the mouth of the Congo. He traveled from Marseilles to Zanzibar (where he contracted 68 Zanzibaris to help in his work).

At Gibraltar, Colonel Maximilian Strauch, appointed Secretary General of the Comité d'Études du Haut-Congo by Leopold, informed Stanley that he was to go ahead with arrangements for construction of a wagon road around Livingstone Falls. He was to erect a string of trading stations up the river. Leopold, who was sole "director" of the Comité, also authorized Stanley to create a Confederation of Free Negro Republics in the Congo River Basin, "each station would regard itself as a little republic. Its leader, the white man in charge, would himself be responsible to the Director-General of Station who in turn would be responsible to the President of the Confederation. The President will hold his powers from the king." Leopold was conniving—strategically planning—a coup; however, he hastened to add, in a later letter that "The King, as a private person, wishes only to possess properties in Africa. Belgium wants neither a colony nor territories." That is to say, Leopold was now purchasing a vast territory for his own uses. These occurrences were well known to Casement when reviewing the development of the Belgian Congo, and he made pertinent use of them in his report for the British government.

At any rate, Stanley, in spite of any misgivings he might have had, went ahead with his duties. On 14 August 1879 he reached the estuary of the Congo and headed for Boma. Here he was able to recruit 170 local blacks and fourteen Europeans. Work on the wagon road began on 1 October 1879. Vivi would be the first station. As roads were built, the boats and heavy equipment would be hauled to the next station. It was at this time that Stanley got the nickname Bula Matari—Smasher of Rocks, for his determined drive to smash a way through the jungles. By February 1880 he had set up the Isangila base, one hundred forty miles from Stanley Pool. It was expensive in human lives: six Europeans died and twenty-two Africans. Stanley himself—often wracked with fever and taking enormous doses of quinine, suffering from tumors, bed sores and palsy—slogged back and forth along the thirty-eight miles of road. At last, down to a hundred pounds and dosing himself with up to sixty grains of quinine dissolved in a glass of Madeira wine, he appeared to be near death himself. He miraculously revived.

Brazza, hurrying down from Gabon in the north, was intent on hoisting the French tricolor on both banks of Stanley Pool. The two explorers met, rather cordially. Brazza had managed to secure the other side of the Congo for the French by a rigged treaty. This *fait accompli* infuriated Leopold in Brussels; he considered Stanley "stupid to the highest degree" for having allowed Brazza to get there first. Stanley, he said, should have shot Brazza outright and ended the matter there instead of showing himself "as gentle and tractable as those wretched savages that have to be civilized." (These gentle and tractable people would later be enslaved, mutilated, driven into the forest to starve, when Leopold's agents found they were useful as rubber gatherers. Casement in his later report would describe their plight, in a fashion similar to Livingstone who had invariably noted the conditions of the natives under the threat of the Arab slavers.) Money was growing short and Leopold was sinking huge sums from his personal fortune into the scheme of the Congo. Perhaps Stanley could charge a toll for travelers on the road he had built? Trade was necessary, in order to recoup his considerable losses—and those of other investors: colonies, even private ones, should ideally be profitable.

But Stanley was having problems with the natives. The Senegalese Sergeant Melamine, left in charge of the fort on Stanley Pool when Brazza left for Europe, had convinced the local natives to refuse to sell Stanley food when he arrived. Stanley retreated from the north, attempting to deal with the chief on the left bank, Ngalyema, who had prospered since first meeting Stanley in 1877. "During the four years that had elapsed," Stanley wrote, "he had become a great man ... grown richer by ivory trade," and he had also become powerful in the region "by investing his large profits in slaves, guns and gunpowder." Ngalyema was about thirty-four, well-built, proud and evil. They swore blood brotherhood, drank toasts in palm wine, exchanged gifts. But the chief did not want a permanent settlement to be set up by the Europeans in his territory. They palavered for weeks over the question, while Ngalyema suggested he might be more tractable if he could be assured of gifts such as a particular japanned tin box; some fathoms of cloth; iron boxes; a few cases of gin; guns and gunpowder; Stanley's best black suit; Stanley's Newfoundland dog. Stanley called the chief's bluff, scaring the wits out of him in a hokey confrontation, and went on to establish Leopoldville. The road to the Pool was completed in 1881. Fifty tons of equipment and stores were hauled up the road, along with the parts of the paddleboat the *En Avant* which was assembled and launched on the river. A fourth station was built between Ngalyema's village of Ntamo and another village called Kinshasa. From here the Congo was navigable for a thousand miles, making the whole Congo Basin accessible to trade—exactly what Leopold had intended. Stanley's drive, his powerful control of men and circumstances, his dedication to his job—all these combined to make his assignment on the Congo an incredible success. Leopold, however, was incensed by his lack of ruthlessness. The French had now taken control of the other side of Stanley Pool and they could not be dislodged.

Falling ill, Stanley was taken unconscious to Vivi. He handed over his command to the naturalist Peschuel-Loesche whom Leopold had hired to carry out scientific work for the Comité. Stanley believed that the three-year contract with the Comité superseded the five-year contract with the Association Internationale. Leopold would correct this misconception.

The wily Leopold met with Brazza in Brussels and tried to hire him in order to forestall the French claims in the Congo. The Frenchman could not be persuaded. "Doubtless the King of the Belgians ... gave his millions with the sole aim of civilizing the savage tribes ... [but] if it was a good thing to get hold of the Congo, I would prefer that it was the French flag, rather than the Belgian 'international' flag, that floated over this splendid African territory." The French parliament ratified the French Congo Treaty. Brazza, in spite of his feud with Stanley, showed himself courteous and unresentful, making an impressive conciliatory speech at a banquet given by Stanley on 20 October 1881 after his return to Europe.

"Surely, Mr. Stanley, you cannot think of leaving me now, just when I most need you?" Leopold whined in Brussels. The work in the Congo had to go on. Although General "Chinese" Gordon, having resigned in the Sudan, expressed interest in working for Leopold, his collaboration had not been assured (and never would be). The king insisted that Stanley return to the Congo at once. So in November Bula Matari went back to the Congo reluctantly.

The naturalist Peschuel-Loesche had meanwhile allowed the whole operation to disintegrate into a shambles.

2

Roger Casement, a strikingly handsome boy of seventeen, had gone from studying for the Civil Service to working as a junior clerk in marine shipping. He hated the job. He was a romantic. He had followed the newspaper reports of the African explorations, of the struggle for colonial territory, and his imagination was aflame with fantasies—fed by the reports that were regularly coming into the office of the Elder Dempster Shipping Company concerning the development of West African trade He was having early sexual encounters in

Liverpool with its busy docks as well as Dublin and London—all of which had their share of fairly visible sodomites. Male prostitution had been common—though not so common as female (a vast majority of whom were adolescents); there was also ready flesh on the streets. The strict Victorian moral code rarely affected the "lower" orders or the military. Before the "cleansing" campaign of 1837, disastrous in terms of human suffering, there were thriving boy brothels in London—and, when these were closed, Piccadilly, public parks and lavatories, railway stations and the streets swarmed with available youths. Later, shelters would be set up to help these "boy sodomites" who often combined poorly paid work for "trade" of a different kind. Rehabilitation was rarely successful.

Soldiers and sailors were another story. In 1865, out cruising, J. A. Symonds picked up a grenadier off Leicester Square. He visited a male brothel in 1877 conveniently near the military barracks in Regent's Park. Cadets and subalterns were indisputably involved in homosexual prostitution. (Public school boys were also among those out on the streets.) Venereal disease rates among the military in 1860 were 369 per thousand, with most contagion originating with female prostitutes. Licensed or "regulated" prostitution had been attempted—but the Contagious Diseases Acts failed to attract enough support in Parliament. The Purity Campaign, on the other hand, made a vicious effort to clamp down on all adolescent sex. Brothels were shut. The age of consent was raised to sixteen—a disastrously stupid idea, even in the minds of some Lords. The traffic in young girls—many of whom came from King Leopold's Belgium—withered. All types of sexual activity between males (not just sodomy but also mutual masturbation and other indecencies) were outlawed, irrespective of age. This was at a time when in many other civilized countries any punishment for such acts between consenting adults was abolished. England was particularly fascist in comparison with the Continent, where countries moved near the end of the century toward a more humane—or more socially sensible—attitude. Masturbation (self abuse or self pollution) was a looked upon as exceptionally catastrophic from the point of view of both the English church and medical authorities: from the 1860s masturbation was attacked as the cause of degeneration in the next generation. Self abuse was even to become one reason for expulsion from public school—where all kinds of sexual activity were generally rampant: sex between boys at Eton was in fact "the old hereditary vice"—but not only at Eton. Certainly in view of the prohibitions, fears, punishment, ostracism, outright hate inspired by masturbation, it no doubt diminished in intensity ... or did it?

Homosexuality was another thing. Often encouraged by social bathing in the nude, furthered by mutual curiosity and sleeping naked together at school, "homosexuality" as classification was a relatively recent invention by the Puritans. The word came into use in 1869, to cover a variety of acts, not just anal intercourse (sodomy) but oral intercourse (fellatio), but even mutual masturbation. "Homosexuality," in effect, became a catchall term for a socially detrimental disease. As for homosexual solicitation, flogging was introduced in 1889 for such incitements—a delicious punishment, perhaps, for some. (General Sir Eyre Coote a former member of parliament and Lieutenant Governor of Jamaica was caught at Christ's Hospital in a flogging and groping sessions with fourteen- and fifteen-year-old boys.) But sex is difficult to legislate; what is not witnessed might as well not exist. No laws, no threatened punishments, kept the telegraph boys, the boys on the street, ambulant vendors, stable hands, young scholars of all ages, cadets, guardsmen, police constables and assorted aristocrats from carrying on as usual. Sodomy did not go out of style: it may even have increased in intensity because it was forced to go underground, though not as far underground as the Chinese in South Africa.

Meanwhile, in the British empire in general—among colonial populations whose customs were more accepting of sexual variations—the British military, commercial agents, even missionaries, were indulging themselves without fear of reprisal or punishment. Of course you had to be careful, especially with fellow expatriates who might resent your wallowing in native flesh and accuse you to the appropriate authorities. However, many small groups of understanding men lived and worked together in tight little societies, sharing the same "vices" in India, Malaysia, Egypt, Africa, everywhere throughout the world, in fact. The British behaved "differently" when abroad. Expatriate life was a liberation.

3

It was not so with Stanley, who was "innocent"—ostensibly chaste, self-righteous, idealistic—during the whole of his adult life. Love and marriage had escaped him, as had sex.

In August 1883, he set off upriver with a flotilla of three steamboats and one whaler, heading for Stanley Falls and collecting, along the way, the signatures of native chiefs to the treaty providing the legal basis for the Congo Free State of Leopold. It was not a carefree journey; they passed deserted villages, smoldering ruins, settlements burned down, the population in terror, the same conditions that Casement would note, with alarm, two decades later. The Congo had been "opened up" by Stanley—but opened up to the increased depredations of the economic slavers. In eleven months a 35,000 square mile area had been devastated. Sickened, as Casement would be sickened later by the same kind of circumstances, Stanley on 10 December 1883 left the Scots engineer Binnie with provisions and a contingent of thirty-one askaris to return to Leopoldville. His contract was ending and he intended handing over to General Gordon (who, as it turned out, would never arrive in the Congo, since he had been ordered by the British government to return to the Sudan, where he would die a year later at Khartoum). Leopold had hired Colonel Sir Francis de Winton in General Gordon's place. On 8 June 1884 Stanley put the reigns into de Winton's hands. At the end of his five-year assignment, he left twenty-two garrisoned stations on the Congo, with roads, a short stretch of railway, a fleet of steamboats on the river and guaranteed sovereignty through treaties with the natives—a viable political and commercial framework on which the Congo Free State would be able to build later.

In Washington, meanwhile, Leopold's man, General Harry B. Sanford—with whom Casement would later be involved in the Congo—was lobbying for American support for Leopold. He found sympathetic ears in Congress and in the administration of Chester A. Arthur. It helped that Stanley had signed treaties with the Congo chiefs: this made the Confederation of Free Negro Republics similar to the US-supported state of Liberia. It also helped that Stanley was considered a Yankee (although he only became a naturalized American citizen on 15 May 1885.) Leopold's African Congo flag, blue with a gold star, was duly accepted by the US as that of a "friendly government" on 22 April 1884. This little coup was, to Leopold's satisfaction, followed the next day by a treaty with the French formally recognizing Leopold's holdings in the Congo. The king had been scheming hard to prevent an Anglo-Portuguese treaty recognizing Portugal's sovereignty over the mouth of the Congo. Bismarck also—at the instigation of Kaiser Wilhelm (another of Leopold's difficult relations)—balked at the Anglo-Portuguese treaty. (Germany was in a cantankerous mood, disputing Britain's claims to Fiji and Samoa about the same time.) Bismarck, with France's acquiescence, called for a conference to be held in Berlin on 15 November 1884 to bring the powers into agreement on the colonization of Africa.

General Sanford was one of the two official US delegates to the Berlin Conference. Stanley attended as an observer, with the title of Technical Advisor to the Americans. The Congress ended on 24 February 1885, with delegates from Austro-Hungary, Belgium, Britain, Denmark, Holland, Italy, Norway, Portugal, Russia, Spain, Sweden, Turkey, Germany and the United States of America formally agreeing to Leopold's personal dominion over 900,000 square miles of the Congo Basin. France got 257,000 square miles of river basin. Portugal got 351,000 square miles. By 29 May 1885 Leopold declared himself King-Sovereign of the Congo Free State which was to remain, in name only, a free trade zone.

4

Casement during the 1880s was making frequent voyages out to West Africa. There were exciting spots in the Dark Continent, he was told, where life was "arranged" to suit special tastes. The Oil Rivers Protectorate, for example, was a tight little society where sodomy—from all reports—was commonly accepted. Sodomy among the native tribes was of course not unknown. The young Roger Casement, on his first assignments to West Africa as purser on Elder Dempster ships, most certainly had been sodomized on board the vessel and at the many ports of call. During his later assignment in the Oil Rivers Protectorate his tastes would become more diversified. African territories were a sexual frontier, wildly different from Ireland and England, and they allowed him—with discretion—to do what he wanted to do, freed him from restraints. This is clear from the surviving diaries.

The young Irishman was already preparing for a career on the dark frontier. Back home, he was always on the streets. It was even possible that Stanley had caught sight of him, or might even have spoken with him. If the young Irishman had been a woman, however, the great explorer would as usual have been inexplicably tongue-tied. He showed no such reticence with boys. In London, Stanley had now moved into an apartment in New Bond Street. He was accompanied by a black youngster from the Congo, Baruti. Soon another boy moved in—a former apprentice bag-maker named William Hoffmann, a seventeen-year-old of German extraction, who was to be "valet-housekeeper." Hoffmann had no previous experience as a valet or housekeeper but he was willing to learn. Stanley had caught sight of him at his hotel, where the boy was making a delivery, and had been "taken" by his good looks. Soon after this, Stanley confronted Hoffmann with the offer to come to "care for" him on a full time basis. Take care of him Hoffmann did—in a relationship that was to last for years and ended only with Stanley's death.

Stanley's two-volume bestseller, *The Congo and the Founding of Its Free State*, appeared in 1885. Casement would read it a few years in the future, with cynical disdain for the lies and half-truths. The book was dedicated "to the generous monarch who so nobly conceived, ably conducted, and munificently sustained the enterprise which has obtained the recognition of all the great powers of the world." At the last, Leopold reneged on his promise to make Stanley Director-General of the Congo Free State, awarding him, instead, the Order of Leopold and an extension of his old contract, this time as consultant, at $5,000 a year. Stanley didn't need the money. His needs were of a different sort.

5

In 1892 Casement was back in West Africa after a spell in Ireland. This time he went out to the Oil Rivers Protectorate, the notorious "frontier" region where sodomy was the rule. He did well there. "I entered the Service there," he wrote, "not in a consular capacity, but in a branch of the public service that was administered by the Foreign Office through consuls and vice-consuls." On 31 July 1892 he was appointed member of staff of the Survey Department and became, at the age of twenty-eight, Assistant Director-General of Customs at Old Calabar." This was an excellent apprenticeship for the Consular Service. The commissioner administering the Oil Rivers territory was General Sir Claude MacDonald, who (in his customary style) wrote a splendid report of Casement's work: "It would be difficult to find any one in every way more suited to the work of exploration." Exploration meant research into the feasibility of trade; and Casement made three tours into the interior of the Calabar district which proved satisfactory—during his third trip he had been welcomed by the tribes along the Cross river, opening up the country to the East. His reports if not outstanding stylistically were adequate and presented information bearing on what would be a British consul's commercial concerns.

The administration of the Oil Rivers Protectorate was in the hands of the Consular Service and Casement often acted on their behalf. From his position at the Customs Department he went on to become General Service Officer. Although he lacked a university education, his experience—and his social background—fitted him ideally for a position as representative of the British Government in Africa. The official British opposition to slavery and the possible use of government service as a vehicle for reform made such work attractive to an idealist like Casement. Even a half century after the abolition of

slavery in England, it was still prevalent in many parts of the African continent. One form of slavery or another could still be found in many parts of the
world and would continue to be widespread in spite of laws and reform. Slavery was endemic in human societies everywhere.

Pederasty was also endemic in many parts of Africa, not only in the Oil
Rivers Protectorate where Casement would spend three years. In the numerous mining compounds of southern Africa during the late nineteenth century
women were not commonly admitted and small boys were recruited to do the
cleaning and washing, serve as bed-warmers and cooks, and (occasionally after
payment of bride-price or *lobola*) for sodomy as substitute wives. This practice
was convenient to all—the black boys receiving higher pay, bicycles and other
gifts simply for playing the passive role in intercourse (though their ejaculation
during the act was frowned upon). Convenience was not the only reason for
preferring boys: sex with prostitutes carried the danger of venereal disease
which could adversely affect the productivity of the workers. Low wages also
sometimes led to the necessity of laborers sharing a bed or a single blanket,
leading—as in the workhouses of England—to homosexual activities.

The fear of "outsiders" coming to Africa and corrupting the natives was
widespread during the early development of the continent, when, for example,
Chinese were imported as laborers. The Asians were—ironically—accused of
teaching sodomy to the blacks, though it was notorious that sodomy was popular on the Zambesi, on the east coast and other regions, chiefly where the
Portuguese were established: their soldiers and police were devoted to the
practice, as they are to this day. However there is no evidence of anal syphilis
among the Chinese bugger-boys (usually actors playing in the Chinese theaters and notorious as male prostitutes) and certainly no public scandals as
there were in urban Johannesburg, where sodomy was flagrant. The Chinese
were "discrete" in relations with the little Kaffir boys. They did their little
deeds in secret, in disused mines, out of sight, in the dark.

Empire meant a loosening of moral restrictions, when men came into contact with cultures with attitudes sexually less restrictive and a good deal more
"interesting" than those at home. Not that promiscuity and sodomy were rare
in England, even when the law was extreme in its punishment for unnatural or
indiscriminate acts. The authorities were known to overlook certain uncomfortably human facts. Love-making among young men in the army and (notoriously) in the navy was accepted as unfortunately common—and only
condemned when distasteful, such as in flagrant mutual masturbation. Contact with Arab civilization at many ports might have tended to encourage sod-

omy, but the army and the navy were already traditionally reservoirs of boys who both at home and abroad were available for fun.

There was always a troubling risk of venereal disease, however. Statistics for VD are accurate and readily available from official sources. They show a marked increase in infection among soldiers and sailors stationed abroad. Not all this disease was acquired by contact with female prostitutes, anal gonorrhea being common among boys.

Casement was in Africa during the 1880s and 1890s, when he was in his twenties, in frontier areas where "unnatural" tastes were often openly indulged. When he went to work for the Survey Department the Oil Rivers Protectorate he was twenty-eight. He may have been introduced to buggery by the Europeans there, but this is doubtful. He was almost certainly already sexually promiscuous, to judge from a reference in his 1903 diary. His taste in boys with enormous endowments is notorious in the entries that escaped the flames. His diary entries are peppered with "huge" and "enormous"—and he often gives measurements.

Leaving the Oil Rivers Protectorate in 1895, he arrived at Margherintemple in June of that year. He was now practically an old Africa hand. His reports, published in February, had brought him to the attention of the Foreign Office. He had a reputation. Whitehall recognized his value. It seemed probable that he would go out to Uganda on a Foreign Office mission. Times were tumultuous. War with the Boers was imminent. In June the Conservatives were returned to power under Lord Salisbury who acted as his own Foreign Secretary. He was looking for experienced men available for British service in Africa.

Suddenly Casement was ordered to hold himself in readiness to go out very soon on a new assignment. "I may have to sail for the Cape in a week or ten days," he wrote.

Casement was appointed HM Consul in Lourenço Marques. The new posting would be to Delagoa Bay, a neutral port on the edge of the Transvaal, linked to Pretoria by rail. His consular duties included monitoring developments in Portuguese East Africa. It was vital to determine the number of arms shipments passing through the area. The usual qualifying examinations were dispensed with—this was Lord Salisbury's prerogative. Career diplomats would make clear to Casement later that he had entered the Consular Service through favoritism and simply because of his experience in Africa. This however was not unusual at the time. His uncle Edward and numerous others had served as consular officials without a university education or extensive train-ing—consular work being for the most part related to trade and, at any rate, not directly related to "diplomacy" per se.

After a stilted reply to Lord Salisbury, accepting his assignment "with grat-itude," Casement went out to Lourenço Marques and set up shop. He imme-diately began issuing a steady stream of extensive reports, letters, memoranda and cables, which must have overwhelmed his superiors. His "real" consular career had now begun. In his new post he showed himself to be officious, demanding, frustrated by inefficiency, and verbose in his recommendations and complaints.

Like the privileged "upper class" to which he almost belonged, Casement had nothing but contempt for "trade."—shopkeepers, business people, money-grubbers. Yet most of his work with the Foreign Office over the next twenty years would be to further the interests of British trade. His supplied the facts, even though they were often imbedded in complexity. He was always a man with a mission. He was both ambitious and pushy, to judge by his official cor-respondence.

Casement continued to be periodically sick, or "seedy." He suffered from malaria and assorted complaints such as headaches, dizziness, extreme fatigue. He was chronically constipated and had piles. Occasionally he took to his bed with fever. He had inherited the Africa of Livingstone and Stanley, the Africa of sickness and death. Like Livingston and Stanley he had endured rejection, abandonment. He too he had begun to use evasion as a tactic, if not to the same extent, and at times—to be intensified much later—actual paranoia, common in cases of malaria.

6

This was Casement's Africa. These were the myths he absorbed—as did Con-rad, whose *Heart of Darkness* dealt indirectly with the events of Stanley's last expedition and, probably, the death of Jameson.

In mid-January, when Stanley was sitting down to write the story of the Emin Pasha Relief Expedition, Casement had been in Africa for some seven years. He was an experienced clerk and organizer, duties which—in spite of their boring nature—were good experience for the job of consul; and he knew the natives well. When in 1895 he was appointed to his post in Lourenço Marques, Britain's position in colonial Africa was solidly established. That year she annexed the territory of Kenya. Zanzibar became a British protectorate. Trade was opening up, often utilizing the vast network of routes that the Arab slavers had established over the centuries. The great powers were basically at peace with each other for the time being. Leopold however was still scheming to take over the southern Sudan. He had kept the Lado enclave in his hands, but the project was hopeless. He had spent over thirty million francs on his obsession in the past fifteen years.

Consul Casement

1

Swami, the Woman's God, or Monafuma, Son of a King: these were the titles, according to his early Fred Puleston, his early friend in the Congo, given Casement by the natives. Edward Glave and Herbert Ward were also close associates of his in the African service who would later write descriptions of young Casement. In working for the Congo Free State it was said that those involved in the development of the country had to face the same hazards as Stanley and Livingstone—"savage cannibal tribes; unpredictable weather—frequent storms; stifling hot days followed by chilly nights—and menacing wild beasts: buffaloes, leopards, crocodiles and swarming insect life" that made life a torment. In fact, things were a lot better by the end of the century. Casement, throughout even difficult periods maintained his sensitivity to the conditions of the natives and even to animals. He was so "emotional, tender and sympathetic" that, when his beloved fox terrier got its stomach ripped open by a wild hog, he was unable to control his feeling and wept like a girl. (Puleston wrote this fifty years after the fact, in his memoir *African Drums*, dedicated to Stanley and to Casement.) In Herbert Ward's *A Voice from the Congo*, published in 1895, he describes Casement: "A tall handsome man of fine bearing: thin, mere muscle and bone, a sun-tanned face, blue eyes and black curly hair. A pure Irishman ... with a captivating voice and a singular charm of manner. A man of distinction and great refinement, high-minded and courteous, impulsive and poetical." Much the same might have been said of almost any member of the little group of expatriates.

On the Sanford Expedition, however, Casement had been criticized; the reasons are not obvious. He had the mentality of the modern aid worker, but without the sophistication: "making friends with the natives; I liked them, poor souls—and they me." Different biographers disagree about Casement's early movements and the dates, when and why he resigned, how long he spent in each assignment, if and when he traveled to the US on the "lecture tour" with General Sanford. The Foreign Office records are more helpful after 1895.

Africa was a turmoil of mixed intentions and conflicting interests at the end of the century.

The Fashoda incident directly involved the Congo. The British Foreign office had been alerted by Casement that the Mahdists were being supplied arms through the French Congo. On his way to his post in Loanda in December, Casement reported that "considerable numbers of French officers and men, and large quantities of ammunition, said to be destined for the Bahr El Ghazal, have been recently dispatched. A French contingent led by Marchand proceeded from Brazzaville to Fashoda in 1896, after the Conservative government in Britain had sent out Kitchener to reconquer the Sudan from the Mahdists in the name of Egypt. The decisive battle of Omdurman—in which Sir Hector Macdonald took heroic part (further "heroics" with boys in Southeast Asia will come later)—on 2 September 1895, left 50,000 of the enemy dead against fifty of Kitchener's forces. The Mahdi's tomb was broken open; the corpse was mutilated and the head sent as a souvenir to the unfortunate General Gordon's nephew. Kitchener moved south to oppose the French. The confrontation with Marchand was a farce. After weeks of hesitation the French withdrew unconditionally.

The British were embittered and frustrated by their lack of trade in central Africa. Leopold, in breach of the Berlin agreement to grant permission to private concessionists in certain areas of the Congo, now imposed heavy import duties. Foreign traders in general were effectively excluded from the Free State, often by force of arms. In 1895 an English trader, Charles Stokes, working in the southeast area of the Congo Basin, was arrested by Captain Lothaire as a gun runner. Stokes was summarily tried, with no hope of appeal, and hanged. The British Government was outraged, all the more so when an American missionary, John B. Murphy, reported that Stokes had been trading with the natives, a practice which, it seems, was punishable by death. Trade was effectively limited only to the State. The Belgians thus held a monopoly in the ever-increasing, and extremely lucrative, rubber trade.

Information was received about the Belgians' methods of rubber collection: "Each town and district is forced to bring in a certain quantity to the headquarters of the *Commissaire* every Sunday. Rubber is collected by force; the soldiers drive the people into the bush to collect it. If they will not go, they are shot down, and their left hands cut off and taken as trophies to the *Commissaire*." About one pence per pound was given the *Commissaire* on all the rubber he collected. The severed hands of men, women and children, proof that overseers were doing their job by catching slackers, were often smoked to preserve them until they could be shown to the *Commissaire*, according to a Swedish missionary's report of 1897.

None of these atrocities was "unusual" in the Congo Free State. It was a nightmarish place. Casement's uncle, Edward Bannister, Vice Consul in Loanda in 1892 with responsibility for the Congo territories, reported that British subjects from West African colonies were being employed illegally as sentries to ensure the collection of rubber. If they were lax in their duties they were flogged. The Consul was told, when he reported this to the Foreign Office, to confine himself to *commercial* questions. Later, Bannister, alerted that West Africans were being illegally brought into the Congo to work, boarded a ship in order to examine the documents of the passengers. The Belgian authorities were found guilty of trafficking in illegal labor and duly fined. Bannister, an obvious troublemaker, was asked to resign by the Foreign Office, even though the Congo Free State admitted to an illegal act and promised to stop employing British subjects from West Africa as sentries. Leopold's agents simply ignored the growing international outrage and went on with business.

Arthur Parminter gave Reuters an interview in which he described watching the ongoing deterioration of the Congo population. West African sentries, hired for a term of seven years, were responsible for the pursuit of escaping natives—de facto slaves. When they returned from a foray they would hold up a string of severed ears as proof of their success and receive congratulations from the *Commissaire*. Edward Glave (who would die in an attempt to follow in the footsteps of Stanley's explorations) also wrote a revealing report which unfortunately fell into the hands of the Free State. Some of Glave's papers survived, however, and were published in the *Century Magazine* in 1897. The Free State, he wrote, was "wringing rubber from these people without paying for it." Natives were flogged with a *chicotte*—a whip made of hippo hide in the shape of a corkscrew, its edges as sharp as knife blades. Escape brought mutilation or death, he added, confirming the findings of Parminter and others. Casement remembered Glave with affection, and wrote a poem on his death.

"The officials are but men," was one excuse made for the perpetrators of these atrocities by Casement's former employers in the Free State. King

Leopold could hardly be blamed, as Stanley implied in the introduction written to a book on the Congo by his protégé Guy Burrows: "what great gratitude the civilized world owes to King Leopold—for his matchless sacrifices on behalf of the inhabitants of the region.... [W]ho can doubt that God chose the King for his instrument to redeem this vast slave park?"

There was now a powerful reform movement in the House of Commons. Lord Salisbury, acting under pressure from the Anti-Slavery Society, opened a special Congo Atrocities File. An official investigation was called for. Casement would not in any case be sent to prepare such a document—Major Pulteney was now Consul there. Reports indicated that trade was being channeled through Matadi and Boma, load after load of rubber arriving on its way to Antwerp. The import-export figures were strangely skewed. The few imports coming into the Congo were mostly guns and ammunition. The Upper Congo was effectively cut off from the civilized world. Forced labor had replaced slavery. The profits of the rubber concession run by Lothaire reached well over four million francs per annum.

But the protection of the African aborigines would have to wait.

2

Trouble was looming in South Africa. On 29 July 1898 Casement was transferred as Consul for the Portuguese possessions of West Africa, based in São Paulo de Loanda (where his uncle Edward had preceded him). However, on 9 October 1898 the Boer War erupted and he was reassigned immediately to Lourenço Marques, a more strategic post—vital to the Boers as the only port available to them for the import of military supplies. It was Consul Casement's job to keep an eye on the shipments of arms.

Casement wanted to take a more active part in the war. While in Lourenço Marques he put together a plan for a military expedition to blow up the railway line to Pretoria to stop arms arriving in the Transvaal from Delagoa Bay. A contingent of 540 officers and men was dispatched to Swaziland, accompanied by Casement. But Milner suddenly called the maneuver off and recalled them. Casement would be awarded the Queen's South African Medal for his efforts in the war.

Casement was assigned at Cape Town as Intelligence Officer after the aborted expedition. (Cape Town was not a bad assignment for the young Irishman, given his tastes in well-hung boys and the notorious reputation for sodomy enjoyed by the area.)

Returning to Lourenço Marques would, Casement considered, be a nightmare: he had grown to loathe the place, and the populace was incensed with the colonial powers. Crowds were stoning the British consulate and persecuting its local employees. The consular quarters were also a mess—the iron ceilings rusting and dribbling debris over the furniture, papers and workers, ruining books and pictures, the floor sagging. Casement had tried to get away from this trash heap. For example, after dawdling at Pretoria for some time on vacation in 1897, he had suddenly demanded home leave, claiming he had to have an operation. Not that he was totally isolated in Lourenço Marques: he had made friends with two Irish peers, Lord ffrench and Lord Ennismere, as well as with Count Blücher whom he would meet later in Berlin, a German with an English wife. Blücher later, in his memoirs, reported what was probably his own vaguely biased opinion of Casement: "All I can say from personal experience, and long friendship, is that I always found [Casement] sympathetic, clever and fascinating ... an exceptional personality. He possessed an absolutely genuine though somewhat exaggerated idealism; nothing whatever would stop him assisting the weaker against the stronger, because he simply could not help it."

In spite of his frustrations and feelings of ennui, Casement never ceased to carry out his consular duties with (often excessive) zeal. The correspondent Poulteney Bigelow said that Casement's flow of information showed that he was the sort of man who was "everlastingly exploring and extricating himself from every imaginable difficulty by superhuman tact, wit and strength.... Mr. Casement knows more of the natives between Basutoland and the shores of Mozambique than any other white man."

But the consular routine was paralyzingly dull: "I find it a severe strain upon my time and temper ... to be forced ... to interview anyone, whether white or Indian, who called throughout the long day at the consulate, often upon trifling business or in quest of unimportant details, sometimes being even compelled to rise from bed when ill to listen to a drunken sailor's complaint, or the appeal to my charity of a distressed British subject."

Since 1897 there had been ever-louder complaints—voiced in the House of Commons—about the sorry state of affairs in the Congo. The Anti-Slavery League and the Aborigines Protection Society had come together to demand an official inquiry. Sir Charles Dilke's speech of 2 April of that year was particularly telling—but had absolutely no effect on the Belgians, who considered the English, quite rightly, to be meddling in their affairs.

The internal conditions in the Congo Free State were not normally within the range of consular involvement, nor was a British Consul responsible for reporting violations of civil rights. A consul, indeed, was in place mainly to protect British subjects in the State, and Casement's first chore was to officially ensure the rights of some workers from British West Africa who had been hired for construction projects. Casement was part of the British Establishment, and was so considered by officials in the Free State and also by King Leopold, who desired good relations with British officialdom. In 1900 the king invited Casement to visit him in Brussels while on his way home on leave.

On 10 October King Leopold received HM Consul graciously, as a former employee. Casement shared the king's hospitality with the Duke of Aosta and Prince Victor-Napoleon, The next day a private interview was arranged, during which Leopold made numerous excuses for the state of affairs in the Congo. Casement was not impressed—though no doubt he had been thoroughly impressed by the high-flying individuals he had become acquainted with at the court.

3

Casement's leave had been arranged because he was ailing. His health continued to be affected by the appalling climate. The list of his complaints is familiar: intermittent fever, extreme fatigue, anal bleeding, intestinal complaints.

On 20 August 1900 he was appointed Consul at Kinshasa in the Congo Free State, a position which now put him on a completely different plane in his relations with Leopold and his officials. The Belgians were frantically squeezing the territory of ivory and wild rubber, enslaving whole segments of the native population. In January 1901 Casement was in Kinshasa, carrying out semi-official investigations of the atrocities perpetrated by Leopold's agents. He was still ailing, however, and was forced to return to England on sick leave by the end of the year. In London he was given additional consular responsibilities, increasing his authority to include part of the French Congo. He had numerous consultations with Sir Martin Gosselin and Gerald Spicer of the Foreign Office to discuss the disintegrating situation in the Congo. The campaign against King Leopold was gaining ground, encouraged by the efforts of journalist and reformer E. D. Morel (who would finally got together with Casement on 10 December 1903 for discussions concerning the Congo atrocities and the campaign for reform). Morel was interested in preventing humanitarian outrages and in abolishing the slave trade and other types of bondage common in Africa. The Belgian contagion was even spreading—the French were reported to be emulating the worst aspects of Leopold's administration in their territories. Morel and others in the Anti-Slavery Society and Aborigines Protection Society considered it essential to put a stop to mutilations, killings, enslavement and associated horrors. Their determined pressure on the Government finally brought powerful men around to their way of thinking.

It was of immediate interest to the British Government to preserve free trade in the Congo, or simply to allow trade. There was little evidence of free trade in the Free State: the state was in fact, as Casement wrote to Lord Lansdowne (who had succeeded Salisbury as Foreign Secretary), "the sole property of one individual, the King of the Belgians." But Lansdowne dawdled and mumbled. Morel and his associates saw no decision on the part of the British Government to interfere in the Congo; nor there was any action on the part of other nations. The Aborigines Protection Society, in view of the stagnating situation, called for a public meeting to be held at the Mansion House on 15 May 1902. The turnout was massive. A resolution was passed calling for the signatories of the Berlin accord to redeem their pledges.

Still the British government hemmed and hawed, worried mostly about the commercial situation, unwilling to antagonize the Belgians.

Roger Casement was always interested in Trade. Trade had been his main interest as HM Consul in Africa, and, in another sense, "trade" had always been his personal concern after office hours. He carried on a vigorous and varied sex life with young men picked up, casually, on the streets. These entertainments went (supposedly) unsuspected by his friends, superiors and associates in the consular service. Casement was assuredly not the only British homosexual carrying on in outposts of the empire; but unlike the majority of his colleagues with the same, or similar, tastes he was addicted to noting down his affairs—tantalizingly brief, pertinent details of estimated cock size and payments, in diary form or in a cash ledger, carefully preserved, along with sketchy details of copulation.

In 1902, when so much was occurring in London which would affect him, Casement was trying—unsuccessfully—to regain his health. He dreaded the return to the Congo. But he did return, this time to a consulate housed in a hut at Boma, which seemed a punishment instead of a post. Soon after reaching Boma he heard of some Sierra Leone men in the Matadi jail, where they were held under grisly conditions. He investigated. Of the twelve originally imprisoned seven died and one escaped. The four remaining were housed in a cell with a cement floor and no bedding, and during the day they worked on a chain gang. They were still wearing the clothes they had on when arrested. Casement managed to get the men repatriated. Lansdowne expressed his disinterest.

In December Consul Casement was recalled to London. He managed to recuperate during this period during a getaway to Ireland, where he had often spent his leave with his family, often giving financial support to his brothers, and to his problematical sister Nina who would later emigrate to America. He also saw his good friend Richard Morten. He cruised Ireland and the London streets successfully. By February 1903 he was off again for the Congo. It would be his last trip out.

The 1903 Diaries

On his way back to the Congo he paused in the Canaries, a familiar stopover, where he enjoyed himself at the casino, socializing with "excellent society," dining out, chatting, playing bridge—and pursuing boys. In spite of his ill health, he was getting buggered regularly, sometimes in the same locales where he was getting buggered eighteen years before as a young man just beginning his career in Africa.

The Lett's diaries for the year 1903 and part of 1904 are invaluable records of a vanished world. Copies of these diaries were distributed to government officials and journalists in 1916, when Casement was being charged with high treason. The pages are starred with X, a shorthand symbol for copulation.

In London, on 14 February he was busy writing, lunching with friends and going to tea with his sister Nina, saying his good-byes and buying supplies for the trip. Then, on 17 February, a day of "bright and glorious sunshine," he had lunch with Nina and observed some troops from Parliament in the Park. Then there comes what must have been a startling entry for those who first combed through the diaries.

February 17th. Writing, then club, dinner with H[erbet].W[ard], then walk, papers (saw enormous, youthful).

On 18 February he did his banking and sent clothes—two packages, hatbox and trunk—to 55 Ebury Street where later his papers would be found and confiscated by Scotland Yard. After a stupid play, "Aladdin," with Nina it was home to bed. On the 19th he got his passage for the Cape Palmas run and saw a performance of *La Bohème*, his last outing in London.

February 20th. [After visiting his aunt to say farewell he heads home.] Back by Frederick St. at Sailor's Home, H. Abrahams from Demerara, 'Arthur' 11/ 6.… Medium, butmu ami, monene, monene, beh! beh!

On 21 February he sailed on the *Jebba*, a ghastly tub of the Elder Dempster Line. The weather was beastly, he writes, and the ship rolled fearfully. However, by the 27th the weather had improved and he was scribbling letters, both personal and to the Foreign Office, and looking forward to his arrival. The ship docked at Funchal at 7:30 on 28 February and he went ashore with immense anticipation. He immediately took his film to be developed at Perestrello's, a photography shop he knew from former years. The boy there had changed immensely, and for the better.

February 28th. Perestrello as in September 1897, on 'Scott' with photos. Grown tall, eyes beautiful, down on lip, curls. On shore with Reid to Careno [Hotel]. At café in square, and coffee and offered.… [After lunch with Bailey, walked in the Alameda], types, dark, distressful, then gardens at 4.… Out at 8 to Old Town, same place as in Feb. 1885, 18 years go, then to Square. Two offers, one doubtful, the other got cigarettes, same I think as in Alameda in afternoon.

In the evening, he had a couple of whiskeys and visited the Casino—as he would daily—and lost one milreis on roulette. On 1 March he made social visits, went to gamble at the Casino again, and cruised the avenues.

March 2nd. Delightful, beautiful creature coming down by stream at tramlines.… 19—cigarettes—clubfoot.

He turned in early, visited the Square off and on, marked time until his voyage out.

March 4th. Smoked too much y'day. Walked up hill to Mount Church. Beautiful there. John Hughes, an Irishman, at Hotel. Beautiful types at Carro and Belmonte [hotels]. Stayed all day there, lunching with Reids, nice waiters.

March 5th. After lunch to Mount by train, beautiful not there.

March 6th. Young P in cab Belmonte Hotel. Looked camera, took photo, asked, White said Homas de Arminestreda Veirra ... Walked about all day. Beautiful there. José, Correiro de Monte.

March 7th. Went Perestrello's with roll of film for developing to try and get [photos for boy of] Veirra de Machicos done, asked his address. Told out by Groves Hotel, so walked there. Quinta Nures. Lovely spot.... [Then afterwards to Perestrello's again, to ask for Machicos address in Funchal.] Saw very beautiful near Casino at shop door and again at bridge when going back to lunch ... Tomorrow and Agostinho about 17 ½, segunda feira [for the second time].

In the evening he went to Grove's Hotel at 9 for dinner and saw many people there, dancing and gambling. He dropped a couple of pounds at the tables and then went on to Connelly's where he met the lieutenant from the *Don Carlos*. "[S]plendid. Then suivant in gardens with Senhora—Quinta? Bestante there. Miente frio, many times $4,000." His assignation with Agostinho for the next day was, however, to be frustrated, much to his chagrin. On 8 March he went back to the Mount with the photos for the Veirra boy; he visited the *Don Carlos* and later went to the Casino for dinner and to play roulette (losing $2,500).

March 8th. Back [from Casino] walking lovely night. No sign of Agostinho. Waited long.

March 9th. Beautiful morning, waiting all morning for Veirra de Machicos but no visit. [To the Casino. Then out afterwards.] Many types, two Ruada Carreira up to S. Pedro and there ... sailor.... Walked home stranded and strong. Lovely night. No Agostinho.

March 10th. To Club. Many beauties there, exquisite eyes.... In Square most of day. [At Casino] came away with 30/-clear and all expenses paid. Home met Alvaro and $2,000 poor boy, 19, is a clerk in an office. Mother a seamstress.

March 11th. [Up to Mount.} At Belmonte, waiter said had given letter to Veirra who would come to Careno to thank me.

March 12th. Went up Mount to Belmonte.... Left four photos for Veirra with waiter and noon and card.

He was socializing a great deal, meeting upper class Britishers, among them the young Duke of Montrose, and playing hard at the Casino, losing and winning intermittently the usual trifling sums. It was raining in Funchal.

March 13th. [In bed till 12. Raining. Visits, meals, Casino, theater, boredom. Then a marvelous meeting.] Agostinho kissed many times. 4 dollars.

March 14th. In bed till 12. [Then to Convent and Cemetery (a popular cruising spot) and to Casino.] Portuguese beauties there.

He is a little worried about his funds being down to about twenty dollars, but his life style is typically comfortable and his habits generous.

March 15th. Still raining. Agostinho and whiskers. [A quick account of his expenditures to date shows a gift of $1000 to Club Foot, obviously a bad investment, and of $5000 to Agostinho, who was much more deserving.] Then after dinner Agostinho, splendid.

On 16 March he was not well and stayed in bed almost all day, but went to the Casino in the evening. On the next day something unpleasant occurred, it appears.

March 17th. Club foot a traitor.

March 18th. Boarded ship for Grand Canary.

March 19th. Going to Grand Canary on the worst ship I've been on yet. Vile Germans on board.

March 20th. Arr. at Las Palmas 7.30. To S. Catalina, charming. Old waiters' faces just same, all welcome one, Swanston at door. To town by tram, many beautiful, out with Swanston [and after dinner to] Cathedral Square. Beautiful and then on bridge followed. No offers. Saw one, that one. Home at 10.15 on foot.

March 21st. Juan 20. [Arrived at Tenerife at 4 p.m. he found letters waiting for him at the Consulate, one from brother Tom who was complaining as usual of business deceptions and money troubles.] Some types at pier head on landing. [W]ent downtown. Filled with Spaniards on Square. Home [by way of] Plaza de Constitución. Sat down and then to waste ground. Came X ..., not shaved, about 21 or 22, gave pesetas 13 about, to meet tomorrow.

March 22nd. Went to Laguna by tram. Broke down. Inocencio there.... Down by 6 tram. Many beautiful in the day. In evening to Square, to Band. Beautiful in white, exquisite.

March 23rd. Fair hair, blue eyes, brown clothes, round about 17.... Enormous at 10 o'clock in Square.... Dined with Olsens, nice waiters. After to Plaza to Avidiva by new road. X ... mu mua ami. Mal umi maudi matuvia brambit, gidkili. 25 note and 13 pesetas.

He was suffering a great deal from the usual seediness. On 24 March he was not well at all. He had gone to the W.C. eleven times, with what looked like dysentery; he was passing a great deal of blood. John barked all night, keeping him awake.

March 25th. X ... 'Mucho amigo' X.... Not at all well. Very bad night between 'John' and dysentery lying down nearly all day. [Dr. Otto had advised him not to go to the Congo, considering the precarious state of his health. However, in the afternoon he was feeling slightly better, so he decided to go out, recklessly.] In street and to Avenida. Juan mua mu ami diaka N. sono 18 p. 20 yrs. Back to Olsens. Pepe, 17, bought cigarettes mucho duen, dia tidiaka moko mavabela mu muami mucho mucho bueno fiba, fiba, X ..., p. 16.

March 26th. Lauro his name. [He made a visit to the *Anversville* on getting up. The Captain will give him the best cabin on board. He went onto the ship about 10:30 after leaving his card on Dom Paco.] Photograph boys there. Bought L same as last year but grown most exquisite. M. Violetta at the Las Palmas, but this one on 'Anversville' too last year. Smiled often. Gave 2,100 p.

in copper. Left Santa Cruz at 11.15 about. Steamed splendidly.... Thought of Pepe X and his pellos of y'day.

On 17 March they were steaming splendidly indeed, making 312 miles by noon, when Casement got up. He read *Le Temps* and stayed in bed most of the day. The trade winds were blowing gently.

March 28th. Manuel Violetta at Jordao Perestrello.... The voyage like all on this Coast is very wearisome. [He makes notes, meanwhile, on the British elections.]

March 29th. Lauro of Santa Cruz. Manuel Violetta gone to Las Palmas. Pepe and Juan again. Stayed in cabin. Feeling very seedy. Bleeding badly after as in Santa Cruz.

It was much hotter as the trip continued, and on 30 March he passed his time sweltering in his cabin, writing letters and musing about the boys.

March 31st. Pepe of Guimar at Tenerife 17. Read Loti's 'Mon Frère Yves.' B boy on board. Read 'Smart Set', very hot indeed. [Poor John was sick with the heat.]

On 1 April in hot weather they passed near Cape Palmas while Casement continued reading trash (*Les Carnets du Roi* "stupid exposition of a beast king"). Then on 2 April the weather became "lovely clear soft, blue delicious sea." There were only about 900 miles left to Banana. On 3 April he writes, "We shd be in Banana by noon on Monday with luck, but Skipper Lovejoy says he cannot enter after 1.30 p.m.... so mardi matin. Alas." His reading was now *La Double Maitresse* by Henri de Regnier. When 4 April came there was a tornado and he notes that there are only 572 miles left to Banana. He is very tired of the ship. On the fifth there was more furious weather and the captain now said that they could not possibly make the Congo until Tuesday morning. After the Regnier novel, he went on to read Marie Corelli's *Soul of Lilith*—light reading indeed.

April 6th. XX. "Accra" enormous in. Beautiful morning. Congo water.... At 12.30 saw the tree-top by Red Point on Cabinda, only 44 miles to Banana.

Captain says will try to go in. Monrovian ... Down and oh! oh!, quick, about 18. Arrived Banana at 4.30.

April 7th. Did not sleep last night. Left Banana at 8.30 for Boma, struck twice on sand, last time badly. Did not see "Accra" again.... Kenboys of Cape Palmas, only a few there. Walked a bit. Lots of letters.

On 8 April he was on board the *Tarquati* headed for Malella and Banana, and from there to Loanda at 5 p.m.

April 9th. Arr. Loanda. [He dined at Julio Caesar's with its "clean waiter" and mentioned an Angolesi lad, but noted that there was "nothing interesting."]

On 10 April he was writing the eternal letters to the Foreign Office and was unable to sleep, sitting up with John. The next day he was at Ambriz and left at noon, eating no food all day. The boat was "dirty and rotten lot on board". On 12 April they arrived at Cabinda, as dead as Loanda and Boma. Everyone was sick and the mosquitoes were vicious.

April 13th. Beautiful morning, getting rooms ready.... This day last year I arrived at Lisbon, and curls and ... in Avenida.

April 14th. This day last year. Another beautiful morning sun and clear. Weather cooled agreeable, got very hot.... Heavy rain and lightning.

On 15 April the boredom continued. He received letters, did busy work, and went to bed after 10 p.m. to read Conan Doyle's "Mystery of Cloomber" which he considered rather good. The next day he wrote the Foreign Office, got a bottle of Irish whiskey and turned in tired.

April 17th. HMS "Odin" arr. Brought news of Sir Hector MacDonald's suicide in Paris. The reasons given are pitiably sad. The most distressing case this surely of its kind and the one that may awake the national mind to saner methods of curing a terrible disease.

General Sir Hector Macdonald was a self-made man. A Scottish crofter's son and a draper's apprentice, he enlisted in the ranks at seventeen in 1870. Stationed in India for some nine years, he was made lieutenant after the Battle of Kandahar (for which he was decorated). He fought in the Afghan war with "Bob"—Field Marshall Lord Roberts—on the march to Kabul. By 1887 he was captain in the Egyptian army. Then, during the war against the Mahdists, he gained fame for his heroism at Omdurman (where we last saw him). Although secretly married and with a son, he had separated from his wife. His "best friend" was a schoolboy from Aberdeen, Alaister Robertson, whose picture he kept with him always. He was at the unfortunate battle of Majuba Hill in 1881 against the Boers. He rose to colonel during the Boer War. He was named honorary ADC to Queen Victoria and later to Edward VII.

In 1902, Macdonald was appointed Commander-in-Chief of British forces in Ceylon. The general, like Casement, was bored speechless by the vacuities of his position and the dullness of the locale. However, there were compensations, notably among the natives, in a culture where pederasty was, if not totally accepted, commonly tolerated. There were catamites at the temples. There were male entertainers—dancing boys—in the rest houses. The charming waiters at the Grand Oriental Hotel were often obliging. There were naked adolescents swimming on the beaches and available for occasional sodomy. There were even Tamil boy prostitutes working the docks in Colombo. You could include the countless slim and attractive children in normal society—often under the age of ten—anxiously willing to have sex or to be observed doing so.

Macdonald soon became friends with the prosperous de Satan family. Some of the planters gossiped among themselves that, inexplicably, the General spent a great deal of time with the two de Satan boys. Rumors circulated as well about a club which Macdonald patronized—whose members included many British and Sinhalese young men of distinctly dubious character. Ceylon was a closed community; gossip, as usual in such circumstances, was the major pastime.

Then, the well-known story: A British tea planter accidentally opened the door of the wrong railway carriage at Kandy and was aghast to discover General Macdonald, half in and half out of "civilian" clothes, having a session of mutual masturbation with three Sinhalese boys. The planter immediately spread the story. In February 1903 a group of outraged clergymen and schoolmasters presented their charges to the governor, Sir Joseph West Ridgeway. In fact, the governor was already aware of such activities—there had been other similar charges which had been hushed up for fear that, if they became known, they would bring down a wave of accusations not only against the Commander-in-Chief but other well-placed individuals. The governor claimed that as many as seventy witnesses could have testified that Macdonald was having sex with numerous schoolboys.

Governor Ridgeway (whose own son may have been a member of Macdonald's intimate circle) wrote that most of the general's victims were "the sons of the best known men in the colony, English and Native." One of the boys had "gone off his head" with anxiety—not from the sexual perversity, no doubt, but from fear that his parents (and everyone else) would find out. Silence was called for. The governor sent Macdonald home, saying that if the general had remained a few days longer the clergy and planters and others who had formed a Vigilance Committee in Colombo would have taken action and a warrant would have been issued for his arrest.

What would Macdonald have gained by staying? "He knew his case to be helpless," the governor wrote. "There was just the chance he might be allowed to retire. If not, suicide remained the only alternative. My action has been so far successful that the revolting details of the case have not transpired and need not transpire unless the poor man's friends are very indiscreet. The danger is that they provoke revelations. However I shall continue to ensure silence."

If the facts came out the resulting scandal might have implicated countless prominent individuals and even, perhaps, the British army. The ramifications were frightening. The governor advised the Commander-in-Chief to take six months off. He advised Field Marshal Roberts who admitted, on hearing of the accusations, that he had known that Macdonald had been given to "quaint practices" in South Africa. Roberts demanded that Macdonald be court marshaled. In London he informed the general that he would have to return to Ceylon to undergo trial. The king met with the accused hero before he left. Macdonald would be allowed to proceed to Paris on his way back to Colombo.

Ridgeway at this point publicly announced in Colombo that serious charges were being bought against General Macdonald and that he would be returning to Ceylon to be court-marshaled. This sensational bit of news was snapped up by the *New York Herald*. The story was published in its Paris edition where Macdonald, putting up at the Hotel Regina, read it the same day. He committed suicide immediately.

Suicide was what the authorities in London and Colombo had most desired, and probably counted on. The Macdonald file was thus closed—probably destroyed—and along it the ramifications it might have had throughout the empire.

Although Casement spoke of Macdonald suffering from a "disease"—a common attitude of the times—he presumably referred, in his diary entry, to the degenerate state of the general's personality. He certainly did not blink at the fact that very young boys were involved (some "victims" were twelve years old, though Macdonald preferred them with pubic hair). Casement himself did not suffer from guilt on that score. His diaries document sexual activities with boys as young as eleven. He did not believe himself in any way tainted by his habits, common in all the parts of the world he knew. Such activities were generally accepted outside Britain. His tastes were a fact of his life, sometimes risky, but by no means "abnormal."

2

Casement went back to his customary consular round, bored as usual—playing tennis (badly, he admitted) and sometimes billiards in the evening—and receiving complaints from British citizens. Fever and craw craw and hemorrhoids were bothering him, the old malaria and bloody stool. He contemplated retirement, but had no money; there was no possibility of pension.

Meanwhile, in London the public outcry against the Congo atrocities could not be stifled. During an especially rancorous House of Commons debate on 20 May 1903, Herbert Samuel brought a motion demanding a conference of the signatories of the Berlin Act. Moved by this assertiveness, Lord Lansdowne sent what was for him an "emphatic" note to King Leopold concerning the matter. The king took his time replying, but finally sent an insulting reply to the British government reminding them of their own dismal colonial record. He noted, as a matter of interest, that Congo trade had increased from ten million francs in 1895 to fifty million francs in 1902, certainly proof of beneficial rule.

Rankled by this reply, the Foreign Office decided to mount a special inquiry concerning the prevailing conditions of the Free State. Casement, as the expert on site, was given responsibility for the investigation and for writing the subsequent report. The American Baptist Mission offered its steamboat, the *Henry Reed*, to help the consul in his task.

The question of confronting the Belgian government with any kind of ultimatum was out of the question at this point. There had to be proof of wrongdoing, as well as an expression of international outrage. Casement would document the atrocities. Accusations against the Belgians, he would find, were invariably founded in fact, in spite of accusations by Leopold's mouth-pieces that they were blatant hearsay.

Later, after reading Casement's report, the unimaginative Lord Lansdowne would declare, with uncharacteristic warmth, "Proof of the most painfully convincing kind, Mr. Casement!"

Casement as a consequence of his investigations suffered from "insinuations" as he called them, on the part of Leopold's men. These were passed on to the Foreign Office. He wasn't worried. "All men are snobs—and they worship assurance and position," he wrote in a letter. "The men I have scorn for are not these—the jackals—but the King of Beasts and his pimps.")

Casement for a while was happy to be back in Africa. In a letter to Richard Morten some time later he says, "The best thing was the Congo, because there was more against me there and far cleverer rascals."

The days rolled on, as they usually did, full of correspondence, inane consular duties and socializing. On 18 April he noted dogfights and headache. On 19 April the rain continued hard and he mentions that he is "Very sorry at Hector Macdonald's terrible end." On the 20th, he was reading *Reminiscences of an Irish R. M.* and finding the book "delicious." He bought four suits cheap. On the 21st he felt extremely tired after another bad night of mosquitoes and other horrors—specifically, a centipede in his bed. He notes on the following day that he could not sleep due to the centipede incident, "Huge thing all over mosquito curtain and then it disappeared and I lay in dread." On the following days he was immersed in routine chores, calling on the Governor, suffering from heat, going for swims and playing snooker.

April 29th. Fever on me—all thro' night. First attack since I came out. Took 16 grains quinine and lay down till 3 p.m.

He decided to travel up the Congo on the *Hirondelle*, which had arrived in port on the 29th. He packed everything and left Cabinda at 9 a.m. of the 30th, arriving in Banana at 4 p.m. John was sick again. They gave him a dreadful room at the hotel in Banana. The sandflies were horrendous and he did not close his eyes all night. Again he adds, "Hector Macdonald's death very sad."

Arriving at Boma from Banana on 1 May, he began the usual routine. He played tennis and billiards to relax from official duties. He worried about John and his canine ills. Letters poured in from the Foreign Office, some of them indicating a growing concern in England about the Belgian Congo situation.

From 2 May the days follow one another dismally. He suffers from the mosquitoes and complains about the constant heavy rains. On the 4th he went into the consulate to work, instead of using his bedroom. On the 5th he walked with "K.B." of Cow, "splendid." He played billiards, determined to improve his game. He received visitors and complaints in his consular capacity. John continued to be sick. He himself was not well, which might have explained in part his ghastly game of tennis and his losses at billiards.

May 9th. A lovely night. "John" ever so much better. "Craw, Craw" troubling me dreadfully.

On the 10th he went to examine the land for the construction of the new consulate. "Beautiful evening. Moon glorious." Then on the 11th he hired masons, wrote letters, sent money off—depressed by the hopelessness of his brother Tom's financial predicament. On the 12th it was a "military musical" morning. Later he played tennis, complaining about his nervous service, then in the evening billiards. Then a note: "Tall, 'How much money?'"

Darkness, rain and busy work. Billiards and tennis continue to take up his free time. On the 14th he gives a champagne breakfast to Trust, his billiards partner, who is now leaving for another post. The same day he receives two important wires from the Foreign Office, indicating that they are finally taking action. By the 16th he notes that both his tennis and his billiard games are improving. He was, perhaps out of ennui, drinking too much beer. He was also out strolling almost every night. On the 18th he "walked till 1 a.m. Stiff evening…. 'How much?' and cigarettes."

May 19th. Saw pelicans at 5.30 p.m. Out on land all morning. [Later more billiards and more beer. The seasons now seem to be changing.]

On 20 May he notes "Dry season, morning cool and excellent." The pelicans, he adds, never fail. Articles on the Congo are appearing in the international press, which is encouraging. After preparing dispatches all day on the 21st, he decides to go to Matadi on the *Albertsville*. On the 22nd, he makes a significant brief note: "X. Left Boma." (This after having getting his hair and beard trimmed for the first time since being on board the *Anversville* at the end of March.

Arrived at Matadi, he finds it is the same old hole. On the 23rd he enjoyed another beautiful morning after having passed a bad night. He bought a bottle of whiskey and left Vanadium with Sims to experiment with on cases. On the 24th he notes the Old Queen's birthday. On the 25th he complains of another bad night and pitiful crying of a dog which had been castrated. "Old P castrated it, he tells me. The boys not castrated, say they are 'Kaidi bene for poor Tinker.'" The South African War medal arrived for him, he mentions with disinterest, via the Foreign Office, on the 26th. On the 27th and 28th the weather continued lovely. He was reading a Foreign Office report on the hardships inflicted on British subjects in Africa. John's health seemed to be improving. He composed dispatches, read old Blue Books on the Congo Treaty of 1882 and '83 with Portugal which never came off, also old correspondence between the English Government and the Belgians concerning recruitment of native workmen on the West Coast. On the 31st he walked to the prison: "just the same as last year. No change save whitewash. No beds, looked in one of the three cells. Bare cement, blankets rolled upon it. Saw no jailer, three police in yard at back."

On 1 June his life goes on in a coma of official duties, writing the Foreign Office, hearing complaints (none of which got any satisfaction from him). The down-and-outers are "often a rotten bad lot." He yarned with the doctor until 9:30 after a walk into Matadi town.

June 2nd. Very cold grey morning. Read Irish magazines. In night dreamed splendid plot of novel, got up at 3 a.m. and sketched it out, wd make splendid story.

The 3rd was a beautiful day and the boat from Boma brought two Foreign Office wires, one in unintelligible government code, the other in cypher, an Africa report about the mismanagement of the Congo. He now determined to go to the interior as soon as possible and to send reports off soon. "The debate in Commons has been terrible attack on Congo States."

June 5th. Left at 7 a.m. [He took supplies of potatoes, onions and rice.] The country a desert, no natives left. [Sleeping sickness was rampant in the area but the decline in population may also have been due to forced transport of natives.] Beautiful cool at Tumba. Dined Alreo. Lovely Ntombe.

June 6th. Left Tumba at 6.30, cold and nice. [A number of] Sona and Grunga splendid. High wind and cool. Congo men now in line instead of coast men, latter very few I'm glad to say.

From the Sale valley to Kinshasa and Leopoldville there was no sign of improvement in the country or the people, "except for a few broader paths to the water, where we swam of old." At Kinshasa there were friendly settlers and comfortable accommodation and the weather was good except for a drenching cold mist on the 8th. On the following three days he wrote and sent dispatches and met with Childs, the Vice Consul at Zanzibar who was on a special mission in the territory and with whom he was able to send off official correspondence. He saw Childs off on the 15th. He received letters from Boma and noted that things were going ahead with the imposition of the Foreign Office, encouraged by his dispatches. He was busy correcting Lord Lansdowne's draft proposal to Brussels and further reports including one on the police at Boma. He often wrote until after midnight. "I have got through a lot of writing for F.O. of late," he notes. "It would make a big book if published."

On the 18th he went to Kinshasa on foot and received a copy of *Punch*, sent by his cousin Gee, which carried an article on the Congo Free State. On the 19th and 20th he writes about the native hospital, "It is far worse than the thing at Boma. Deplorable. I never saw anything like it." There were terrible attacks on the Congo Government in the *West African*. More letters from Tom had arrived, begging for money, "a sorry business for him." On the 21st he spent the morning at church and in palavers with some locals, then visited the cataracts with a group of English travelers and also the hospital again, "The same terrible spectacle," which shocked the women. On the 22nd he was staying with the Gordons at their Mission house, "very comfy," and then on the 23rd received an offer of free passage on a private ship to Chumbiri, which he accepted. On the 24th Dr. Villa sent his boat and he crossed to Brazzaville, which he found a charming place. "It is the beginning of a town, not as at Leo[poldville] only great Govt. factory." He called on the Vice Governor of the French Congo the next day. He liked the Governor. Brazzaville was better in most ways than Leopoldville and there was more freedom there. After consular business he visited Dr. Villa, a charming man, who told him of a recent visit to Molunda where the people on seeing a white man all ran away and had to be coaxed back. Much of Casement's time was involved with taking testimony from various individuals. He got food poisoning. He suffered from ill health in general.

July was taken up by the same intense and repulsive work. On 1 July he heard of the Belgian monster Duprez, going home first class after the slaughter of Cellumbiri.

July 2nd. After lunch with Dr. Villa at 2.30 got off round French bank. Beautiful Dover cliffs, lovely view. Camped on Island in Pool at 6.30 about. Hippo downstream. Saw three pelicans feeding, close to us. Also saw a beautiful Egyptian ibis, black body, white wings; a lovely fellow in full flight over us for his home in the woods below Dover cliffs, white-winged too.

The 2 July entry is an unusual one since he rarely makes any kind of direct observation of natural phenomena. Diaries are curious things; they often display characteristics that are unintentional. "Secret" diaries are especially interesting, but different individuals have different kinds of secrets. Charles Darwin, for example, kept a secret diary, but its entries are very different from Casement's. Darwin is concerned to keep his religious doubts a secret, to keep his flashes of truth to himself: "It is absurd," he writes in one heretical passage, "to talk of one animal being higher than another.... People often talk of the wonderful event of intellectual Man appearing—the appearance of insects with other senses is more wonderful." Of course his brother Erasmus, whose sexual identity was a mystery, no doubt had secrets more like Casement's, unless he was—as some claimed—simply neuter. Nearly all cultures, Peter Gay remarks, "draw some line, more or less distinct, between the personal and public spheres. But nineteenth-century middle-class culture was particularly emphatic about this, making the gulf between private and public as wide as it could manage. In such a culture the diary, or its expansive cousin, the journal, were bound to flourish." Casement was pre-eminently nineteenth century in his diary-keeping and his symptomatically humdrum relations of everyday life—except, of course, for the additional details such as the ones included below.

3

On 3 July they left camp at 6.45.... "Passed Robrick's Grove at 11, wood post at entrance to Pool. On past a state wood post—two French ones and a telegraph post to the bank at 10.30 about, where we anchored for the day, to get wood. Elephant hippo buffalo and antelope tracks, disturbing ibis. An antelope came down to drink in the evening. Passed State barge full of rubber towed by small steamer.

On the 4th he describes the crew of the ship—two Europeans, two wheels, two sounders, three firemen, one waterman, two greasers, seven woodcutters (there are usually a dozen), one sentry, one cook, one washerwoman, three boys, one headman, twenty-five natives. A sizable contingent. This is only one of many such steamers plying the Congo. The ship can carry 20 tons of cargo, exclusive of wood. The voyage continues on the following days.

They reached Chumbiri on the 7th. The place was much hotter than at the Pool, and Casement was happy to change clothes twice a day. He did not like Chumbiri, but met here "old Hairy Bill" who had had a queer life on the river and who will be taken on for the voyage. He now plans to go up river with the *Henry Reed* and hopefully to charter her from the Baptist Missionary Society for his voyage of investigation. On the 9th he was packing and writing official correspondence and getting ready to leave on the *Reed* the next day. He was glad to be leaving Chumbiri where the cuisine was ghastly: "Chicken, chicken, custard, custard, so every day come Sunday. Goddam."

Departure of the *Reed* was delayed because of some female passenger but at last they cast off and the same day reached Bolobo, a "regular town" with lots of people, before 7 p.m. (He notes that Hairy Bill is an excellent chap and a good worker.) In Bolobo he called on Miss de Hailes at her hospital. She complained of the State exactions on the natives. Back at ten from the gathering of the "silent damned" faithful, he could not sleep until 1:30 a.m. owing to the racket made by the Bolobo boys. "A regular Hell this place—by damn damn." On the 12th the goats began bleating at around five in the morning, an awful din. He made his way to church again—there were about 400 people in the congregation, mostly males. At noon he lunched with Miss de Hailes. He was not feeling well the next day, but nevertheless went down to the *Reed* at 10 a.m.

July 13th. All hard at work scraping and painting her. Basakas splendid types. Two magnificent. Hairy B. says he may go with me. I hope he doesn't mean to bring the apple of discord, that would be too much…. Besides sleeping and bathing, etc., nothing important. At State beach photo'd pier and Loanaga—about 9". Young probably Hansen's.

Casement traveled in an official capacity and his private life was rather circumscribed because of this fact. However, he did manage well.

July 14th. French National Fete. Thunder in night. Very cool breeze in morning. This must be Auntie's birthday. Poor wee soul. I will send her a present…. Prayers in evening. Decided not to take Bogindi, Hairy B. goes himself.

On the 15th the Captain called to say good-bye and made some strange remarks on Belgian officers. On the 17th the mails arrived and on the 18th he was busy with official correspondence. Everything meanwhile was in readiness on the *Reed*. The contract stipulated that he would be responsible for compensation if the boat was wrecked. This caused him brief concern. Getting ready to leave, he sent his aunt five pounds and dropped a line to Nina. The ship finally sailed at noon.

On the 21st he met with some Basingili refugees and heard the story of their ill treatment. They were at Lake Leopold now. He walked to various villages, investigating conditions, stopping to overnight in Impoko. He left Impoko for Bonginda at 8, bathing en route, and seeing more refugees. They reached Bolobo and left the next day, the 23rd, stopping at the wooding post on the Island on the French side of the river, where they saw game tracks (probably hippo) and where Casement chatted at length with the eminent missionary George Grenfell. The *Reed* was often stuck on sandbanks, or managed to nudge the shore, and sometimes they ran out of fuel, but the trip was generally free of disasters.

The depopulation of the Congo was astounding. At Lukolela only ninety-three out of many hundreds were left. "Spent pleasant day at Luk. Poor frail folk seeking vexed mortality—dust to dust ashes to ashes—where then are the kindly heart, the pitiful thought—together vanquished." At last on the 28th they struck off into what Casement called the "vague unknown." They reached Itoko, once the home of some 5000 natives, now with an alarmingly depleted population numbering about 600. It rained heavily. On the 31st they reached Bikoro with its State post where Casement met several witnesses of atrocities and saw the plantation that was part of the exploitation of the Domaine Privé: "A horrid business."

August 1st. [Suddenly a memory, in the midst of rain, John catching goats, the deadly chore of writing up a draft of his visit.] Roman soldier Coliseum. August 1900.

August 2nd. First to church and then ... X.

On the 3rd they left Itoko for Ituta. The *Reed* passed other steamers at all stages in their voyage. There was incredibly feverish commercial activity on the rivers, indecent when you consider that it was built on the exploitation, mutilation and enslavement of thousands of African natives. By 5 August Casement complains of fatigue, while still jotting down testimony from the natives. On the 7th he was writing up his notes. As they progressed the villagers would usually flee, but finding they were mission people soon returned. He notes that flogging seems to have stopped but depositions continue of major atrocities, "dreadful." At Bikoro on 13 August he learned that five people with hands cut off had come to show him, but hearing that he was to leave at daybreak they turned back and did not reach his camp. He dispatched a canoe, urging them to come on.

He was feeling sick, physically and emotionally. Few bright moments punctuated the trip. Once an officer admitted punishing soldiers severely for mistreating natives, but this was rare. The whole area was filled with ruined villages and ruined lives. On the 16th they spent a quiet day at Bolingi. Casement walked on to the native town and remembered the unfortunate E. J. Glave who had served with Stanley—Casement had met him while on the Sanford Expedition. Africa was a continent of suffering and misfortune.

August 20th. Left camp for Lulanga. Tube burst in boiler. Repaired.

On arriving at Lulanga he found letters from the Coast and down country. "Underwood V. Consul Boma congratulates me on my appointment to Lisbon." This is a surprising entry, and shows that he was aware that he had been earmarked for the consulship at Lisbon from this early date. Lisbon was considered a real plum of an appointment for a career man in the Foreign Service—but not for the likes of Casement, in spite of the intensity of the cruising there and the abundance of willing and well-hung boys. (He would later take the Lisbon post, reaching there in November 1904, but would stay only about a month. His rejection of the "generosity" of the Foreign Office would, in their eyes, be considered a slap in the face.)

On 21 August he took more testimony, noting the fine Bulele and Mongo people with their "good straight limbs and nice faces." It poured during the night and all morning of the 22nd. After more questionings he bought a leopard skin and took his leave of Bolongo ("dead") and went on to Banginda where he visited missionaries and their wives. He was finishing up Bentley's *Plunder of the Congo*. He walked into Boginda and further down, sleeping in a good room on shore. The morning of the 24th was lovely. "Three Stripi came standing looking at 'John' and 'Major' pulling incessantly, locus standi lussi."

This day he made a tourist purchase of sixteen black-dyed Bangola dresses and on the 25th left for Ijumi, noting that he was now reading a Guy Burrows book, probably *The Curse of Central Africa, and the Belgian Administration*, a sensational exposé which had led King Leopold to instigate a libel suit against the author. On the 26th he went up channel to Ijumi, then the next day entered Lulanga and proceeded upstream to the Ikau Mission. He met briefly with the Lowens and the Jeffreys, missionary couples. Taking leave of them, he was soon back aboard the *Reed* and plowing ahead in spite of snags and mist. On the 29th they were at the Kongo stream just below Ngwere. At Bongandanga he called on Lejesme and examined the rubber market which turned out to be nothing but guns—about twenty armed men were in evidence. "The popn. 242 men with rubber all guarded like convicts." The next day was quiet. He saw sixteen men, women and children tied up and at his intervention the youngsters were released. "Infamous, shameful system." The last day of the month was spent with the Lejesmes at a large plantation, where in the evening he attended a dance organized in his honor. "Poor souls. I was sorry for it, of all the forced enjoyment I ever saw this took the cake."

September 1st. My 39th birthday here up the Lopori in the heart of Africa indeed.... Terrible oppression of these poor people.

On 2 September he saw more prisoners and took testimony from many. The *Reed*, struggled slowly upstream for days. He hoisted the consular flag to avoid being stopped by government patrol boats. They many steamers and received letters indicating that things were moving ahead in England. On the 6th he met with wounded and mutilated people and took depositions; the witnessed overwhelmed him with their stories and implored his help. The country was beautiful and varied but he had few moments to observe it. On the 10th he notes the land beyond Ikilamba as "grassy plain with smoke of frivolous grasses hanging in trails." On the 11th he left for Stanley Pool and after a long run reached Bolobo. At the Pool he met Grenfell. After spending the night at Chumbiri he left on the 14th and on the 15th was at Brazzaville. He crossed over to Leopoldville at once and spent the whole night writing the Foreign Office. The next day he returned to Brazzaville on the *Reed*. There he heard shocking stories of the mutilation and ill-treatment of natives in the French Congo. The whole of Africa had seemed to have gone mad. He was "very tired and used up" due to the excitement and the emotions of the past few days. The *Reed* was leaking. Writing all day on the 17th in Brazzaville he asks himself what the future holds for him. His life seems like a nightmare journey into hell.

On the 18th good Dr. Villa called and cheered him up, listening to his story of what he had seen upriver. The doctor was furious on hearing about the atrocities Casement had witnessed and begged him to continue his work. In spite of headache, fever and now a nagging toothache, Casement went on writing, "wanting [sex] certainly" at the same time. He was complaining of deafness (due to so much quinine) and his eyes were troubling him, but not as much as they would later in the Putumayo. The food was depressing: "'Les Cloches de Corned Beef,' Opera in 365 Actes. The daily chop bill on the Congo.

On 21 September he finally left for Kinshasa and arrived there at 1:50, going to the Malets' to dinner. This is the day he gave poor John a "fearful hiding, broke my stick over him." His nerves were shot.

The diary entries for the next few days are brief, with writing, waiting, chatting with Dr. Villa, sending packages to Matadi and hoping that Hairy B. will arrive so they can get off. He sent the Lowens 18 bottles of beer. On the 24th he paid off the crew, "all good lads," and was ready to head for Matadi in the morning.

Arriving at Matadi at 3 p.m. on the 25^{th,} he was met by a contingent of several English settlers. In the evening he made a copy of the letter to the Governor General of the 12th in which he detailed the miserable condition of the interior. "Richard Koffee took letter at 9 p.m. and returned with answer and then we talked and he said 'Yes—true Massa, a big one and I swear God Sir,' and so to bed at last." Cryptic, as usual. Tired after writing most of the night, on the 27th he went by launch to Boma, arriving there at 5.15 p.m. and went straight to the consulate to bed, to sleep badly.

The next day it was on to Banana, and then on the 29th on the *Hirondelle* to Cabinda where he found little new in the sleepy town, visited his old quarters and holed up while it drizzled without cease.

October 1st. Sent Nisco a case of Port wine. To call on Gov. of Cabinda. Walked up Hill. Cabo Verde Sentry.

The *Benguela* arrived at 11 a.m. from Loanda on the 2 October. He booked passage for himself and three boys and John, a total of $30,500. The *Benguela* was, thank God, a comfortable ship and Masanba, Mawuki, Charlie and John all bunked together forward. They reached Ambriz in the morning of the 3rd

and Loanda at almost midnight. The next day he visited the consulate, climbing over the wall to get in. He promptly installed himself, sending a wire to the Foreign Office saying he would be staying several days. He dined with Dobritz, an old friend and the German Consul. After dinner they talked at length about the Congo. On the 5th he received a wire from the Foreign Office ordering him to stay at the Pool. He notes that Hardwick, a young entrepreneur, changed one pound of gold for $5,000—an excellent indication of exchange rates at the time.

October 6th. Beautiful day and night. Band in evening—walked and talked with Dobritz, Brock, etc.,…. Saw en route enormous with moustaches.

The days were pleasant now and he relaxed a bit, often feeling "hopelessly lazy." He dined out often with Nisco and Dobritz, chatting over whiskeys, going over to the Island to playing tennis, swimming. He notes listening to the band concerts in the evening, on the 8th adding "To dinner—certainly huge and after sans incident to bed with 'John' snoring fearfully." He forwarded with Hardwick (grinning drunkenly) a report to the Foreign Office including Dobritz's views on the African situation. Hardwick was, he noted on 10 October, "only a boy—but rather a decent boy" if often tipsy, and he babbled openly to Casement about himself and his ambitions.

October 11th. [To the Island for tennis, he sailed home and after a nap went out for a walk.] Cabinda enormous 'adios etc.' and then to dinner with Nisco, Souza and Dobritz—enormous.

October 12th. Stayed in all day. Twice enormous at dinner came to me. XX. To dinner at Frazao's—big on right—waiting with 'John' and Charlie.

On the 13th he dined with Dobritz and was home by 10.30 and on the 14th went to Frazao's again as usual for dinner. There was a big surprise in store for him there.

October 14th. Walked with Dobritz and then to Frazao's. [F]ound Joe H. of Accra (Sept 1901) here at Loanda as waiter. Ah! Me! Big one transferred to both sides holding 'John' and whiskey.

From the 15th he was in communication with the Foreign Office and clearing up back work at the consulate. The Foreign Office wanted to publish the Grenfell statement about the Commissaire of Protection being useless, but he advised them to wait until he could get permission. He was suffering ill health again. On the 18th he spent all day in bed. The next day he was well enough to get up, but stayed home writing dispatches. In the evening he went to dinner at Frazao's.

October 19th. Went down to dinner Frazao's. Big was bigger—about 9" and awfully active. Earnestly at it again.

On the 20th he received wires telling him to come home to prepare his Congo Report. On the 21st he wrote Ed Morel about Congo. He was also writing Poulteney Bigelow on the same subject and to Joseph Conrad. He asked Morel to forward copies of his pamphlet to them.

October 21st. Shall (D.V.) go by 'Rápido' on 8/9 Nov., due at Lisbon on 26th, but am not decided.

On the 22nd he seemed to be feeling better. He sent his Congo boys home. He dined with Dobritz, enjoying delicious turtle soup. He dined with the consul again on the 23rd. Dobritz was feeling ill, probably from overindulging in turtle soup. Life was picking up for Casement as he readied himself to leave. He observes on his voyage over to the Island, on the 25th, "enormous Ambundu stroke oar." On the 26th he mentioned that the British note to the European Powers concerning the Congo situation had been published, in which he was referred to as a "Consul of extensive African Experience." A letter arrived the same day from Morel. On the 27th and 28th he dined with Dobritz and the two talked for hours about the future of the Congo.

October 28th. 'Portugal Rápido' in from Lisbon. Dined with Dobritz.... H., big at last.

The following two days were very bad and he spent them for the most part in bed. However, he did manage to go out for dinner with Dobritz. He was also well enough to go to the Island for tennis on 1 November but complained of being "very tired after tennis, bath, sports, two and a half hours standing." On the 2nd the bells of all the churches were pealing. He wrote out fourteen official letters. In the evening he was fit enough to attend a farewell party for Dobritz who was leaving he next day for Benguela. The entries for the next few days include reports of dinners at Frazao's, lovely walks at night and wires from the Foreign Office urging him to come home at once to prepare his official report on the Congo.

He decided on 5th to leave on the *Zaire* and the next day installed John and Charlie on board. By the 8th they were steaming toward Santo Thomé, which they reached on the 9th. Here he met friends and took long walks and finally was off on the *Zaire* for Lisbon on the 12th, making about 300 miles per day. Life on board was unremarkable. On the 16th he stayed up all night reading *The Woman in White* by Wilkie Collins. They passed numerous steamers. It got hotter and hotter in his cabin until finally he decided to bed down in the smoking room. On the 21st they finally passed Las Palmas at about 9 p.m. The next day they were plunging through heavy seas. On the 23rd he discovered that he had somehow mislaid his diary but found it again at last. On the 24th they were at Cintra 7 a.m. and three hours later docked at Lisbon. He dined on shore and later took a long exploratory ramble in familiar surroundings.

November 25th. Dined with self at Central, walked. Spanish type X.

On the 26th he lunched at the Legation and the next day boarded the *Ambrose* of the Booth Line for Liverpool. At noon they were off Finisterre. The weather deteriorated, "beastly, gale and sea." On the last day of the month they reached Liverpool. He took the night train to London.

December 1st. Arrived London. To Stores and then to F.O. where saw many men.... They are a gang of stupidities in many ways. Ordered to make my report at once. Cold coming on.

His cold got worse. Lord Lansdowne asked to see him on the 3 December at Lansdowne House, where he duly made his report. It was very well received, "Proof," Lord Lansdowne said, "of the most painfully convincing kind, Mr. Casement." Arrangements were made through the Foreign Office to supply him with a typist ("typer" or "typewriter" as he calls him) who finally arrived on the 9th to get down to work. Casement dictated (as not far away Henry James would also be dictating to *his* typist).

December 5th. Typer came and hard at work all day. Began dictating my report.... Many letters and various people seeking to interview me, including Reuter's Agency.

December 6th. Very busy on report with typer. Did 6,000 words today and revised a lot. Dined at Comedy Restaurant. First time there in life. Porter good, excellent dinner, French chef, then walked. Dusky depredator huge, saw 7 in. in all. Two beauties.

December 7th. Very busy again, got now some 15,000 words of report typed since Saturday. At it all day. Papers full of my Congo journey. [He strolled in the evening, successfully.] Dick, West End, biggest and cleanest, *mui mua ami*.

From the 8th to the 10th he continued dictating, revising, editing with his typist, as well as getting out to dine. On the 10th Morel called, meeting him in person for the first time after exchanging so many letters. They talked until two in the morning and Morel bedded down in the study, leaving after breakfast. This same day Casement had dinner at the Comedy again and took a long walk. The next evening, after long labors on his report, he dined at Gatti's Adephi and strolled home in the rain.

Casement was being attacked from several quarters as well as praised. He was anxious to protect himself. Morel wrote again, to warn him. The *African World* announced that the "curious particulars of Mr. R. Casement's tour" would be published after it was issued by the government.

December 15th. Very busy finishing notes all day, got mostly all thro'. At Victoria, beautiful fat type.... Supper at Press Club and home tired.

Villiers told him that he wanted Casement's report out before the end of the month. It was in fact, so far as Casement was concerned, already wrapped up. However, Villiers was as usual indecisive and evasive. He mumbled that the report was not likely to come out until February when Parliament was due to meet.

December 18th. Lunched with Cust at United Service. *Beautiful* there. X uniform.

He visited the Mortens on the 20th and on the 21st was off to Dublin.

December 22nd. Bad crossing. At North Wall. Went Bray. Francis Naughton not there, back to Westland Row. At Harcourt Park, J.B. grown greatly in all ways. £1.6/-—Xmas. Dinner at Dolphin. Home to hotel, nice fire in bed and off to sleep. J.B., £1.8/-, came, handled and also came.

The next day he went to Belfast where he saw a "fearful" performance of *Uncle Tom's Cabin*. On Christmas Eve he reached Ballycastle where, disappointingly, there was no one to meet him. The house had changed and he was miserable on Christmas Day, but managed to do some additional work on his report. On the 26th he received praise from the Foreign Office for his report; Farnall wrote that it "could not be better, admirable both in style and substance." By the 28th he had finalized his draft and sent the report off. Then he went to Portrush to see Nina. On the train, "Beautiful got in with sister at B'mony. The next two days at Portrush were pleasant, but the world was in turmoil and war seemed ready to break out on several fronts.

December 30th. Japan and Russia still threatening peace, but war likely to end their instigations.

On New Year's day, 1904, he was with Cunninghame Graham at Dernster after talks at the Foreign Office in the morning with Farnall and Villiers about his report and the state of the Congo in general. On the 2nd he wrote to Morel again and lunched with Gerald Spicer at the Carlton Grill. He was back to socializing but seems bored by it all.

January 3rd, 1904. Went to Conrad at Pent Farm, Sanford, near Hythe, and spent a delightful day with him. Back by last 8.20 train and home to bed.

He visited the Foreign Office, dined at the Café Regina, and on the 5th went to Liverpool, traveling 2nd class, to see Morel. Coming back via Chester he met Lloyd George in the train and talked with him at length of the Congo and other things. On the 8th he made the final revisions of his report and dined again at the Café Regina and went home without incident.

There is a note here in the diaries, floating free from the often loathsome details: *Sept. 15, 1903. 'John' on 'Henry Reed'. 'A thing of beauty is joy for ever, Innocence personified.' Sitting down evening. Lovesongs and water lilies, and wearing with enormous paws the mystic darkness into speech.*

The Congo Report

On 11 December 1903, Casement formally submitted his Congo Report to the Marquess of Lansdowne. The report would be extensively edited and revised (Casement would have said emasculated) by the Foreign Office. They would remove all specific references to individuals, and disguise place names by the substitution of letters.

Casement's narration was simple.

He had left Matadi on 5 June 1903 and arrived at Leopoldville on 6 June. He remained there until 2 July, then left for the Upper Congo in order to begin investigating conditions for his report. He returned from his trip of investigation on 15 September, having spent some two and a half months visiting several points up to the Lolongo river junction, ascending the river and its principal feeder the Lopori to Bongandanga, reaching as far as Lake Maretumba.

He was particularly interested in contrasting the present state of the country with that which he knew quite well sixteen years ago. He visited familiar places and was stunned by the changes that had taken place.

During these years the Congo Free State had constructed permanent stations, well ordered and impressive, at many points along the river and inland. There was a fleet of forty-eight State steamers navigating the main river, making regularly scheduled stops. The country, in a word, had developed remarkably in less than two decades, helped in great measure by the railway that connected Stanley Pool with the ocean ports, running through the sterile country bordering the cataracts. Whole areas that had once been thickly populated, however, were now nearly deserted.

There was no single reason for the depopulation of the Congo, but one of the main and incontrovertible ones was the rapid spread of sleeping sickness. Casement mentioned the disease as "one cause of the seemingly wholesale diminution of human life." He observed that "Perhaps the most striking change ... was the great reduction everywhere observable in native life. Communities I had formerly known as large and flourishing centers of population are today entirely gone; or exist in such diminished numbers as to be no longer recognizable." The southern banks of Stanley Pool were formerly home to some 5000 Batakes; when Casement reached there he found only a hundred or so. The native huts had simply vanished. Only a few European houses remained.

His report contains a description of a native "hospital" that he visited, and the patients he spoke to there. While mentioning in an aside the Government establishment where scientists were carrying on bacteriological studies in well-ordered clean surroundings, he contrasts the three huts where natives were treated, or abandoned to die.

"I found seventeen sleeping sickness patients, male and female, lying about in the utmost dirt. Most of them were lying on the bare ground—several out in the pathway in front of the houses, and one, a woman, had fallen into the fire just prior to my arrival ... and had burned herself very badly. She had since been well bandaged, but was still lying out on the ground with her head almost in the fire, and while I sought to speak to her, in turning she upset a pot of scalding water over her shoulder. All the seventeen people I saw were near their end, and on my second visit two days later, the 19th June, I found one of them lying dead in the open."

Against these grossly inhuman conditions, the State workshops responsible for maintaining the steamers were a model of impeccable efficiency. The "brightness, care, order and activity" of the Government were impressive, making him wonder why some efforts of the kind might not be made to help the sleeping sickness patients, if nothing else simply by building a proper hospital. Even the Government stores were solidly constructed—but of course they were important elements in the trading structure of the State.

Produce was brought downriver direct to the railway trucks, and then by train to Matadi. The State had a stranglehold on the transportation system. The companies holding concessions in the State were prohibited from shipping goods or passengers outside their specific area. If they did they were forced to pay a tariff comparable to that charged by the Government steamers. As a consequence the Government ships were chronically overcrowded. Casement had made a booking on the *Flandre* but it was due to leave with twenty European passengers who would have to sleep on deck because there were no available cabins. This absurd state of affairs in his case were solved by being granted free transport through the kindness of the Director of the Société Anonyme Belge du Haut Congo who offered him comfortable passage as a guest of the State on one of their steamers.

The Foreign Office was worried about naming names. They were also worried about the highly charged comments that invariably found their way into what should have been Casement's "objective" reports. Lansdowne and his officers went through these reports and edited them carefully, in order to avoid confrontation with individuals or with the Belgian Government. Most specific references were dropped and initial letters were substituted, making for an odd and strangely blunted, even "unreal," narration. Place names were particularly important—but were simply deleted; the officials in the Foreign Office had blanc mange for brains.

Casement stayed four days at F. He had visited this once thriving and healthy settlement in 1887, at which time there were between four and five thousand inhabitants. There were now only about five hundred. The life of the villagers was miserable. The telegraph line, running through the town-lands and linking Leopoldville and Coquilhatville, had to be maintained clear of destructive undergrowth. Although the telegraph road was useful as a public path between villages, cutting back growth and caring for the line in general was a heavy burden, especially for a diminished population with other pressing needs. The chore was obligatory—but without compensation, or at least payment had not been received for over a year now. Besides this, the men of F were forced to cut wood for the steamers, work difficult and time-consuming, and underpaid.

Payment was in brass rods, the common currency in the Congo; a clumsy and filthy specie.

"The reasons for the decrease of population at F ... point to sleeping sickness as probably one of the principal factors," Casement wrote. "There has also been emigration to the opposite side of the river, to the French shore.... Where formerly [the natives] were accustomed to take long voyages down to Stanley Pool to sell slaves, ivory, dried fish, or other local products ..." they are prohibited such activities today.

Both the slave trade and the native canoe convoys had vanished; the first had been vigorously suppressed by the Congolese Government, the second had followed the demand by the Government stations for firewood and supplies, leaving the natives nothing to sell or barter. At F the male inhabitants rarely left their homes except as required by the Government, to clear brush, to cut wood or to serve as soldiers. There was one other reason: to carry supplies of food—considered a "tax"—to the nearest Government station, for the European staff there. These supplies were notably goats and chickens, a number of each assessed per fortnight, which meant that the region was scoured for fresh meat that became more scarce. At Bolobo the pressure from the Chief of Staff caused actual armed expeditions to go out to "requisition" food. These expeditions did not simply round up animals, they massacred villagers to get them. One example: at the end of 1900 an armed party traversed a small village, killing seventeen, mostly men, and tying up ten others, taking them away as prisoners until a payment of sixteen goats had been received. They wiped the villages out. The raiding party took forty-eight goats and 225 fowls. They pillaged the houses and then burned them down. Damage was estimated at 71,730 brass rods (3,386 Fr), which included 20,500 rods (1,025 Fr) as compensation for the people killed. (The worth of a human life was estimated at 1,000 rods while that of a goat was 400.) When compensation for this outrage was requested by the villagers the Government Commissioner from Stanley Pool showed up and paid 18,000 rods—levied as a *fine* for misconduct on the part of the officer responsible for the raid. Subsequently the officer was transferred to another post and finally sent back to Belgium. The villagers made do.

Bolobo itself was once an important station with a population of 40,000, mostly of the Bobangi tribe. When Casement visited, there were only 7–8,000 inhabitants left. The Bobangi had once been keen traders and navigated the river at considerable distances. Now their large canoes had vanished and the men spent their free time hunting hippopotamus on the river. There was no cottage industry. There was no ivory, and no rubber, in the area; however, food supplies were still demanded of them. Their services were required for wood-cutting, paddling, telegraph route maintenance. "If a local official has to go on a sudden journey, men are summoned on the instant to paddle his canoe, and a refusal entails imprisonment or a beating." Women were also summoned to weed kitchen gardens, neglecting their own gardens and homes.

Important internal migrations had taken place to avoid maltreatment or the impossible demands of the Government and its representatives. Casement noted a large influx of natives from the L district, in the Domaine de la Couronne located 120–150 miles away. He visited the area, spending three days visiting two large villages. Half of the inhabitants were immigrants from the Domaine de la Couronne who had fled to avoid ill treatment from the Government. They claimed they were often killed for failing to bring in a certain amount of rubber; some simply died from starvation in the forest, trying to collect their quota and without adequate food to sustain them in their labors.

This visit Casement found valuable, for the information on the state of mind of the natives, and the dilemma of people uprooted and living among strangers. One of the towns had 71 houses inhabited by the locals; 73 were inhabited by the intruders from the Domaine de la Couronne. The newcomers were industrious, simple people—skilled at weaving palm fiber into mats or cloth, working brass wire into bracelets, chains, anklets, forging knives. Casement carried on long interviews with the people there:

Casement:	Why did you leave your homes?
Native:	Because of the rubber tax levied by the Government posts.
Casement:	How was this tax imposed?
Native:	Each village had to take 20 loads of rubber. [Indicating the size of a load] As rubber got scarcer, the white man reduced the amount. We had to take these loads in four times a month.
Casement:	How much did you get paid for this?
Native:	We got no pay. We got nothing.
Native A:	Our village got cloth and a little salt, but not the people who did the work. Our Chief ate up the cloth; the workers got nothing.
Native B:	It used to take ten days to get the 20 baskets of rubber—we were always in the forest to find the rubber vines, to go without food, and our women had to give up cultivating the fields and gardens. Then we starved.
Native C:	Wild beasts—the leopards—killed some of us while we were working away in the forest and others got lost and died from exposure and starvation and we begged the white man to leave us alone, saying we could get no more rubber but the white men and their soldiers said: 'Go. You are only bests yourselves. You are only Nyama (meat).'

Native D:	We tried, always going further into the forest, and when we failed and our rubber was short, the soldiers came to the town and killed us. Many were shot, some had their ears cut off; others were tied up with ropes around their necks and bodies and taken away.
Casement:	How long was it since you left your home, since the trouble you speak of?
Native:	It lasted three full seasons and it is now four seasons since we fled and came into this country.
Casement:	How many days is it to your country?
Native:	Six days of quick marching.

Several natives informed Casement that the Chiefs of the tribe were unable to do anything to help. They were simply hanged, while the people themselves were either killed, starved or worked beyond endurance.

Casement:	How do you know it was the white men themselves who ordered these cruel things to be done to you? These things must have been done by the black soldiers without the white men's knowledge.
Native:	The white men told their soldiers, You kill only women, you cannot kill men. So then the soldiers when they killed us [pointing to the private parts of Casement's bulldog] cut off those things and took them to the white men who said, It is true, you have killed men.

An old Chief told him: "We used to hunt elephants long ago and there were plenty in our forests, and we got much meat; but Bula Matadi [the white men] killed the elephant hunters because they could not get rubber, and so we starved. We were sent out to get rubber, and when we came back with little rubber we were shot."

Casement:	Who shot you?
Chief:	The white men sent their soldiers out to kill us.
Casement:	How do you know it was the white men? It might have been only those savage soldiers themselves.

Chief:	No, no. We sometimes brought rubber into the white men's stations…. When it was not enough rubber the white men would put some of us in lines, one behind the other, and would shoot through our bodies.
Casement:	You were killed in the Government post by the Government white men themselves or under their very eyes?
Chief:	We were killed in the stations of the white men themselves. We were killed by the white man himself. We were shot before his eyes.

Casement thought that there had been some exaggeration on the part of the natives, and some possibly false statements. He continued asking questions. There were also communications from various other sources—witnesses of the atrocities who wanted their stories known.

One witness reported: "After a few hours we came to a State rubber post. In nearly every instance these posts are impressive, some of them giving rise to the impression that several white men live in them. But in only one did we find a white man…. At one place I saw lying about in the grass surrounding the post, which is built on the site of several large towns, human bones, skulls and in some cases complete skeletons." On inquiring the reason for these horrors, the witness got the answer that, "[W]hen the bambolete [soldiers] were sent to make us cut rubber there were so many killed we got tired of burying, and sometimes when we wanted to bury we were not allowed to."

Casement:	Why did they kill you so?
Witness:	Oh, sometimes we were ordered to go and the sentry would find us preparing food to eat while in the forest, and he would shoot two or three to hurry us along. Sometimes we would try to do a little work on our plantations, so that when the harvest came we should have something to eat and the sentry would shoot some of us to teach us that our business was not to plant but to get rubber. Sometimes we were driven off to live for a fortnight in the forest without any food and without anything to make a fire with, and many died of cold and hunger. Sometimes the quan-

tity brought was not sufficient, and then several would be killed to frighten us to bring more. Some tried to run away, and died of hunger and privation in the forest—trying to avoid the State posts.

Casement: But if the sentries killed you like that, what was the use? You could not bring more rubber when there were fewer people.

Witness: As to that we do not understand it.

Casement explored a number of areas, once densely populated and fertile. He found desolation: untended farms, neglected palms. From State sentries he received confirmation of what had happened, there was no reason to hide the facts. The Domaine de la Couronne during the last seven years had become a hell on earth.

He left Bolobo on 23 July. This time he traveled in his own hired steam launch with a local crew. He made his way along the French shore and then on 25 July he arrived at Lukolela, where he stayed only briefly. In 1887 there had been about 5,000 inhabitants; today there were under 600. The reasons given by the natives were: disease, sleeping sickness, lack of food, raids by soldiers to recruit forced labor, exactions levied on them such as the rubber tax and requisitions for food by the white men.

A concerned missionary stationed at Lukolela, Reverend John Whitehead, gave Casement letters to take to the authorities. On his way down river, however, Casement did not have the time to follow up the information laid out in the letters; but verification seemed beside the point. Reverend Whitehead wrote to the Governor-General of the Congo State, discharging, so he said, his duty to the State and to His Majesty King Leopold II, "whose desire for the facts in the interest of humanity have long been published." The facts included the following: "The population in the village of Lukolela in January 1891 must have been not less than 6,000 people, but when I counted the whole population in Lukolela at the end of December 1896 I found it to be only 719." He went on to say that at this average rate of decrease the population should have been at present about 400 (the date of the letter is 28 July 1903). But the last count shows that only 352 are left, and the death rate is obviously increasing. "I note also a decrease very appallingly apparent in the inland districts during the same number of years; three districts are well-nigh swept out.... Very soon the whole place will be denuded of its population. The pressure under which they live at present is crushing them; the food which they sadly need themselves very often must, under penalty, be carried to the State post, also grass, cane string, baskets for the 'caoutchouc'." The last three items do not appear to be paid for. The Chiefs are imprisoned, put into chains for the shortage of manioc bread and caoutchouc. "… [T]he officials of the State have never attempted even the feeblest effort to assist the natives of Lukolela to recover themselves or guard themselves in any way from disease."

At Lukolela there were only eighty-two men in the village. The rest had been detained as workers. Twenty desperately ill people were seen by Casement; and when he next passed by nine of these had died. The natives now considered the white man as their natural enemy. "Some have sworn to die, be killed, or anything else rather than be forced to bring in 'caoutchouc', which spells imprisonment and subsequent death to them…. [They] conclude they may as well die first as last."

The Reverend Whitehead made several suggestions in his letter to the Governor-General, among which were: relocation of the remainder of the population to higher ground, which is healthier and better—after clearing—for gardens; isolation of persons with sleeping sickness downriver, but to be supplied with food and care; burial of the dead, with the graves located far from houses and dug at least a fathom deep; better latrines; feeding from common vessels to be stopped; encouragement of hunting, fishing, blacksmithing and other traditional activities, with women caring for the gardens; property ownership by natives; an end to compulsory labor; recognition of the authority of the Chiefs; appointment of sentries to make sure reforms are carried out.

A second letter, of 7 September, concerned a number of atrocities. The Reverend mentions a report made by him on 16 August 1902 to the Commissaire Général at Leopoldville concerning the murder of two men. This murder was committed by a soldier who was taking the men, in chains, and another prisoner—an unchained boy—to fetch water. When the soldier took a chicotte from a house they were passing and began to beat the boy, he ran off. The soldier, furious, then shot the others. There were witnesses to this murder. They were sent to Leopoldville to denounce the crime but there they were given the usual Government run-around, left without food and shelter and finally were lucky enough to be returned home by mission steamer. On 6 March 1903 the Reverend reported seeing at Mibenga a Chief named Mopali of the Ngelo imprisoned to force his people to bring in more rubber. The chief had head wounds and his mouth was swollen from a blow—these were the result of maltreatment while he was in chains ands forced to carry firewood.

M. Lecomte had asked for witnesses. Nothing was done. When the reverend returned some time later and inquired about the Chief he was told that he had died—but actually the man was simply in hiding. His feet had been slashed (which hadn't been noticed before) and he probably was permanently crippled, dragging himself along on his buttocks. People said that at first they were required to bring in five baskets of rubber and to make them increase the number to ten they threw Chief Mopali in chains. Now they were demanding two more.

On 17 August at Mibenga Chief Lisanginya declared that after giving his tax of eight baskets of rubber, M. Lecomte had said that was not enough—three others being needed. A chain was placed around the Chief's neck, soldiers beat him with sticks, and he was forced to cut firewood, carry heavy loads, haul logs. In the morning he also was required to empty the slops of the white men into the river; on the third day he was made to drink from the slop jar by his guard, a soldier named Lisasi. Released after the three baskets were produced, the Chief was ill for days.

Then on 21 August Mr. and Mrs. Whitehead met a man called Mpombo who after taking ten baskets of rubber to the post had been told that more was required. They chained him up and treated him roughly, breaking his left wrist, badly bruising a finger of his right hand; he had a large sore from a beating, his back was also bruised and his left should had been slit with a knife; his left knee was also bruised and his feet swollen from being thrashed. The man's mind was disordered from so much suffering.

The Reverend describes the mode of slavery at the post: "[A] man for some reason … commences work at the post; he completes his term, and he is told he cannot have his pay unless he engages himself another term or brings another in his place."

Casement went from Lukolela to O where in the autumn of 1887 he had seen a lively community containing 4–5,000 people. Of the three villages in O nothing remained; they had been replaced by a large "camp d'instruction" where some 800 native recruits from various parts of the Congo were being trained by a Belgian Commandant and eight European officers. Casement was politely welcomed by the Commandant who boasted of being comfortably off, with food in abundance supplied by natives of the surrounding Irebu district on the chief navigable channel of the Congo opposite the estuary of the great Ubangi River.

From Irebu it was only twenty-five miles to Ikoko on the north shore of Lake Mantumba, where he spent seventeen days, visiting lakeside villages.

A Statement is appended to the Congo Report in regard to the condition of the natives at Lake Mantumba during the period of the rubber wars which began in 1893. The disturbances arose from attempts by the Government to levy a rubber tax and only ended about 1900, by which time the native population was reduced by 60 percent. Only at present were people returning. From 1893 to 1901 the Congo State began a system to compel natives to collect rubber, with the stipulation that they were prohibited from going outside of their district and selling to traders. Soldiers were given free rein to see that the system was enforced. The population lived from then on like hunted animals, hiding in the bush, afraid to build homes or make gardens.

The enormous decrease in population was due to people fleeing to the French territory, from outright war in which men, women and children were killed indiscriminately. Some were carried off, ostensibly to a far camp; they never returned. Many young men took refuge in the missions. The death rate was enormous: "Ten children were sent from a State Steamer to a mission, and in spite of comfortable surroundings, there were only three alive at the end of a month. The others had died of dysentery and bowel troubles contracted during the voyage; two struggled on for about fifteen months but never recovered strength and at last died. In less than two years only one of the ten was alive." The natives were debilitated because of the meager and irregular food supply and were unable, as a consequence, to resist disease. The birth rate also decreased—women did not want babies as a burden, and pregnant women could not easily run away from the war. The black soldiers were responsible for arbitrary shootings. They would take off the right hand of their victims as evidence of their faithfulness to the Government. "[C]anoes have been seen returning from distant expeditions with no white man in charge, and with human hands dangling from a stick in the bow of the canoe, or in small baskets—and being carried to the white man as proofs of their courage and devotion to duty."

The statements given Casement were full of "war" and "atrocities"—those trying to hide from the soldiers, were usually unsuccessful, and were taken prisoner or killed.

A young girl, Q, told Casement about how she had survived. "The soldiers ran quickly to the place where we were and caught my grandmother, my mother, my sister.... Several of the soldiers argued about my mother, because each wanted her for a wife, so they finally decided to kill her. They killed her with a gun—they shot her through the stomach. [S]he fell and when I saw that I cried very much, because they killed my mother and grandmother and I was left alone."

R talked to Casement of different battles in the "war." R ran away with two old people, who were caught and slaughtered. He was then forced to carry the effects of the old people along with their hands, which the soldiers had cut off. The soldiers went into the bush to find the villagers hiding there, and killed a mother and her four children. They tied up some people; they killed many others. "They got my little sister and killed her and threw her into a house and set fire to the house."

S, escaping with her little sister, was caught. "We might keep them both," the soldiers said. "The little one is not bad looking." Another said, "No, we are not going to carry her all the way, we must kill the younger girl." So they put a knife through the child's stomach and left the body lying there. They took S to the next town where the white man, C.D., had told them to go. She was threatened by the men and thrashed because she could not find manioc for them. The corporal said, "We must not kill her; we must take her to the white man." So they took her and showed her to C.D. Now the soldiers asked C.D. for an old woman, one of three they had caught. They wanted to eat her. C.D. said take her. They cut the old woman's throat, divided her into pieces, and ate her. S acted as a guide for the men; but they found few people wherever they went. At one town "they killed a lot of people—men, women and children—and took some as prisoners. They cut the hands off those they had killed, and brought them to C.D. They spread out the hands in a row for C.D. to see and count.

U told Casement about many encounters and miraculous survival. "[T]hey killed ten children, because they were very small; they killed them in the water. Then they killed a lot of people, and they cut off their hands and put them into baskets and took them to the white man. He counted out the hands—200 in all; they left the hands lying. The white man's name was C.D." When U was a prisoner and working outside, "a soldier came and said, 'Come here' and when I went he wanted to cut my hand so I went to the white man to tell him, and he thrashed the soldier.... On our way, when we were coming to P, the soldiers saw a little child, and when they went to kill it, the child laughed, so the soldier took the butt of a gun and struck the child with it, and then cut off its head.... One day they killed my half sister and cut off her head, hands and feet because she had on rings."

Casement concludes that "a careful investigation of the conditions of native life around the lake confirmed the truth of the statements made to me that the great decrease in population, the dirty and ill-kept towns, and the complete absence of goats, sheep, or fowls—once very plentiful in this country—were to be attributed above all else to the continued effort made during many years to compel the natives to work india-rubber. Large bodies of native troops had formerly been quartered in the district, and the primitive measures undertaken to this end had endured for a considerable period. During the course of these operations there had been much loss of life, accompanied, I fear, by a some-what general mutilation of the dead, as proof that the soldiers had done their duty."

He added that only now were some village inhabitants returning to the region. Villagers when they learned of the approach of Casement's steamer, ran away in terror. "Fear of this kind was formerly unknown on the Upper Congo; and in much more out-of-the-way places visited many years ago the people flocked from all sides to greet a white stranger." Now women snatched up their babies, bits of food, and ran away into the jungle.

The European Chief of the P post said that the same alarm was shown everywhere. When you went on a peaceful mission only a few miles from home, the villages were deserted and it was impossible to get in touch with anyone. The reason for this fear of the white man, he said, strangely, was that, "these people were great savages, and they knew themselves how many crimes they had committed, they doubtless feared that the white man of the Govern-ment was coming to punish them for their misconduct."

There were victims of mutilations everywhere. Two were especially noted at Mantumba. "One, a young man, both of whose hands had been beaten off with the butt ends of rifles against a tree, the other a young lad of 11 or 12 years of age, whose right hand was cut off at the wrist. This boy described the circumstances of his mutilation.... [A]lthough wounded at the time he was perfectly sensible of the severing of his wrist, but lay fearing that if he moved he would be killed." Of six natives who had thus been mutilated all but one had died.

The day Casement left Mantumba five men with their hands cut off came from across the lake to talk with him; he just missed them.

The notes that Casement appends to the report are always startling. One native, for example, had both of his hands beaten, not hacked, off.

Casement: How did you lose your hands?

Native:	State soldiers came and attacked my town, burning and killing. They came led by a European officer. They took prisoners and tied them up. They tied their hands very tight with native rope and then the prisoners were left in the open, in the pouring rain all night. The thongs contracted and their hands were swollen terrible by the morning. The thongs cut to the bone.
Casement:	What did they do then?
Native:	There were eight of us prisoners. Two were killed during the night. Then they saw that my hands were useless, so they beat them against a tree. Then they released me. The white man could see what they were doing. He watched, drinking palm wine. Later my hands fell off, and the villagers returned and found me.

On 14 August Casement visited the State camp at Irebu again and told the officer in charge his story. He emphasized that this brutal act had occurred under the eyes of a fellow officer. "Impossible!" was the answer; however, Casement got assurance that an inquiry would be made. On his return from the Lulongo River, he indeed found that the Commissaire Général of the Equator district had proceeded to Lake Mantumba and was undertaking a judicial investigation. The boy in question had been taken to Bikoro, provision had been made for him and he was given a weekly allowance.

At B Casement found a twelve-year-old boy with his right hand gone. The boy said it had been cut off by Government soldiers some years before (when he was perhaps five), an assertion confirmed by relatives. The soldiers had arrived at B from Coquilhatville by land, through the forest, led by a white officer. The boy's father and mother were killed before his eyes—then a bullet hit him (he had a scar at the nape of the neck to show) and he fell unconscious to the ground. When he woke his hand was being hacked off. He had felt the cutting but had been afraid to move.

Here Casement took the names of six others. One, an old woman, had fled with her son when the village was attacked by the soldiers. When he fell dead she fell down beside him, fainting; when she woke they were chopping her hand off. She made no sign. They also cut her son's hand off. The taking of hands was not a native custom, Casement adds, before the white man came, "it was the deliberate act of the soldiers of a European administration, and these men themselves never made any concealment that in committing these acts they were but obeying the positive orders of their superiors."

From Lake Mantumba he went on to Coquilhatville for five days, traveling along the banks of the river with the natives. Today, there were only isolated settlements, reduced in number from the thriving villages he had seen before. There were no goats, sheep, fowls to be had; formerly there had been a bountiful supply, along with fruits and vegetables. Food for Casement's crew was hard to find. The tax of food and firewood for the steamers at Coquilhatville had drained the surrounding area; sentries were also quartered on villagers, an added burden. One of these sentries Casement spoke to was from Bussira, hundreds of miles away, and this was his third term of duty with the *force publique*—he could not live in his home village because of the rubber tax. These "taxes" were levied fortnightly or even weekly and were simply contributions called *prestations annuelles* established by authority of Royal Decree of the Sovereign of the Congo State, dated 1901, "requiring the establishment and upkeep by native Chiefs of coffee and cocoa plantations." Casement nowhere saw or heard of such plantations. There did exist such plantations, without doubt, but were the property either of the Government or some European agency. The Royal Decrees made provision for investiture of native Chiefs. There was a copy of the *procès verbal* deposited in the public archives including the name of Headmen, the number of houses in each village, the population, a list of products to be supplied (e.g. maize, sorghum, palm oil, ground nuts), stipulating besides the required *corvées* of workers or soldiers required and the description of lands to be cleared. No accurate records were kept, the natives were ignorant of what was actually demanded of them by law. As for the population, no census had been taken for years. One village which had once been large now had only six adult households, eleven huts, and a population of twenty-seven. Casement was brought to the village by a boy of seven who was the property of a certain official who had acquired the boy in exchange for a fine of about 1000 rods (50 Fr).

The journey was intensely depressing; Casement was never entirely well. He finally left Bongandanga on 3 September, steaming down the Lopori and Lolanga and arriving at J. Here he interviewed a sixteen-year-old boy whose right hand had been hacked off by a sentry of the Lulanga Company who was quartered at the village. This sentry had also murdered one of the Chief men. The boy had been shot in the shoulderblade and was, as a result, badly deformed. A familiar story: he had fallen down after being shot and when he woke the sentry was cutting off his hand to take to the Director of the Company at Mampoko. Was a complaint made to the authorities? No—no good would come of such a complaint.

Another boy at J had been mutilated in the same fashion by the same sentry. This boy had been in hiding and now begged Casement to go with him to the main town to determine the truth of his story. "In the morning," Casement wrote, "when about to start, many people from the surrounding country came in to see me. They brought with them three individuals who had been shockingly wounded by gunfire. [T]he soldiers had entered [the village] to enforce the due fulfillment of the rubber tax." Two men had been shot through the arm; a small boy of six had a hand missing. No white man had accompanied the soldiers from the La Lulanga Company but the villagers had sent to inform the white man about the attack. No one knew what punishment had been meted out to the guilty men, if any.

The report is a steady accumulation of similar detail. One man was brought in with an arm shattered by a gunshot, at the same village a small boy had his left arm broken in two places from gunshots; the wrist had been shattered and the hand was wobbling about useless. This had been done by a sentry who had accused them of taking rubber to Mampoko without first showing it to him and paying a "commission." When witness went to the Director of the company he refused to return with them to check the story. Returning to the village they found that the wounded man and boy were tied to a tree. The sentry asked 2000 rods (100 Fr) for their release. All complaints about such treatment failed. The villagers had ceased even to complain to the authorities, fearing that they would not be believed. "They thought the white men only wished for rubber, and that no good could come from pleading with them." The La Lulanga Company was particularly vile: the company soldiers pursued villagers for the rubber tax, hunted people down and cut off their hands.

Not only were villages attacked, whole villages were also relocated. A group of natives told Casement that their village had been transferred from the south bank of the river to a spot near the company factory. This movement of a whole community was at the command of the Commissaire Général who personally ordered them to work daily at the La Lulanga factory. The women were taken away and to get them back, a fine of 10,000 rods (500 Fr) was levied. The villages wanted Casement to help them return to their homes.

Casement asked one Chief why he hadn't gone directly to the Director to complain of sentries beating him and his people. The Chief showed Casement a tooth, dropping out, saying "This is what I got from the Director four days ago when I went to tell him what I now say to you." The white man, he added, frequently beat him and others.

Another man had been ordered by the Director to serve as one of the porters of his hammock during a journey inland. The man told the white man that he could not go, since he was finishing building a new house, but offered to find a substitute. The Director then ordered the man's house burned down. "I lost all my belongings in the fire," the villager said, "and then I was tied up and taken inland and loosed when I had to carry the hammock."

Others, hearing Casement was in the area, wanted to talk to him, but he was pressed for time. "I proceeded in a canoe across the Lulongo and up a tributary to a landing-place.... Here, leaving the canoes, we walked for a couple of miles through a flooded forest and reached the village of K. I found here a sentry of the La Lulanga Company and a considerable number of natives. After some little delay a boy of about 15 years of age appeared, whose left arm was wrapped up in a dirty rag. Removing this, I found the left hand had been hacked off at the wrist and that a bullet hole appeared in the fleshy part of the forearm." He then went to find the culprit—followed by a crowd of natives. The guilty sentry appeared, carrying a rifle. "The boy, whom I placed before him, then accused him to his face of having mutilated him. The men of the town ... corroborated the boy's statement." The man denied responsibility, saying it must have been some other sentry of the company. The crowd assured Casement that this man was the worst of the lot. Several individuals even said they had witnessed the deed. "I took the boy back with me," Casement wrote, "and later brought him to Coquilhatville, where he formally charged the sentry with the crime, alleging to the Commandant ... that it had been done 'on account of rubber.'" The sentry was later arrested and charged.

"The fact that no effort had been made by these people to secure relief from their unhappy situation impelled me to believe that a very real fear of reporting such occurrences actually existed among them." That everything the natives asserted was true, Casement could not believe; however, "in spite of contradictions, and even seeming misstatements, it was clear that these men were stating either what they had actually seen with their eyes or firmly believed in their hearts. No one viewing their unhappy surroundings and hearing their appeals, no one at all cognizant of African native life and character, could doubt that they were speaking, in the main, truly...."

As for "security"—there were large numbers of "forest guards" in the service of various companies, these not being Government concessions must hire their own police. For example, the A.B.I.R. Company had at least twenty stations, with factories directed by Europeans, and each maintained a "protective" armament of some twenty-five rifles. This company alone thus had an armed force with over five hundred rifles and an unlimited number of cartridges. These "forest guards" had very effective cap guns and Casement bought "the skin of a fine leopard" from a hunter who had shot the animal the previous day.

The system of quartering Government guards in villages was once common but had been abandoned. The Government practice of employing native soldiers in isolated posts had not however stopped, in spite of the Governor-General's explicit instructions, as recently as 7 September 1903 (the period Casement was in the Congo), that no black troops were to be employed unless they were accompanied by a European officer. In this official circular, the Commandants and officers of the *force publique* were required to rigorously observe the "oft-repeated instructions ... forbidding the employment of black soldiers by themselves on the public service."

Nevertheless the number of European officers was limited; they could not always be with their men. The territory was vast. "The ramifications of the system of taxation ... show it to be of a widespread character, and since a more or less constant pressure has to be exercised to keep the taxpayers up to the mark ... a certain amount of dependence upon the uncontrolled actions of native soldiers ... must be permitted." The most important article of native taxation in the Upper Congo was unquestionably rubber. The Governor-General, Casement adds, also distributed a circular (included in the report) exhorting officials to be on the lookout for fraud on the part of the natives to avoid payment.

Casement asks an important question: Is the Congo State a trading company or a Government? The instructions in such circulars "would be excellent if coming from the head of a trading house to his subordinates, but addressed, as they are, by a Governor-General to the principal officers of his administration, they reveal a somewhat limited conception of public duty. Instead of their energies being directed to the government of their districts, the officers therein addressed could not but feel themselves bound to consider the profitable exploitation of india-rubber as one of the principal functions of Government.... The praiseworthy official would be he whose district yielded the best and biggest supply ... [and] the means whereby he brought about the enhanced value of that yield would not, it may be believed, be too closely scrutinized."

On his return in December from Coquilhatville to Stanley Pool, Casement met with a group of natives fleeing to French territory. Unable to pay the State taxes, they would be forced into chain gangs, so they were attempting to get away. Casement could not allow them to accompany him, but he told them they were in their rights, could navigate the Congo freely—just as freely as he himself—and that there was no law on the books in the Congo State saying that they could not go wherever they wished, even to French territory. He had no idea what had become of the group, or whether they got to safety or not.

Edited by the Foreign Office—most specific names of places and individuals deleted, the writer's personal views omitted—the report was rendered toothless, or as toothless as possible, and duly published as a government Blue Book. The Congo Report is not what today we would consider well documented, but it is a work of polemical force—and served, as Morel and the members of the Aboriginal Protection Society were quick to admit, as a reminder to the world that atrocities such as those reported by Casement would not be tolerated.

Leopold Again

1

The Case for Leopold is still open. Historians consider him a "monster"—but he was not atypically bad. Encouraged, perhaps, by his family connections—royalty throughout Europe was related to him by blood, his cousins, nephews, his aunts and his sister had been placed on thrones in England, Portugal, Russia, Mexico. His father might have ruled England. He himself might have reigned in Spain, had he married the Princess Isabella. "In the course of the long and intricate negotiations," Lytton Strachey writes, "there was one point upon which Louis Phillipe laid a special stress—the candidature of Prince Leopold of Saxe-Coburg. The prospect of a marriage between a Coburg prince and the Queen of Spain was, he declared, threatening to the balance of power in Europe.... King Leopold was firmly fixed in Belgium; his niece was Queen of England; one of his nephews was the husband of the Queen of England, and another the husband of the Queen of Portugal; yet another was Duke of Wurtemburg." Later, the contagion of the house would continue to grow through alliances with Queen Victoria's children.

Leopold II deserved to rule an empire, in his opinion, even though, like the old queen, he was only a "constitutional" monarch. If worse came to worse he could simply *purchase* an empire with his personal fortune. This, in fact, was what he eventually did in the Congo, where he was allowed to rule—after numerous machinations—as absolute monarch over a *Domaine privé*. It was not a profitable business, this empire, but he planned to make it pay eventually. He even solicited the support of the Arab traders, as well as enlisting the efforts of Stanley, in an attempt to extend the frontiers of the Congo to the Upper Zambesi, Lake Nyasa, Lake Victoria and the Upper Nile. He achieved, with money, the collaboration of the Arabs. But the Congo did not become a money-making proposition until rubber began to return enormous profits. This took time.

From 1885 to 1895 the king's losses had to be made up from his private fortune, though he was helped by a lottery loan in 1888 and another loan, interest free, in 1890 for $5 million. The Belgian Government could either demand payment in ten years time or annex the Congo.

Leopold broke the pledge he had made to the state by borrowing an additional $1,250,000 from A. de Browne de Tiege, offering as guarantee a chunk of the Congo. Even at that he faced collapse of the whole enterprise in 1895. If it had not been for rubber, the Congo would have been untenable as a colony, in spite of the Belgian monopoly in ivory and raw materials. Leopold was a gambler; he was not interested in the progress of civilization—despite his mawkish phrases about helping the natives into the modern world. Ivory was one way to make money, but it was swiftly supplanted by rubber after 1895. In that year the Congo exports of rubber were 100 metric tons, rising in 1896 to 1,300 metric tons; in 1898 that figure almost doubled, to 2000. Incredibly, by 1901 the Congo was exporting 6000 metric tons of rubber a year, about one tenth of the world production. Leopold's Domain had yielded only 150,000 francs in 1880; in 1901 it yielded 18 million francs, ample support for additional loans and an immense surplus which was used to pay for magnificent public works such as the Arcade de Cinquantainaire in Brussels, the Tervuren Museum and construction projects at Ostend. Between 1898 and 1908 rubber would represent $80 million in exports against only $25 million for all other products. The money supplied by the Congo transformed the Belgian capital. Not surprisingly the Belgians did not consider Leopold II a monster.

In respect to the discrepancies of imports versus exports, Morel was the first to point out what these represented. Imports should have been higher than exports as in all developing countries, but for example in 1902, with a falling population, exports were three times those of 1897 and imports $600,000 less than the year before. Between 1898 and 1908 imports were about half of exports and three quarters of all imports consisted of administrative materials, military supplies and public works. E. D. Morel, like Casement and his uncle Edward, worked for the Elder Dempster Line, which enjoyed what was almost a monopoly in Congo trade. His job included making periodic trips to Antwerp and Brussels as company representative (he was a French speaker and naturalized British citizen as of 1896). He had extensive and frank discussions with Belgian officials concerning the Congo. During his work he made studies of West African affairs, not only the Belgian Congo but the French Congo, and was appalled at what he found. This led him to initiate a campaign for reform. He resigned his post at Elder Dempster to become a full-time journalist, founding and editing the *African Mail*, in which he carried on his work against the conditions prevailing in the Congo. He found immediate support in the Anti-Slavery League and the Aborigines Protection Society. Casement's reports would prove invaluable in his program.

2

The numerous reports, many from British missionaries, concerning the atrocities being committed in the Congo by agents of the state did not faze King Leopold. He had ready excuses. "If there are abuses in the Congo," he declared in 1899, "we must make them stop. These horrors must end or I will retire from the Congo. I will not allow myself to be spattered with blood and mud." However, the system did not change, since any change might affect revenue. The king paid journalists in England and America to support him with articles. His counselors pronounced the accusations unjust and exaggerated. The king reacted violently against his critics.

In 1895 the Congo was bankrupt. At that time King Leopold reluctantly agreed to its annexation by Belgium. However, since there was no outright majority for annexation in the parliament, the only option remaining was another government loan. In 1901 the king again opposed annexation, and only in 1905—with the outrage growing in Britain—was the topic revived. During the Boer War the Belgians were naturally on the side of the Boers and sentiment in the country was anti-English. King Leopold detested E. D. Morel, whom he accused of being paid by Liverpool merchants to write his slanderous reports. Only in 1904, with the publication of the Casement report on the Congo atrocities did Leopold, supposedly alarmed, send out a special commission to investigate. The committee returned a confirmation of Casement's findings, much to the king's annoyance.

At long last, in December 1906, the question of annexation came up again. The reformers had won a moral battle. The United States now supported Britain in calling for an international conference to suppress atrocities and abuses against the natives in the Congo. Leopold continued to resist annexation. It took two years to bring it about. The Fondation de la Couronne had to be ended, and the systematic siphoning off of Congo resources to Belgium. Formal annexation finally took place on 15 November 1908. At this time the king ordered the destruction of incriminating documents in the Belgian archives in Brussels, including evidence that might have illuminated the part Stanley played in his criminal game. The king would die on 17 December 1909, leaving a trail of bogus companies and secret bank accounts, as well as the Niederfulbach Foundation with vast assets. His will disposed of a personal fortune of only $3 million, but the true value of his estate was actually more like $16 million. The Niederfulbach Foundation alone received $9 million in stocks and bonds.

3

In June 1913, as Europe slid inexorably toward war, the Congo Reform Association was dissolved. There was no reason, Morel himself admitted, to continue agitating for change, in view of the reforms that had rapidly come about. The Congo reform movement had had an extensive effect in the colonial policy of other nations. Brazza, in the French Congo, had been encouraged to make similar studies. He had found horrors equal to those in the Congo Free State. "Ruin and terror," he reported in messages sent home, "terrifying depopulation, universal exodus." With Brazza's death in Dakar, Senegal, in September 1905, conditions remained static. But by that time wild rubber collection was declining swiftly and Asian plantation production would soon replace it.

4

Meanwhile, for some years now there had been intriguing stories of atrocities like those in the Congo or worse, draining out from the darkness of the Amazon forest where wild rubber was producing millionaires at the expense of native populations.

After a few missteps, a stint at home, loose ends, Roger Casement would soon be back in Rubber Country.

Red Rubber in the Amazon

1

Rubber was a phenomenal product with a multiplicity of uses. Raw rubber, or latex, was extracted from the Hevea tree which grows up to a hundred feet high. In the wild, rubber stands may number around 300 to the acre. The Amazon area was the first important area for rubber collection and the Amazonian natives were master workers. Hevea brasilensis and Hevea benthamiana are native to the Amazon. When wild rubber was the main source of raw material these trees produced the best latex. (They are also the original sources of the millions of acres of plantation trees in Asia.). Techniques of gathering latex are simple and have been the same for hundreds of years. The liquid latex is gathered as it drips from grooves cut in the trunk of the tree. Later this "milk" is coagulated, smoked and built up layer by layer. Smoking makes the rubber strong and durable; if not smoked it will rot. (Modern methods of tearing and pressing the rubber with heavy rollers make this smoking unnecessary.)

The French scholar explorer, Charles Marie de la Condamine, off to South America to measure an arc of meridian on the Equator, crossed the continent and traveled down the Amazon to Pará in 1743. He remained there to study the natural history of the region and returned to France in 1745, carrying with him samples of rubber, which was looked on as a curiosity. He proposed making waterproof clothes of rubber; a workman produced a traveling case of the material for his scientific instruments. Later, Freneau described rubber collection techniques in use in Guiana. He also made several suggestions for possible uses, and sent samples home.

By the end of the century rubber trees had also been discovered in the East, but the Amazon was the first successful producer. In the early 1800s, rubber

93

shoes were being exported to Boston; in 1850 up to a half million pairs arrived. These were mostly supplied by the Pará Indians When the vulcanization process was discovered in 1839, an increased demand for rubber was created. In 1860 the US bought 1,670 tons, and prices continued to rise. Rubber production became so important in the northeast of Brazil that normal crops were neglected and staple foods such as beans, farinha, maize had to be imported to feed the rubber workers. Production could not keep up with the demand.

The Amazon was crowded with wild rubber trees, but access was often difficult in an area covering 2,722,000 square miles. The Amazon River was navigable by steamer, however, so the trade had a ready means to export the product abroad. Territories on the Amazon tributaries were loaded with rubber trees, which were native to almost the entire region—northern and central Brazil, Bolivia, Colombia, Ecuador, Peru and part of Venezuela. The Indians were exterminated or enslaved by the rubber companies, an easy job since, with the expulsion of the priests from Portuguese and Spanish colonies, they had been often left in a state of dependence, set adrift. "Timorous, servile, helpless," they clung to settlements. Their numbers had also been thinned by wars, disease and absorption into white society. Forsaken until the times of the rubber boom, from then on native rubber gatherers became key factors in production.

In the 1850s steamers began regular trips on the Amazon. In 1853 the Amazon Navigation Company had three wood-burning steamers on the main stream. In 1857 seven steamers were transporting rubber, cacao, and Brazil nuts down the river for export. Ocean-going liners from London and New York now began service upriver to Manaos and Iquitos (2,300 miles from the sea). During the Civil War, demand grew for rubber. Ironically, while America was fighting a Civil War to free the slaves, thousands of South American Indians were being enslaved for the production of rubber to be exported to the north. Tin masks, the bullwhip, iron collars were used to control the Indians. Children and young girls were sold to the rubber men, reluctant workers shot. Native huts were torched, those fleeing were shot down, recalcitrants left to rot in the stocks. The Putumayo was not the only area affected by such inhuman exploitation. All over the Amazon the competition was intense.

By 1883, Brazilian rubber exports had doubled, to over 11,000 tons; in 1890, Brazil exported 19,000 tons of the world total of 29,000. By 1903, when exports of Congo rubber were beginning to decline, Amazonia exported over

30,000 tons per year to supply the necessary material for the automobile industry, enough to allow the mass production of tires which began in 1910.

Bolivia was second to Brazil in amount of rubber produced; next came Peru, which mostly produced an inferior kind of caoutchouc, exploiting the Castilloa tree. Much of the Putumayo production was of "weak fine" rubber from Hevea guyanensis. Slave labor was considered "necessary" in order to ensure a profit, so Indians were rounded up in all rubber-producing territories. Shipments were normally cleared through Manaos or Iquitos, where Casement was based during his investigations of the conditions in the Putumayo. The rubber boom crested in 1910–1913 (when it was bringing in over $3 a pound)—creating an orgy of spending before the inevitable crash as local supplies petered out and plantation rubber from Malaysia and Sumatra entered the market. The major operators were companies such as J. G. Araujo of Manaos, known as the King of Rubber, the Suarez brothers in Bolivia, J. C. Arana of Peru who had begun as a peddler of Panama hats and ended by claiming 14,200,000 acres of land in Colombia and Peru. Various Swiss, German, French, British and American companies operated in the region, often in league with local producers.

2

Casement would arrive in the Putumayo at the height of the rubber boom. Over 1600 ships a year were calling at Amazonian ports. The cost of living in Manaos, the rubber capital, was four to five times higher than in New York. (Casement would eternally grumble about his awesome expenses.)

The tax on rubber (up to 30 percent) provided the money for Pará's wide boulevards, electric lighting, municipal water system, impressive harbor works, streetcars, advanced sanitation, hospitals. There were opera houses on the edge of the jungle, cafés, theaters, casinos, luxurious bordellos. The traffic in white slaves boomed; European whores arrived by the shipload (many direct from Brussels). Manaos, on a level of opulence comparable to that of Pará, was internationally renowned as a venue for opera, "high" culture and lavish entertainment, dance, delights of French cuisine and moral degeneration—a latex frontier. Iquitos, the capital of the state of Loreto, became almost overnight the second busiest Peruvian port after Callao, with paved streets, an opulent three-story hotel, a narrow gauge railroad for freight, three newspapers, electric lighting, immense warehouses and floating docks, elegant restaurants, and a very active Malecón. Iquitos was the capital of J. C. Arana's Peruvian Amazon Rubber Company.

Reports coming out of the Amazon at that time are interesting. Various writers note that the bachelorhood of the tappers led to "bestiality and other perversions." Some were even "Depraved hermits [who] dreaded visitors bringing disease." In Bolivia, Peru and Colombia the tappers—white, red or mongrel—were treated even more brutally than were the Brazilians. "No one could leave the company service. There was no rendering of accounts." Any deviant act could be committed with no fear of reprisal. Much of the rubber gathering was the work of small gangs, contracted or enslaved by itinerant adventurers who were often simply criminals in search of easy money. Some producers worked independently, but often in fact were enslaved by the Arabs or Moroccans who ran the village trading station.

It was said that during the boom years the native slaves of the Putumayo accounted for 25 percent of all Peruvian production. This was worth about $5–7 million on the London market.

As for the atrocities, these were the same as those committed elsewhere in the Amazon.

3

The enslavement of the Huitotos, the most docile tribe of the Putumayo region, began early on. The natives were initially willing workers, and gathered abundant latex. However, the quality of the rubber was not high and more intensive gathering was necessary to make a profit. This led to the agents cheating their workers, fixing arbitrary units to be gathered, and then to outright oppression. Julio César Arana's company was the paramount offender. Arana had begun as a mere peddler trading out of Yurimaguas on the Huallaga. He eventually achieved a navigation and trading monopoly on the Igaraparaná and Caraparaná rivers, which flow southeast to join the Putumayo. He offered ready credit to Vega and Company, Colombian rubber producers, and, when they were unable to pay, he bought them out. Arana had a sharp eye for business.

During the rubber boom attempts were made to subjugate the Andokes, Boras and Ocainas Indians. Not all tribes, however, proved to be as easily subdued as the Huitotos. (As recently as 1974, Survival International discovered the remaining 120 Andoke Indians. "In 1974 at the invitation of Survival International, the Anti-Slavery Society.... shared in an operation to free the

Andoke, an Amerindian tribe in Colombia, who were working for a rubber merchant to whom they stood in perpetual debt.... The tribe numbers 120 persons [today]. These are all that are left of the Andoke nation which in 1905 was estimated at 10,000 and was then enslaved and reduced by the Peruvian Amazon Rubber Company, Limited." By now they are probably extinct.)

"Uncivilized" aborigines as far as the Japuri were in the service of Arana and Brothers. After buying out the Colombian concern, Arana set up the Peruvian Amazon Company, Limited, incorporated in London, capitalized at $5 million (the J.C. Arana and Brothers Company had been capitalized at only $400,000). This consortium now took over the eight million acres of J. C. Arana and Brothers. The area was now under company control, aided by the Peruvian army, half breed "racionales," hired gunmen from Barbados and native overseers called "muchachos." By 1910, 10,000 Indians were under the company's authority. Some 4,000 workers were massed in twenty collection zones. There were hundreds of sentries, assorted gunmen, Barbadians, and aborigines working in the control, punishment and massacre of the Indians. As many as 20,000 Indians had already been exterminated, according to common gossip in Iquitos. Arana was not "directly" involved in company operations, however, by this time. He visited the Putumayo rarely, being principally concerned with the high life and the political scene in Lima. No one of importance in the Peruvian Amazon Company, it seemed, was directly involved in the atrocities committed in rubber collection—neither Lizardo Arana, nor Pablo Zumaeta (Arana's brother-in-law) nor Abel Alarco (another partner and brother-in-law) nor the managing directors sitting on the board in London. These men only hired those involved in the atrocities committed against the Indians. They claimed later that they were unaware of wrongdoing. They were interested only in profits.

In a gradually declining production cycle, from 1908 to 1910, the atrocities took on a feverish and uncontrolled character.

4

Atrocities, it came out later, had been commonplace since the very beginning of the commercial exploitation of rubber. They were a matter of official knowledge in all of the Amazon countries. Missionaries in the region had often reported cases of murder and slavery. These reports found their way into documents submitted to the Peruvian congress in Lima. There had also been details published in newspapers in Bogota, Manaos and Lima concerning massacres in the Putumayo. In Iquitos, Benjamín Saldaña Rocca published specific charges in his fly-by-night scandal sheets, *La Sanción* and *La Felpa*, which appeared irregularly. Rocca even brought charges in court—but the Arana company simply brought *counter* charges. (Rocca later was expelled from the area and took a job as reporter for a Lima newspaper, *La Prensa*.) The articles in *La Sanción* and *La Felpa* were read by a young American, Walter Hardenburg, who had been kidnapped by Arana's men along with a friend with whom he had been traveling. Hardenburg later published several sensational articles based on these reports in the London muckraking periodical *Truth*.

Reading Hardenburg is a trip to the past. *The Putumayo: The Devil's Paradise. Travels in the Peruvian Amazon Region and an Account of the Atrocities Committed upon the Indians Therein* is a fat, old fashioned volume, with soft paper and big print and the plates are wonderfully real. The introduction mentions Casement and quotes Jorge von Hassel in respect to the Huitotos: "Some of them have accepted the industry of collecting rubber—accepting 'civilization' offered by the rubber merchants, others have been annihilated.... [A]lcohol, rifle bullets, and smallpox have worked havoc among them in a few years."

Roundups of Indians, Hardenburg says, have become common, and "King Dog does but give place to King Stork." Barbarities, he adds, committed by the rubber merchants upon the Indians of the Ucayali and Marañón were brought to the attention of the Peruvian Government in 1903 and 1906 by the missionaries and presented to the Ministry of Justice, to no avail. The "peaceful Indians were put to work at rubber-gathering without payment, without food, in nakedness; they were flogged until their bones were laid bare when they failed to bring in a sufficient quota of rubber or attempted to escape, were left to die with their wounds festering with maggots and their bodies used as food for the agents' dogs." The Indians were mutilated in the *cepo*, or stocks, cut to pieces with machetes, crucified head downwards, their limbs lopped off. Target shooting for diversion was practiced on them. They were doused with kerosene and burned alive, both men and women. All of these charges come from *La Sanción* and *La Felpa*, the news sheets published in Iquitos. The stories are familiar.

There had been many reports of atrocities in the Putumayo region. In July 1907 the first published reports had appeared—those of Benjamín Saldaña Rocca in Iquitos, before he was expelled in 1908 and went to Lima to work for *La Prensa*. The reports in *La Sanción* were a series of testimonies, some anonymous; but a declaration of 29 August 1907 was sworn before a notary public. Actually *La Sanción* became, in modified format, *La Felpa* as it continued to bring out mounting charges against the Peruvian Amazon Company. The issue of 5 January 1907 carried descriptions of horrifying mutilations, torture and sadistic acts; the men involved incriminated themselves. In Manaos *O Jornal de Commercio* published additional accusations of Peruvian atrocities on 2 June 1908—reports picked up and published two days later in the *Provincia de Pará*. The latter article was read by Casement.

Hardenburg is particularly affronted by the "callousness of human suffering" on the part of the Spanish and Portuguese. He says that the torture of Indians for diversion (*por motivos frívolos*) is typically Spanish. His opinion of the natives is that they are "grown-up children" a common view and one shared by Casement. In an article published in 1912 in *The Contemporary Review*, Casement wrote, "… in the forest the wild men, it might be thought, were equally its natural denizens. Yet nothing became more clear the more these Indians were studied than that they were not children of the forest, but children of elsewhere lost in the forest—babes in the wood, grown up, it is true, and finding the forest their only heritage and shelter, but remembering always that it was not their home." Certainly, however, the beauties were there, the singing and the dancing, the colors. "While naked in body, slim, beautifully shaped and proportioned, colored like the very tree-trunks they flitted among like spirits of the woods—their minds were the minds of civilized men and women. They longed for another life—they hoped ever for another world." At the same time he also had a lively antipathy toward the blacks—the Barbadians, British subjects, hired by the Peruvian Amazon Company as sentries. The Barbadians were responsible for some of the worst abuses.

Most of Hardenburg's story, mostly hearsay, never fails to fascinate. He describes the Indians who "although short and small, are tough and strong and are of an agreeable reddish, coppery hue. The average height of the men seems to be about five feet; the women average from two to four inches less." They are timid and bashful. Their language is a sing-song Quechua. Later he describes the "Putumayo Indians"—the Huitotos—less agreeably, as "short, broad and strong but generally lazy and shiftless." Nearly all suffer from *carate* (skin disease). Both sexes pull out their eyebrows and lashes. the women are uglier than the men and paint on their faces blue and pink geometrical figures. They pierce the ears and nose with bamboo tubes and wear bracelets on their arms made from the chambria (Atrocarium) palm to ward off rheumatism.

Both sexes wear a kind of "night shirt" without sleeves. They drape themselves with pounds of beads. Their diet is diverse, including game, birds, vegetables, wild yucca, farinha.

5

Hardenburg was an American railway engineer. He and a friend, W. B. Perkins, left the Cauca Valley Railroad in Colombia, intending to seek better work on the Madeira-Mamoré Railway. (A disastrous idea, to judge by an early report by Casement on the type of labor needed there; the climate was deadly for both white and Chinese labor: "The 'darkie,'" he wrote, "and I mean the pure article, not the nigger, mongrel or half-caste of Brazil, but the pure-blooded, vigorous native African is the only type of humanity that can successfully grapple with hard work, hot sun and Malaria at the same time.")

The two friends decided to go off on a lark, crossing the Putumayo by canoe during late 1907 and early 1908. Reaching Mocoa after traversing the Andes, Hardenburg and Perkins faced an immense region disputed by Ecuador, Colombia and Peru, lying between the Napo and Putumayo rivers to the Atlantic. The dense selva was criss-crossed by trails, originally used by the missionary priests to travel from village to village.

Hardenburg and Perkins traveled with abundant supplies and baggage. They were fascinated by the Amazonian rain forest, impressed by the wildlife. They carried a cask of aguardiente and periodically tapped it, happily floating down the river—camping, singing, getting drunk, stripping naked to swim in the muddy waters. It was not a safe voyage; they had to be constantly cautious of dangerous currents, careful to avoid semi-submerged logs and floating debris. Hardenburg gives the reader views of the landscape, simple but sensuous. He offers data on the different kinds of rubber gathered. *Caucho negro*, which once abounded in the upper Putumayo but is now scarce because of the onslaughts of careless caucheros—if notched appropriately it could be tapped over an indefinite period. The other type, *jebe* or *siringa*, is more valuable, and both kinds are being planted. On one of the plantations of the Arana company they saw several thousand rubber trees; these were now two to four years old and flourishing, according to Hardenburg. The plantation rubber, however, was not nearly as important as the wild kind in terms of total production.

Hardenburg and Perkins planned to continue to the Caraparaná and from there by launch to Iquitos. Lots of aguardiente got drunk and, except for a few mishaps such as getting stuck on a mud bank far from the stream when the river level fell, all went well until they reached the central Putumayo region. There, at La Unión station, Don Fabio, the assistant manager, invited the boys to stay over. The place was a pleasant garden, with vegetables and fruits of all kinds growing in profusion. They also observed about 1000 *arrobas* of rubber awaiting shipment. The trader was selling manufactured goods at exorbitant prices to the Huitotos, the forest people, Hardenburg notes. Their guide also told them that the Peruvian manager treated his people "very badly." (The manager worked working for the Peruvian Amazon Company which not long ago had forced the Colombians out.) If the Indians did not bring in a sufficient amount of rubber—judged by weighing—they were flogged, shot or mutilated at the will of the man in charge. Forty-five Huitoto families collected for Don Fabio. Hardenburg observed these people, noting the women with their prominent periform breasts and the genitals of the men, "compressed and tied up so they never reach their normal development."

Hardenburg also mentions the *Chupe de tabaco*, the sucking of tobacco, a ceremony in which the Indians stick their fingers into a thick pot of black juice made of the tobacco plant and then suck the juice off. Possibly coca was added, but intoxication invariably followed. Indians gathered around the pot for hours, sucking and debating, making speeches and yelling with agreement, discussing important matters, blending oaths with hallucination. The ceremony was always followed when any agreement was about to be entered into with the whites. Hardenburg describes the ritual—but probably never actually saw it—and his description agrees with to that of other observers. He also describes the Indians' living arrangements: "As a rule, several families live in one house, each, however, having its own particular fireplace, furniture, and domestic utensils, generally limited to a few small bamboo stools and benches, several earthen pots, some baskets, various kinds of paint, a quantity of gourds used as plates, etc., a few primitive musical instruments, such as rude drums, bamboo flutes, and bone whistles...." The Huitotos have been "enslaved by the 'civilizing' company"—the Putumayo Amazona Company—and are constantly employed in the extraction of rubber, leaving them no time for cultivation. As a consequence their only food is a small quantity of yucca, plantains and grubs, *chonta* palm, and wild fruits. Many die of starvation. Because of overwork, ill treatment, disease and poor diet the numbers of the Indians were diminishing alarmingly, Hardenburg says; "unless something is done to protect them, this noble race of aborigines will ... soon disappear completely, as have so many others in the region of the Upper Amazon."

The use of coca was common, both among Huitotos and "whites." The leaves of the coca plant were toasted, pulverized and mixed with the ashes of the burnt leaves of another plant to take away the bitter taste. Inserted into the mouth, rolled up under the cheek, the coca was kept there sometimes all day; the juice was swallowed. Coca was widely used throughout the region as a stimulant and helped in feats of endurance. Hardenburg himself used coca and found it "useful."

The Peruvian army was instrumental in taking over the land from the Colombians. The army was everywhere, often indistinguishable from the men working for the Peruvian Amazon Company, with which they had a "special relationship"—Arana, living in Lima, was an influential politician by this time.

6

Suddenly, the *Liberal*, one of the Peruvian Amazon Company's large launches—and the one on which Casement and the Commission of Inquiry would later travel—appeared on the river. There were sixty soldiers on board. A Peruvian gunboat, the *Iquitos*, also appeared. Hardenburg and Perkins were arrested, obviously because they were thought to be rubber traders invading the territories of the Peruvian Amazon Company. Their assertions of being American citizens were ignored as irrelevant or untrue. Hardenburg was taken aboard the *Iquitos*, where he was kicked, beaten, insulted and abused by the Captain, Arce Benavides, and a pack of company employees. Perkins was kept behind.

Perkins was taken to El Encanto station, where he soon witnessed the massacre of a dozen peones, and the rape of Pilar Gutiérrez, in an advanced state of pregnancy, dragged from her hiding place in the bushes and allotted to a sentry to who took her off and violated her, accompanied by her agonized cries. Sick and dying natives were lying about the station at El Encanto, thrown in the river when they expired; backs with the "*marca de Arana*"—deep scars made by the bullwhip; plump girls from eight to thirteen years old kept as "concubines" and traded from one man to another until they were murdered or flogged and sent back to their tribe.

There is something sinisterly erotic about all this.

7

The feverish collection system was destroying production at the source. The *racionales* were responsible for assigning the quota of rubber for each Indian. The Indians used their machetes to gash frightfully "every rubber tree they can find, frequently cutting them so much and so deep, in their frantic efforts to extract the last drop of milk, that vast numbers of the trees die annually." The milk, drying on the trunk, was gathered in strings later and carried in baskets to the Indians' huts. There it was placed in a *quebrada* and beaten to remove impurities, wound up in large rolls, dried to a blackish color. This rubber was weighed at the station. "The Indians know by experience what the needle of the balance should mark, and when it indicates that they have delivered the full amount they leap about and laugh with pleasure. When it does not, they throw themselves face downwards on the ground, and in this attitude await their punishment." As in the Congo, chiefs of section were paid no salary but received a commission on the amount produced.

Hardenburg lists the atrocities committed in grim detail, repeating the facts as reported: The Indians of the Putumayo are forced to work day and night with no pay except for food; they are kept in nakedness; they are robbed of crops; women and children are used to slake the lascivious desires of the overseers; some workers are sold as slaves in Iquitos from $20 to $40 each; they are flogged, their bones laid bare, and resulting sores are left to fester; they receive no medical treatment but are left to die, are eaten by maggots or are thrown to the dogs for food; they are castrated and mutilated (penises, ears, fingers, arms and legs cut off); they are tortured, crucified head down; their houses and crops are burned to the ground for amusement; they are cut to pieces, dismembered with knives, axes and machetes; their children are snatched up by their feet and their brains dashed out against tree trunks and walls; the old are killed; they are shot for amusement or soaked in kerosene and set on fire.

Finally set free by the Peruvian Amazon Company, Hardenburg and Perkins spent weeks waiting for compensation from Arana for their stolen luggage and supplies. During this time they made inquiries about the company and were provided by Saldaña Rocca's son with the original texts of declarations published in *La Sanción* and *La Felpa*, as well as other unpublished reports accusing the Peruvian Amazon Company of countless atrocities. Hardenburg took this evidence to the acting US Consul in Iquitos, Guy T. King, but was given no satisfaction. King said that the US Government already had received reports of local conditions from his predecessor, Charles C. Eberhardt.

Hardenburg hastily put together a book, containing reports, declarations and complaints about the Peruvian Amazon Company, along with background material on the canoe trip by the two young Americans and their kidnapping by the "soldiers" of Arana. He took his book to Britain and attempted to get it published. Many of the passages in *The Devil's Paradise* Hardenburg lifted from the pages of *La Felpa* and *La Sanción*. Since so much of the book was obviously hearsay, publishers in Britain were aware of the risks involved in bringing it out. No offers were made. However, Hardenburg finally contacted the Anti-Slavery Society, where the Reverend John Harris (a colleague of Casement's who had worked with him on the Congo revelations) advised the young American to publish in *Truth*. The result was a series of sensational articles. Casement read some of these while working as Consul-General in Rio.

Hardenburg was right about the British Government being concerned, both directly and indirectly, in the Putumayo atrocities. The Peruvian Amazon Company was incorporated in London. The Barbadians employed by the company were British citizens, and they were involved in some of the worst horrors. The whole of the rubber output of the region was placed on the British market, which constituted an additional excuse for intervening; trade was still the major interest of Britain abroad. The culmination of the campaign by the Anti-Slavery Society and the yellow press resulted in the Commission of Inquiry with which Casement traveled during his investigations of conditions in the Putumayo for his subsequent official report.

8

Another, closer, look at the "monster" Arana, founder of the Peruvian Amazon Rubber Company, might show a less horrible face. The descriptions available are all from those who hated him (except for the laudatory articles and honors from the Peruvian Government). Julio César Arana was the same age as Casement. Born in 1864 at Rioja in the foothills of the Peruvian Andes, he had had to struggle to survive on the frontier. The Select Committee later questioned him on his origins. He was not an educated man. He began his career as an itinerant peddler in the Upper Amazon about 1881, when he was barely seventeen. By 1890 had formed a successful partnership with John B. Vega. Amalgamation with a French firm in 1892 had lasted until its liquidation in 1896. Arana first bought rubber from the Putumayo in 1899 and in December 1901 joined with the firm of Larranaga Ramires, established at La Chorrera on the river Igaraparaná, later the headquarters of the London registered Peruvian Amazon Company. It was a good time to do business in the area. Arana's story is one of struggle and success in the face of harsh conditions.

"I entered into business relations with the said Colonies exchanging merchandise for rubber, buying up produce and making advances," he explained. "[The] Indians on the rivers Igaraparaná and Caraparaná had resisted the establishment of civilization in their districts ... [but] from about the year 1900 onwards the Indians became more civilized, and a system of rubber collected by the Indians for European merchandise sprang up between the Indians and the said Colonies. From the time my business in the Putumayo district gradually increased, but by slow degrees."

Arana took his brother Lizardo into partnership, and his two brothers-in-law, Pablo Zumaeta and Abel Alarco. They traded successfully under the name J.C. Arana and Hermanos until 1907 when capitalization was increased by forming a limited company in England. The Peruvian Amazon Rubber Company was incorporated in October 1907 with a capital of £1 million with Arana and Alarco on the board, Arana as Managing Director, along with a Frenchman and an Englishman. In 1908 the word "Rubber" was dropped from the company's name.

One helpful aspect in company operations was the close relationship that Arana had nurtured with the Peruvian government (he would later become a Senator). Many "colonies" along the Putumayo had been claimed by Colombia, but by 1906 Arana had taken over the whole 12,000 square mile area, acquired at the cost of £116,700. At this point Peru and Colombia submitted their territorial dispute to Pope Pius X. Consequently both countries agreed to withdraw their military authority over some 200,000 square miles. However, the Peruvian President, José Pardo, favored the establishment of company rule as one way of asserting sovereignty. He supported Arana's commercial interests in the Putumayo.

Arana considered it important to advertise his rights, and those of Peru, in the Putumayo. A French explorer, Eugene Robuchon, was hired at company expense in 1904 to prepare a kind of general survey, later published as *En el Putumayo y sus afluentes (In the Putumayo and its Tributaries)* proving that the Putumayo belonged to Peru. During his research Robuchon died mysteriously, leaving his report unfinished. Rey de Castro, former Peruvian consul at

Manaos and a close friend of Arana, edited Robuchon's book from his notes and diaries. Twenty thousand copies were printed in Lima 1907 and appeared as a semi-official document. The text and the many photographs reproduced in it constitute a fascinating picture of the Putumayo Indians, of their conditions of life. But something is wrong here. The bodies of the Indians are displayed naked, almost as objects, cannibalized by the Kodak; and the white men carry Winchester rifles while the Indians are unarmed.

They might well carry rifles for protection, since cannibalism was so widespread in the Amazon, according to some reports. Robuchon, writing in his diary, spoke of skulls hanging from the roofs. Indians with plugs of coca stared at him with glistening eyes and whacked his back in friendly fashion, and they surrounded his hut: he kept his rifle ready. Robuchon also kept his camera ready—and it was just possible that he began to photograph not only naked girls, groups of young naked men, and communal houses but the mutilated bodies and the bodies of the dead killed by company agents. Then he would indeed be "capturing" truth; in which case he himself would have to be eliminated. Which is arguably what happened to this recorder of semi-scientific materials, unless the placid Huitotos themselves simply cut him down and devoured him. (Yet he "married" a young Huitoto girl who was later sent to live with his family in France.)

En el Putumayo y sus afluentes, whether written by Robuchon or crafted by someone else, is candid, describing the Indians "objectively." "The chest is broad. The breasts are elevated and flung back, giving an air of nobility. But the superior and inferior members, particularly the latter, are little developed.... It is interesting to note their peculiar way of walking, especially that of the women. The habit of carrying their babies on their backs gives them an inclined position which they keep all their lives. The feet are turned inwards so that when they walk the muscles close against each other, giving the appearance of modesty.... The genital organs of the men, covered by a belt of fiber which constrains them, never achieve their normal development. The member is small and with a tendency to be always covered by the prepuce which is very large and covers all the glans. In the women there is no anomaly. The breasts are periform and stand out, even with the elderly, in whose case they lose their volume but never hang."

There is something very sad here, and something distressingly familiar.

9

By 1905 Casement had become famous. But he had his usual troubles. His brothers and sister were demanding; he worried about them, helped them—when he could—with money and moral support. During his periods of home leave he lived at various lodgings in Ireland and Great Britain, never establishing himself. His priorities were mixed. He felt immense responsibility for the Congo reform movement, was heavily involved; yet actions were being taken that soon obviated his continuing labors. What could he do now that he had an international reputation as a reformer and humanitarian? He was looked upon in the Foreign Office as an asset, yet his fame was a kind of disability. He had, of course, to be rewarded for his efforts. A well-known member of the consular staff could not be given a secondary post in some foreign hole.

Then there was Casement's increasing involvement in the Irish question. Home Rule seemed to answer his need for a crusade. During 1905 he had become friends with Alice Stopford Green, who was a catalyst for his nationalist sentiments. Alice Green was phenomenal. Through her teens she was almost blind, but managed to get an education at home and even taught herself Greek. Later she had an operation that restored normal sight—but she never lost her ability for total recall. After her father's death the family moved from Ireland to London. In 1874 she married John Richard Green, the historian, who since 1869 had suffered from tuberculosis. Following his death in 1883 she continued his work on the history of the conquest of England. She would go on to publish numerous scholarly and historical studies. Her salon in London was frequented by "advanced" thinkers such as Florence Nightingale, May Kinsley, Bishop Creighton, H.A.L. Fisher, the Humphrey Wards and Winston Churchill. During the 1880s her home was a haven for Home Rule fanatics. Casement was invited to meet Mrs. Green soon after he wrote her a letter—dated 24 April 1904—on behalf of the Congo Reform Association, asking for her support. She was fifty-four. He was forty. In Mrs. Green's parlor the talk was frank, and often anti-British or anti-Establishment. Casement reacted positively to such an environment and expressed his own informed criticism of British imperialism, character and commercialism. The Great Question for the Irish, especially since the turbulent 1880s, continued to be Home Rule. In America, millions of Irish immigrants vehemently supported Irish independence. The Irish Nationalists inside and outside Ireland were generally ignored by the English, who were uncomfortably aware of the economic interests in the balance. Britain controlled Irish wealth, and independence—in the view of the landlords—was thus always out of the question "for the time being." The British Empire, in process of slow disintegration, still held out, inspired by trade and longstanding commercial interests.

Gladstone, a "parson perverted" as Henry James called him, a religious monomaniac and self-righteous moralist, had became ever more intent, in his senility, to drive the Home Rule Scheme through parliament. Ireland was on the brink, he believed, of outright revolution. England could not continue subjugating Ireland without risking self-destruction. The Home Rule bill failed. Gladstone, the Grand Old Man, was out in 1886.

These frustrations only exacerbated the Irish problem and encouraged Irish separatists toward radical action. The brilliant Parnell had seemed to carry the whole country with him. The 1889 trial, in which he was accused of having condoned the Phoenix Park murders in Dublin in 1882, was sensational, the evidence shown to be forged by Richard Pigott (with the collusion of members of the British government). Then Parnell was destroyed by the scandal of his private life.

It seemed year after year that Home Rule would have to come eventually. In 1895 the Conservatives were out again—making no difference nevertheless to official attitudes toward Irish Independence. The Home Rule question continued to affect English politics and Anglo-American relations—but enthusiasm tended to fade periodically while the Irish, brawling among themselves, lost their impetus to move ahead toward self-rule. Conflict with America developed over a border dispute in British Guiana and Venezuela, developing into a journalistic drama that pushed Home Rule into the background, and suggesting that war might even be possible with the United States. In political circles in Dublin and London, however, Irish activists continued to mouth their loathing for Britain and the Empire, planning—actively organizing—outright revolt. They were aided by money and encouragement from across the Atlantic.

Casement's extreme anti-British statements and his fame as a reformer gave him a certain cachet in Alice Green's salon. He became a part of an influential clique of Irish renegades. The Irish Question provided an answer to Casement's need for a campaign to right what he saw as an obvious wrong—the "enslavement" of the Irish by the British and the denial to the Irish of their claim to self rule.

10

In view of Casement's outstanding job in the Congo, the Foreign Office had assigned him to one of the best consular posts in the service, that of Lisbon. It was a cushy and prestigious situation, one that career hands dreamed of getting. But Casement was not interested in spending the rest of his life as a distinguished clerk. He was also ill; but then he was frequently ill, suffering from complaint or another, the price of long African service.

After spending only about a month at Lisbon he requested sick leave and was seconded without pay. Notified of the award of the C.M.G. for his distinguished service in the Congo, he spoke of the honor flippantly. He was contemptuous of honors, or so he appeared. He was seriously considering retirement or a second career. Yet who could retire with no income and no investments? He had come to another "crisis" in his life. The only answer would be to go on working—but where?

He was posted this time to Pará, which was a disappointment—a backwater city on the Tocantins River with a population of about 100,000—but the Foreign Office (outraged that he had given up a "plum" which might have gone to someone else) told him it would be temporary, until something more appropriate could be found for an officer of his caliber. He had almost had the consulship in Haiti, an excellent posting, if not as good as Lisbon, except that a more "deserving" individual got it as a reward for services rendered to the state.

Pará was definitely not a pleasant posting. The former consul there, Richard Rhind, had had to be carried away, dead drunk. The office was a shambles when Casement arrived in February. He arranged to move to the building of the London and Brazilian Bank. (The bank would have second thoughts about their tenant later, when the stream of sleaze began arriving, and the Pará manager would be goaded to get rid of the consulate.) While resting from the entanglements of British drunks and wasters, Casement got to work on the chaos of his archives. He made lengthy complaints to the Foreign Office, and endless requests for reform in the consular service. His obsessive neatness, his passion for the right paper of the right size and the right envelopes, his lengthy reports were noted as a "sin of commitment."

The locals of "mixed races" he abhorred. In a letter of April 1907 to his cousin Gee he wrote: "Brazil and Brazilians are vile. I can't bear them—mud-colored swine!" He hated above all their Parisian affectations and their superficiality. His view of half-breeds was extreme; in March 1908 he wrote to

Lord Dufferin about "hideous cross-breeds—of Negro-Portuguese with, up here in the Amazon, a very large admixture of native blood. Altogether the resultant human compost is the nastiest form of black-pudding you have ever sat down to.... The Brazilian is the most arrogant, insolent and pig-headed brute in the world, I should think." These attitudes and opinions reflect his position, his self-esteem and the comical side of British relations with coloreds.

Casement did not maintain himself apart from society. He was a respectable member of the British expatriate community. When transferred to Santos he lived in a "settlement" in Guaruja on the healthy seaward side of the island of Santo Amaro, where he often stayed at the leading hotel. Santo Amaro was a lovely resort, with good accommodation, broad beaches, a deepwater port, and sailors.

11

By the end of 1908 Casement requested sick leave. On his way home, he passed through Barbados in the British West Indies. It was a depressing voyage, in spite of the occasional contact. He had, off and on during the same year, considered resignation. He was sick of the Consular Service, which, he said, was "only jobbery and corruption." Back home, he stayed with the Berrys, old friends, and made inquiries about possible positions outside government service. In May 1907 he had had a tentative job offer with the Mozambique Company, as Inspector of Finances, but negotiations fell through.

Then he was offered the position of Consul-General in Rio de Janeiro. He accepted immediately. His official life would not after all change for a while.

The Rio consulate that he took charge of on 22 March 1909 was over a cookshop, with its accompanying odors and heat, reached by way of two flights of an obscure and narrow staircase, humorously described by Ernest Hambloch in his memoirs. But it was in the center of town, near the Custom House and—although noisy—convenient to the usual clientele. Casement did not set up living quarters in the city itself but located in Petrópolis, the affluent suburb where the British Legation and the international diplomatic corps were established. (Petrópolis is where, some time later, Elizabeth Bishop lived with her Brazilian lover, Lota de Macedo Soares, and battled her own demons, mostly the bottle.) Petrópolis was the spot for Consul-General Casement: it had been founded by the Emperor Dom Pedro, and was the sanctuary of many old court families, decidedly the most distinguished place to live, socially, and the most pleasant climatically—free of the stifling heat and dust of the city. Casement viewed his new role as more "diplomatic" than consular and fame, his Irish charm and his fascinating conversation gave him immediate entree to the choicest circles. The official dispatches continued to flow—some critical, especially from the British Minister, Cheetham, who reported later—pettishly—that Casement had not played a sufficient part in the social round. "He lived," Cheetham said, "too retired a life, and did not take quite the position in the colony which would have been the most useful." Casement, at 44 a very young Consul-General, probably avoided the Minister's company as much as possible. His anti-British pose had grown increasingly vocal by this time. The Consul-General's surprisingly untypical anti-British comments were noted by the Baron von Nordenflycht, the German Consul-General, with whom Casement became friendly. In letters to Irish nationalists and sympathizers he let himself go, in spite of the fact that he was an official British representative. Reports indicate that he seemed to be losing touch with the realities of his situation. Hambloch describes how, during a cocktail party, Casement angrily swept vases of flowers off a table during a tirade. At a party given by the general manager of the Leopoldina Railway, Knox Little, Casement, the British General-Consul, delivered an embarrassing anti-British speech.

All was not consular boredom in Rio, as his diaries show.

The 1910–11 Diaries

January 13th. Gabriel Ramos. Last time—'Polpito' at Barca at 11.30. To Icarsby 'precisa muito'. 15 or 20$. X deep to the hilt. Also on Barca the young caboclo (thin) dark gentleman of Icarsby, eyed constantly and wanted, would have gone but Gabriel querido waiting at Barca Gate! 'Polpito'—in very deep thrusts.

January 20th. Valdemiro—20$

From 20 January until the 24th he was sick in Petrópolis, traveling down to Rio on consular business, but actively pursuing his personal goals at the same time. His entries exhibit notable gaps.

January 24th. Valdemiro Rua 20$.

February 28th. Deep screw and to hilt. X 'poquinho'. Mario in Rio 8 ½ + 6" 40$. Hospedaria, Rua do Hospicio. 3$ only FINE room shut window lovely, young 18 and glorious. Biggest since Lisbon July 1904 and as big. Perfectly huge. 'Nunca veio maior!' Nunca.

He went on leave, beginning 1 March 1910, heading for Sao Paulo. First, he had, he notes in his diary, pressing business with a boy in Buenos Aires. He would never visit Rio again.

March 2nd. Arr. S. Paulo. Antonio. 10$ Rua Direite. Dark followed and hard. Teatro Municipal. Breathed and quick, enormous push. Loved mightily, to hilt deep X.

March 3rd. Saw Antonio at Café watering plants.

He traveled to Santos on the 4th to see Parminter, who had been a member of the Sanford Expedition and whom Casement was to help not only at Santos but also in London in 1912. He stayed in Santos until the 8th, when he left for Buenos Aires and his pressing business with the boys.

March 11th. Arr. B. Aires and on shore to the Hotel of before Algerian.

March 12th. Morning in Avenida de Mayo, splendid erections, Ramón 7$, 10" at least. X in.

March 13th. Saw Ramón get off tram at Zoo and sit down on seat and read pencil under ear, watched long and then on to Station, back at 10 p.m. met Ramón at Palace after sailor with request of fleet. Ramón 10$ to meet tomorrow.

March 14th. Ramón. At Zoo entrance and Ramón to breakfast at Restaurant there, no it was in Chocolate House and name written on paper and his pencil mine gave 20$. Again at night.

Tuesday, 15th March. Ramón. Breakfast Restaurant and at Plaza Hotel at 11 p.m.

From the 16th till the 20 he was at Mar de Plata, then on the 21st returned to Buenos Aires.

March 22nd. Ramón at Zoo again and in the Bosquet afterwards, by train to Belgrano and back.

March 23rd. Ramón X in, 4 this year. To La Plata and lunch at Hotel there. Lay down for an hour and then to gardens and tea and back at 5.30 train. At Club and arranged to go San Marco tomorrow.

He was at San Marco from the 24th, returning after what seems a wet, interesting but obviously uneventful stay, to Buenos Aires.

March 27th. Returned to Buenos Aires at Station and sailors again.

March 28ᵗʰ. Ramón. At Zoo and lunch and walk to gardens of Palermo.

March 29ᵗʰ. Ramón. Left for Mar de Plata but sick of night train so stayed behind, many types, especially Martinez of Entre Ríos.

On the 30ᵗʰ and 31ˢᵗ he was at Mar de Plata, then in Buenos Aires again on 1 April.

April 2ⁿᵈ. Wrote Ramón.... Met sailors of fleet and others. At club with 'Amethyst' officer. [This day he drew £80 and book passage on the *Veronese* for Liverpool. He regretted leaving Ramón, and his memories of the boy would haunt him.]

April 3ʳᵈ. Last time Ramón, at Tigre. At Hurlingham and then to Tigre with Ramón from Belgrano, never again. Saw last time at Belgrano.

April 4ᵗʰ. Left Buenos Aires in 'Veronese' wrote to Ramón from Montevideo.

April 5ᵗʰ. At Montevideo, posted letter to Ramón. Sailed at 4 p.m.

April 11ᵗʰ. At Bahía. Type at night on board. Stevedore.

April 23th. At Las Palmas. Three types, one beautiful.

April 24ᵗʰ. At Tenerife, all day, gardens and type.

On 25 April he left Tenerife after a pleasant day. By the 30ᵗʰ they were approaching Land's End and on 1 May arrived at Liverpool, where he got the train to London and spent the night at the Euston Hotel. His career was going to take a strange and drastic turn.

Having enjoyed his trip so far, anxious as he had been to get away from his duties in Brazil, Casement had a few days to get his "legs" before crossing to Dublin on 18 May.
The death of King Edward on 6 May gave his visit a somewhat ironic twist.

May 3ʳᵈ. Earl's Court, Greek £1.0/0.

On 6 May he was at the Foreign Office, where Tyrell mentioned that the King was critically ill, probably on his deathbed. On 7 May King Edward's death was announced to the press and the nation went into mourning. From 8 May until he left for Dublin on the 18th, he socialized, dined out, went to the theater and to the opera, visited the Exhibition numerous times, saw Gee and Nina.

May 12th. At Caversham with Gee. Milano Francesco £1.0/0.

May 19th. In Dublin.

May 20th Sent Ramón a postcard from here. In Dublin at Zoo. King's funeral service but did not go.

May 21st. In Dublin. In Phoenix Park and lovely, X where F. Cavendish killed.

Dublin is rather hot, but boring. He knows his way around.

May 26th. In Dublin. 'See it coming'. To Belfast, John McGonegal, huge and curved up by Cregagh Road, met by chance at clock tower and off on tram. It was huge and curved and he was awfully keen. X 4/6.

On the 27th he was at the Gresham Hotel and then on to Richall Castle. He was looking forward to meeting Millar, an old friend with whom he had an excellent arrangement.

May 28th. Left for Warrenpoint with Millar. Heated and huge enjoyment both enjoyed. He came to lunch at G[rand] Central Hotel. Turned in together at 10.30 to 11—after watching billiards. Not a word said till—'Wait I'll untie it' and then 'Grand'. Told many tales and pulled it off on top grandly. First time after so many years and so deep mutual longing. Rode gloriously, splendid steed. Huge, told of many. 'Grand'.

May 29th. At Warrenpoint and Rostrevor. Enormous over 7 ½" I think. Asked after friend, repeatedly. Millar again. First time he turned his back, 'Grand' back voluntarily.

May 30th. Left Warrenpoint to Belfast together. [He sees friends in Belfast. Then he goes on with his arcana.] 'It's Grand' Green jersey at 11 at hotel, did not.

May 31st. At Belfast. To Grant's ring with Millar.

On 1 June he was in Belfast, not doing much but writing letters, some to Rio, and relaxing. From the evening of 3 June until the 10th he was at Bally-castle. Then he was off to Cushenden. He saw Biggar, the solicitor and friend who was to keep many boxes of private papers until the very end, when he opened them, found they contained masses of details concerning Casement's secret homosexual activities—and placed them on the redeeming bonfire. The next entry was curious to say the least.

June 13th. Left Cushenden [with "young driver, 19, on 29 Aug next"]. Tiny wee Jack McCormack talked Irish in road. To Dobbs' to lunch—on to Cole-raine by 6.51 train—to Cloth Workers Arms. Lovely room. Millar and Argentine sailors. XX.

On 14 June he was at Portrush during the day and then home by 6.10 to find a letter from Millar, one which it would be interesting to read, no doubt concerning their late adventures. On the 15th on he was at Tara staying with Harris and family. Then on the 17th he was at Ballycastle, staying at Margher-intemple. Here he received a letter from the Anti-Slavery people about the Putumayo River and the Amazon Rubber Company. He answered by wire and also wrote.

The Foreign Office was interested. Officials there had read the sensational accusations by the American Hardenburg and were being pressured from many sides to do something. However, caution was called for. There was a clear reluctance to act on the basis of reports by an American with no official credentials who was publishing sensational stories in a "radical" reform maga-zine. Accurate reports and specific information were needed, not merely jour-nalistic articles. There had, in fact, been other communications concerning the Putumayo and the conditions there involving British subjects.

June 20th. Left Ballycastle at 4 train, Millar to dinner at N. Counties Hotel, splendid. Gave Millar pin for tie. Stayed till 9.30 and in Room XX.... In deep and warm.

On the 21st he was at Belfast and went for lunch to Castle Dobbs, returning "with medical student in train, charming view and nice face." Back to London on 22 June, he went again to the Exhibition.

June 24th. To dine with Conan Doyle. Morel there and to 'Speckled Band' after. 1 a.m. H.B. 10/-, and Jamaica 6/6 =16/6.

He continued his usual rounds toward the end of the month. At the Exhibition on the 27th, he noted succinctly, "Greek. Fled." Nothing much happened. Life went on.

July 1st. In London. Welsh Will. Splendid 6' 3 ½" 10/- and Japan [exhibition].

He was at the Savoy from the second of July.

July 6th. Left Savoy for London. To Gloucester Road and lovely type X to Bolton Gardens and home.

His days passed in dining out, writing letters, gabbing with friends. On the 11th he attended a testimonial for Morel. He wrote to Tyrell to say he "had heard I was to go to Putumayo and was ready if Sr. E. Grey wished it." On the 12th he packed up to go to Ireland but got a wire from Tyrell asking him to call the next day at the Foreign Office.

July 12th. To Welsh Will but too late at 9 p.m. on and many types.

July 13th. [At the Foreign Office, for talks in the afternoon with Tyrell concerning the deteriorating Putumayo situation, later with Mrs. Green to discuss Irish independence.] To F.O. and Mrs. Green. Sir. E. Grey was decided to send me to Putumayo.

Matters were advancing rapidly. On the 14th he booked passage on a Booth steamer for Pará on the 24th. He spent the 15th looking over relevant papers at the Foreign Office, but that was not all, Hyde Park was hot.

July 15th. To Brompton road and Albert (10/-) X in Park. Then M[arble] Arch and fine type in Park but fled and home at 12.50. 15 ½ years Albert. Albert 10/-.

He left for Dublin on the 16th, feeling very tired after London, arriving at 6:30 in the morning and early at it.

July 17th. In Phoenix Park after dinner to Zoo. Fine type. Stiff.

In Ireland until the 20th, he then returned to London and on the 21st was again at a testimonial for Morel and on the same day for lunch with Doyle. He makes a brief accounting, as usual noting minor expenses, which usually included gifts made to his tricks. On the 22nd and 23rd he was winding up personal affairs and no doubt thinking of familiar scenes in Madeira as well of his upcoming trip to the Peruvian Amazon.

Casement's successor at Pará, George Pogson, had forwarded a report concerning a Captain Thomas Whiffen of the 14th, the King's Hussars, previously believed dead. Whiffen had passed through Pará on 2 June 1909 after intensive exploration of the Putumayo territory. Whiffen had been wounded in the Boer War and, on half pay, was making a trip to regain his health, subsidized by his father. He spent nine months in the Putumayo. During this time he had discovered the death of Robuchon. He had gathered a considerable mass of materials, including maps, photographs, records bearing on conditions of the Indians in the Putumayo. Whiffen was an excellent independent witness who had been helped in his explorations by a Barbadian, John Brown. This John Brown (Casement would later call him a "useless brute") returned with Whiffen to his rented estate at Monserrat, eventually to become Whiffen's "interpreter."

Whiffen is a strange case. He believed the Indians to have an "innate cruelty." They were not, as many believe, "docile" but could be extremely dangerous enemies. The Indian was "extraordinarily negative." The gentle Indian, "peaceful and loving," was a fiction. During the investigations of the Select Committee, later, Whiffen was questioned. He gave an odd story of bribery and intimidation by Rey de Castro and Julio César Arana, who met with him in Manaos before he left South America. They wanted Whiffen to give up his maps and notes made during his stay in the Putumayo, in order—so they said—to publish them as they had those of Robuchon. Some months later, Arana and Whiffen met in Paris at the Nouvelle Hotel. They had lunch together, during which Arana questioned Whiffen about Hardenburg's articles in *Truth*. Had Whiffen been asked by *Truth* to provide more damaging information? Whiffen had not. Two weeks later Whiffen was invited by Arana for dinner at the Cafe Royal in London. Whiffen then told him that he had been asked to write a report for the Foreign Office. Later, after copious champagne, Arana asked how much Whiffen would need to write a report for the Peruvian Government. Somehow, the tipsy captain was talked into writing down a statement in Spanish (Whiffen's Spanish was very poor), including the phrase: "My expenses were £1,400 but I am agreeable and will receive £1,000 as compensation." Sobering up a bit and suspecting a trap, Whiffen tore up the note and threw it into the wastebasket. It was later pasted together clumsily, and—translated into English—presented as proof that Whiffen had agreed to write a report for the Peruvian Government saying he had seen no irregularities in the Putumayo. (Incredible as it seems, Whiffen's subsequently published book did not mention atrocities or criminal conduct of any kind.)

In view of the mounting scandal, the British directors of the Peruvian Amazon Company in England felt compelled to send out a Commission of Inquiry. The Foreign Office was willing to dispatch an official observer—"Some consular official had to go"—and Casement was obviously Sir Edward Grey's first choice, considering his former work in the Congo. If Casement was agreeable, he would accompany the commission when it left for South America.

Casement borrowed Robuchon's book from the Anti-Slavery Society to read on his way out. He also took along Enock's *The Andes and the Amazon* for background information.

July 24th. At sea on the 'Edinburgh Castle'—and missing many meals.

They were to spend four days at Madeira, a particularly pleasant stopover for Casement, as his diary shows.

.

July 28th. Hotel. Splendid testiminhos, no bush to speak of. Good wine needs no bush. Soft as silk and big and full. £1.0/-. Carlos Augusto Costa—189 Rua dos Ferreiros, Funchal. Very fine one, big, long, thick—wants awfully and likes very much. 7/6. João Big £1.12/6. International Hotel. Bella Vista.

July 29th. Hotel £1.0./-. Carlos Augusto Costa £1.0/-. Total L2.10/-. Last time Carlos 9–11, huge extension.

July 30th. Hotel £1.0/-João £10.0/-. Hotel £11.12.6 C.A. Costa £2.10/- = £14.2/6 in Madeira.

They sailed from Madeira on the *Hilary* on the 31[st.] He was unwell at sea. Gambling for small stakes at cards was his only diversion aboard. By 8 August were at Pará where he had dinner with Pogson at the Paz Café (where he saw a "lovely moço"), chatted at length with Pickerell, the American consul, and went out, as usual, to cruise the streets. He had his activities well planned.

August 8th. Arr. Pará at 2, alongside 3.30.... after dinner to Valda Peso, two types, also to gardens of Pração República, 2 types, Baptista Campos, one type. Then Senate Square and Caboclo (boy 16–17), seized hard. Young stiff, thin, others offered later, on board at 12 midnight.

August 9th. Called Pickerell.... Shall I see João, dear old soul! I'll get up early and go to Roy Borbora by 6.51 and wait till 7.30 and all morning till 9. No sleep hardly. Up at 5 on shore at 6 a.m. Lovely moço in train. To Cemetery and lo! João coming along, blushed to roots of hair with joy. Handfast and talked, gave 10$ said he thought it was me To Marco. Lunched Pogson. Dined Barry. Left 10.10 Barry, one type 11.30 too late. Rain and on board midnight. João Anselmo de Lima, 251, Baptista Campos.

August 10th. On shore at 6.35. Met João again at [Cemetery]. He gave roses. Promised to call on him later and he said 'roses'. To stream in forest. Two Caboclo boys there in hut. Bathed and back 'Hilary' at 10.30. Very tired.... Afternoon on shore a minute—too hot. Then after dinner to big square and all over place—including Baptista Campos—but none, altho' several possible types.

August 11th. Out to Ornstein's and on to forest stream and bathed. Huge Caboclo there 40 years. Antonio and Francisco out at Charcoal. Policeman at station. At Zoo and Museum ... Barry and Pogson dined on board with me. Left at 10. With them to Square and all over. No type—but at 12.30 darkie policeman 'em paisana' enormous = $5.

The commission now embarked on a steamer up the Amazon, headed for Manaos and Iquitos to begin their work of investigation.

August 12th. Nice pilots on board—one Paraense boy of 18 or so.

They steamed upriver, planning to reach Manaos in the early morning of 16 August. The pilot boy is an apprentice, Augusto de Maranhos, 18, of Pará. Practicante Augusto is the son of Rubin of the port works. "I like him very much," Casement notes. On the 14th they passed Obydos at 8:30 p.m. Casement had a long chat with Augusto. They passed beautiful cliffs—the ones described in detail by the naturalist Henry Walter Bates in *The Naturalist on the River Amazons*—and Augusto said he knew them well but couldn't remember their name. At Otacoatiarra the Brazilian customs authorities refused to allow the cargo for the Madeira-Mamoré Railway to be offloaded, in spite of the wire from Pará granting permission—"A beautiful instance of Brazilian competency."

August 16th. At Manaos.... Lovely view over bay of Rio Negro.... João up ... Filthy Portuguese vendors. [He goes on shore at 6:30 in the evening.] Gardens by Lycée and Barracks. Several policemen wanting I think. One lovely schoolboy—back and forward several times and at 8.15 to Chambers and stayed all night there in good bed and room.

They left Manaos for Iquitos on the 17th, after Casement refused to meet with the Colombian Consul. He lunched at Dennings and then went out to view the Igarapé Grande, "beautiful water." Manaos he considered, like many, a horrid town. They left on the *Huayna*, a "beastly ship" and "Israel and other passengers on board—including Javari family with boy Luis—17 on 15th July last. Returning home from Lisbon after 6 years." They entered the Solimões with its dark brown water. They steamed along the south bank on the 18th. He complains that there is only one bath and WC for all 17 men passengers. The food is awful. The ship is old and smelly. He chats at length with young Luis. The air and the confined cabin, sweltering, are a torture to him and he suffers from headache. He does not bathe for days. On the 20th they passed the mouth of the Japurá with its high banks, sighting numerous birds, eagles, he says, and gulls. "Indian boy on board," he adds, "3rd class." At 5:30 a.m. they passed Ega, and he mentions Bates in passing, having read *The Naturalist on the River Amazons*.

Henry Walter bates had come out with Alfred Russel Wallace to collect in the Amazon at mid century. (Wallace had left after four years but his friend stayed on for eleven.) Bates had made Ega his headquarters for four and a half years and had lived in a comfortable bungalow in the town, going out from there to collect, at times in excursions of hundreds of miles but usually in the vicinity of the place, where there was an abundance of wildlife, new and exotic plants and animals. The contrast with Consul Casement's lifestyle and interests are sharp. There is a famous moment in Bates's marvelous book which takes place in his description of Ega. In his first year, 1850, twelve months had passed without any correspondence or remittances. Towards the end of this time his clothes were worn to rags and he was barefoot ("a great inconvenience in tropical forests, notwithstanding statements to the contrary"). His servant ran away and he was robbed of all his copper money. But matters improved and his life became wonderfully productive. However, "I suffered most inconvenience," Bates writes, "from the difficulty of getting news from the civilized world down river, from the irregularity of receipt of letters, parcels of books and periodicals, and towards the latter part of my residence from ill health arising from bad and insufficient food. The want of intellectual society, and of the varied excitement of European life, was also felt most acutely, and this, instead of becoming deadened by time, increased until it became almost insupportable. I was obliged at last, to come to the conclusion that the contemplation of Nature alone is not sufficient to fill the human heart and mind." In contrast with Bates, Casement on his Commission of Inquiry seems superlatively affluent and comfortable.

On the 24th he remarks on the many Siphonia elastic trees—some tapped—on shore. On the 25th they passed Boa Vista and then Belém. They were due to arrive in Tabatinga at 4 p.m., he says. He finally gets a bath in the doctor's tub but continues to feel seedy and notes that the *Liberal* (the launch of the Peruvian Amazon Company on which the Commission was to travel) was reportedly on its way to Iquitos with 45 tons of rubber and a lot of sick people on board.

On 26 August they arrived at Tabatinga before noon. He notes the Brazilian military post, with its soldiers "all visibly niggers, the first Liberian Army Corps over again!" They left Tabatinga at noon for Leticia, a short distance upstream, arriving there in just a few minutes. At Leticia he observed "5 Peruvian soldiers off—Cholos—fine chaps, one splendid fellow, gave cigarettes, (also Brazilians from 'Esperanza' high and dry on bank in midstream)—land at 5 all bathing on bank and somersaulting."

Continuing up the river slowly after spending all night at Leticia, they reached Caballo Cocha at seven in the evening. "Huge logs, trees and grass and scum floating past." They will not reach Iquitos until Wednesday morning, he notes with exasperation. The Indians—pure Indians, not mulattos, he notes—on board looked happy although clothed, even the children. "Played bridge with Barnes, Gielgud and Fox," he wrote.

August 30th. [They were now only 114 miles from Iquitos.] There are many more Indians and inhabitants along the Peruvian than the Brazilian Amazon. [He saw two Boras Indians.] Caught young, dark, brutal faces.

August 31st. Arr. Iquitos at 8. All on shore. [He lunched with Consul Cazes and wife and took a room at the hotel 'Le Cosmopolite.' The hotel was dreadful, he said. He chatted with Dr. Paz Soldán who called the reports of atrocities mere fables.] The town is very well situated, but horribly neglected and dirty. The streets atrocious, the houses poor.... Hundreds of soldiers in blue dungarees, splendid looking Indians and Cholos, nearly all are Indians, a conquered race held by Blancos. They are finer men than the Blancos and with gentle faces, soft black eyes, with a far off look of the Incas.

In Iquitos he met and talked with Lizardo Arana who spoke of "the great prospects of the Putumayo, its many Indian tribes, its fertility, etc." Lizardo, representing Julio César Arana, his brother, showed a good-humored willingness to help them in their work. The Putumayo Amazon Company would offer a company launch, the *Liberal*, to take them to the various stations in the area. Expenses would be borne by the company. Casement received a visit from the late Acting French Consular Agent, Vatan, who told him that "the condition of things on the Putumayo had been disgraceful—that the existing method was slavery pure and simple—but that it was the 'only way' in Peru as she exists." It was necessary to civilize the Indians, he added. There were two Barbadians, just back from the Putumayo, who had to be interviewed—and they would prove frightfully open about their part in the atrocities committed—being committed—on the Indians. On 2 September he mentions rereading the sensational articles in *El Oriente* and remarks on a meeting with Dr. Pizarro, with a curious notation on the blotter side facing the diary entries: "Pizarro and Guichard. X."

Frederick Bishop, one of the Barbadians, called on the 3rd to relate the conditions in the rubber camps on the Putumayo, the floggings and slavery and mutilation of Indians. The next day Bishop returned with Juan Guerrido to give evidence to the Commission. Casement dined and played bridge in the evening. On the 5th there was a terrific storm and more depositions, on the 6th still another awful statement by Bishop to the Commission. On the 7th the river continued to rise with the constant downpour. Three Peruvian gunboats arrived with 123 volunteers from the Napo, "Splendid men, all Indians nearly, sturdy and fine, smooth faces, handsome chaps. Poor Indian people." He stayed inside much of this day, reading *Forest Lovers*; it was Brazilian Independence Day. He had dinner with Arana, Zumaeta (Julio César's brother-in-law), Cazes and the four Commission men. Ironically, they drank to the health of Peru while just down the Amazon hundreds of Peruvian Indians were suffering and dying.

September 8th. A lovely day with the river rising over the sandbank. Passengers from the 'Huayna' came up and some were at the forest pool—Morona Cocha—"fine types, one with shotgun, lovely and strong Indian Cholo" [He did little or nothing most of the day and went out for dinner in the evening.] Home at 12 and young Cholo Policeman on Malecón—splendid young Indian.

September 9th I walk Punchana 9 to 10.30 a.m., wretched. No plantation life at all, women bathing in stream. 2 to 4, Cholo soldiers discharging 'America' in blazing sun. Almost all Indians, a few half-castes, all fine splendid youths. One half white muchacho, magnificent display, and a young Cholo with erection as he carried heavy box, down left leg about 6–8" inches. They are far too good for their fate.

The river, along with the local penises, continued to rise, and Casement continued doggedly taking depositions. They were trying to get an interpreter who could speak Huitoto and Boras languages. There was much traffic on the river and on the Malecón. On the 12th he was again unwell and in bed, tortured by mosquitoes. He notes on the 13th Adolphus Gibbs who witnessed Jiménez chopping off the head of a Boras cacique who had tried to escape after two weeks in chains. "Busy writing out depositions of the Barbadians."

On 14 September they left at last on the *Liberal* for the Putumayo, first stopping at Tabatinga/Leticia where they would begin their interviews. The Barbadians by now had deserted. The cook was drunk. "Our interpreter looks a decent muchacho, about 23, wild hair, dark eyes, splendid teeth, etc., and a bright smile. He is half-caste and looks a good sort. Indian pilot a young man, fine chap, and Cholo steersman too." The *Liberal* was comfortable and well supplied. Casement played a lot of bridge, slept—trying the hammock but was cold with no blanket, "not nice." On the 15th he was suffering from sore throat from sleeping out in the hammock. The *Liberal* was nearly swamped near Santa Sophia in a "fearful storm." The Captain remarked that it was the worst storm he had experienced in his fourteen years in the Amazon. At Leticia "Practicante on board. Gave cigarettes nice Paraense moço. On to Tabatinga and Javari" and then the Putumayo. On the way they were delayed by thick white mist off the river and he began to suffer from the old fever. He did note the banks of clay (called Tabatinga, common throughout the Amazon and mentioned in some detail by Bates). There were sand flies and mosquitoes. The diary is eventless. On the blotter side for the 17th, he notes, musingly, "The man who gives up his family, his nation, his language, is worse than the woman who abandons her virtue. What chastity is to her, the essentials to self-respect and self-knowledge are to his manhood." (Is this a quote from his reading or is it Casement himself speaking?) Anchored in the mist on the 19th, he observes herons and the palms. "Passing a new palm the Punchana pilot called 'Pona' a lovely thing. Fox raving about it and well he may. Besides the assai it shoots up its graceful stem with from 6–12 magnificent fronds like those of a hart's tongue fern on top, and then a green budding head to its long stem. Five lovely and different palms growing here close together and in enormous numbers." They caught a small deer in the stream and hoisted it on board, to cage it, not to slaughter it for food. On the 20th they were still 400 miles from the Putumayo This day they arrived at the mouth of the Igaraparaná which gradually began to narrow. At Indostán they reached a desperate settlement of rubber gatherers and were off almost immediately for La Chorrera, the main rubber station of the Peruvian Amazon Company, making stops for interviews and depositions. There was talk of decapitations, the *cepo*, floggings, mutilations. He saw three Boras at La Chorrera with broad scars on their buttocks, 1 ½ to 2 inches broad, "weals for life." On the 26th the *Liberal* left for El Encanto, another station. Casement said farewell to a charming Peruvian engineer he had met on board and who was making a voyage for pleasure on the *Liberal*. The Commission was going on another launch, the *Velóz* to Occidente, arriving there on the 28th. By then Casement was exhausted and slept most of the day. "Andokes for cigarettes at 4 and asked me to give them, looking so gently, poor soul, and fingering anxiously. Has pierced ears. He said several things to me in a soft low voice asking questions,

I thought and looking longingly. I gave him a packet of cigarettes but he did not want to go." He played bridge almost daily. The next day he was writing up a report on Velarde, one of the worst criminals. There would be a dance that night, "promises to be a big thing, lots of Indians arriving from 11 a.m. onwards, the women mostly stark naked, the men (all undersized), some in dirty pants and shirt. Many show marks of flogging. The dance a success—about 1000 present, pathetic."

September 28th. Andokes huge erection in stern at 3 p.m. asleep, 26th Sept. 1910. Small boy on launch.

September 30th. [After interrogations, to the river.] I bathed in river, delightful, and Andokes came down and caught butterflies for Barnes and I. Then a Capitán embraced us laying his head against our breasts, I never saw so touching a thing, poor soul, he felt we were his friends.

The interrogations took place one after the other, with the Commission meeting often. There was gruesome evidence of inhuman treatment of the Indians, almost unbearable to someone so sensitive as Casement. He relaxed with bridge and with observation of the aborigines.

October 4th. At 9 to bath and found Andokes, the light boy and a little boy in the hammock outside bathroom, all doing what Condenhor once said of the boys of Rome, and Johnston of the Nyasaland boys, without concealment! The other servants looking on practically while these three boys played with each other, with laughter and jokes. A fine beastly morality for a Christian Co.

Day follows ghastly day. On the 5th he jotted on the blotter side, after noting that he was feeling lazy and was to leave the next day: "Dreadful nightmare. I yelled for help in night. Waking all house." Well might he have nightmares as he continued recording the evidence of torture, pain and mutilation, the stocks, decapitations, the dashing out of children's heads against tree trunks, rape and sexual outrage and enslavement. On the 6th, leaving Occidente at 9.20 a.m., "The Cholo man servant Pena shook hands with me gracefully this for a bottle of Jameson I gave him…. Many Emperor butterflies—splendid, lots of others." The voyage was as usual mismanaged: there was no planning as in the Congo and no regular meals on board. At Último Retiro the scene was pitiful and depressing. "The vile squalid place is filled with women, concubines of all ages, and is a den of vice and degradation. 18 women making steps to privy under direction of a 'white man'. Three naked as born, rest dressed, but all women...." He took many photos of the Indians and swam in the river and gathered testimony and it rained without cease. He was desperate with an infected left eye, so bad he was almost blind. At Puerto Peruano they found 40 Indians waiting for them. All showed evidence of flogging. On the 12th they reached Entre Ríos, a fine plantation: "O'Donnell the best looking agent of the Co. met yet." Taking testimony daily he began to suffer from depression; his health was deteriorating, his liver was bad. He bathed gratefully in the shallow Cahuinari. On the 16th he left Entre Ríos to visit the Andokes, overnighting on the way, bathing in the river twice in streams of limpid water. The Indians he found starved; they were allotted only a few ounces of rice per day and scrounged crumbs from the table. In the frequent deluges, they made umbrellas of palm fronds. With the Andokes he encountered the monster Normand, who was responsible for all kinds of mutilations and murder. He showed up, "a loathsome monster absolutely filthy." He describes Normand's harem of seven wives, prisoners. Then, "A dance in evg. Of the Boras Indians, who brought in enormous loads of rubber, some of them 140 weight I fancy. Women and children, several women and tiny children flogged." On the following day the Fabrico rubber caravan started, with Casement going along. Some carriers did all right, but one boy was dying with exhaustion and one older woman was unable to continue and dropped out. There is an interesting diary for the 24th: "A large wood ibis at lunch, sailed round and alit close to house. Fox and I saved it from being shot. It was like a stork: a big white bill and broad black ends to its wings." He played on the same day, he added, 33 hands and two rubbers of bridge.

October 25th. [He is reading E. P. Oppenheim's *The Yellow Crayon* to amuse himself.] 4 Boras (a young man, splendid type, a boy of 12 and two women) came down guarded by one armed footpad from Maturas—with 2 loads rubber. I photo'd them and gave a tin of meat. The boy terribly flogged, all over his backside and thighs, enormous weals, a beautiful boy. The young man fine fellow, very light skin. [A boy brought in a deer that day.] Fine muchacho carried deer, beautiful limbs, thighs and chest, light coffee color."

On the 26th he went for a long walk to Atenas from Entre Ríos, making the round trip in about six hours—a total distance of about 24 miles. He swam in the deepening Cahuinari and "Tried banana leaf, caught blue and brown butterfly, magnificent specimen...." On the blotter side he notes: "Bathed at 2–3 in Cahuinari with a boy dreadfully flogged, was a carrier to Andokes.... awful scars, a nice lad of 17 about and six tiny boys, gave all soap, they reveled in it."

October 27th. Normand and Macedo & Co. there with the beautiful Leavine. I go down today with O'D[onnell]. I on horse and he on mule. I made him run [on the walk to Atenas] y'day, but he could not beat me on the hill. I am going downhill! 47th. year and he is only 27.... Left Entre Ríos about 8.30. [He met the Commission for lunch.] Atenas carriers of Commission absolute skeletons—photo'd four skins of bone. Gave meat to them, all the tins I had left.... Caught three splendid butterflies on road, O'D[onnell] and Sealy in fingers—beauties.

On 28 October he was getting ready to leave Entre Ríos to return to Puerto Peruano and catch the *Velóz* for La Chorrera.

October 28th. Left P[uerto] P[eruana] at 7.18. Before leaving the beautiful muchacho showed it, a big stiff one, and another muchacho grasped it like a truncheon. Black and thick and stiff as a poker. [Undecipherable] Lincoln and Occidente muchacho doing same.

October 29th. [At La Chorrera] Boy of launch, also stiff y'day and again this morning, pretending to do it to small boy with huge thrusts, swam in river, which is fully 16–17 feet lower.... Brought things from store and wrote up my diary since Entre Ríos and got various papers in order. [Normand wanted to travel on the *Liberal* but was fortunately prevented by Sr. Tizón.] I washed in the river in morning. The Indian boys are swimming all afternoon, lovely bodies out in the stream, and the girls too, paddling logs across to the island and lying there awash by the hour. After dinner talked two Ricigaros muchachos—one a fine chap. He pulled stiff and fingered it laughing. Would have gone on and the other too. (Keys on chain in left pocket) looking for cigarettes. Awfully exciting and stiff; stiff work. Thought of João and Flores. [On blotter side: "This day last year 'Vaseline' at dear old Icarsby! To think of it!"]

The next day he was busy writing, while the *Liberal* was unable to dock, the river having dropped a foot.

October 31st. Saw Andokes bathing, big thick one, as I thought.... Then saw rubber arrive, huge loads, lots of Indians, fine handsome types of Naimenes

Indians of Sur. Chose one small boy, a dear wee thing named Omarino. His weight 24 kilos in fono [genital strap] and his load of rubber 29 kilos.... A fine muchacho named Aredomi wants to come Very fine lad—would like to take him. He followed like a dog all afternoon. Gave breeches to him. His beautiful coffee limbs were lovely. Promised to take him home if I could manage it. Spoke Tizón. Bought Omarino [for a pair of trousers and a shirt]. More rubber in evg. From Sur, nine or ten tons of it, Marinda at head. All slept under house—his Indians—I looked and saw several, and one boy caressed hand and shoulder....

November 1st. Stiff asleep ones. River still falling in morning. Aredomi I saw for a moment and then no more. Fear he has been sent off.... Saw big ones on Indians at dinner and before.

November 2nd. Up early. Ocainas and others about, and some of the Sur Indians of Marinda, one boy with erection, fingering it longingly and pulling it stiff, could see all from veranda.... Sent Bishop to look for Aredomi.... Bishop reports the boy is over on the Chacara cutting firewood for the launch and I soon saw him. Turned up smiling. [He goes on to note taking testimony from the "monster" Barbadians, writing up his report until 5 p.m. Then he walked after dinner and turned in early. [On blotter side: "Sunday. This day last year Carlos at Icarsby. Evelyn Batson's statement 4. Hallow Eve. Walked till 12 with Aredomi and others. X. Sidney Morris. X. Preston Johnson. X. Augustus Walcott. X. James Mapp 3. Alfred Hoyte 2. Reuben Phillips. Clifford Quintin. X. Allan Davis 1.

November 3rd. Arranged with Macedo to take Aredomi, he has no objection. [He is now arranging to leave. The Atenas carriers arrived—horrendously emaciated, ashamed of their physical state.] Busy all day over the accounts of the Barbados men.

November 4th. Commission went to Sur at 7.30, I followed at 8 with Sealy carrying coat, etc., and Aredomi small tula. Took names of the buried at cemetery. Found orchid on road. Arr. Sur 9.30 and bathed, Aredomi carrying clothes, showed huge. Told him to bathe too—and he stripped. No fono on. Carbolic soap—glorious limbs, a big one.... Returned with Sealy and Aredomi at 4.

[Aredomi was now determined to accompany Casement back to England, along with Omarino, whose "purchase" Casement had now arranged. Although Aredomi was married, his physical attributes probably convinced Casement that he might be a good choice.]

November 5th. [Bishop has informed Casement that the store has been broken into by Boras Indians. A contingent is sent off to search for the thieves.] Bathed with Aredomi in hill stream, second time. [Aredomi's wife and brother had arrived and his wife wanted to accompany him to Europe, definitely impossible, Casement notes.]

On 6 November he notes that the downpour has continued. Aredomi's wife is spending all day with him now. The *Liberal* is not in. He bathed in the river. On the 7th he got signatures from the Barbadians, who are not totally bad but also victims of the Company who charged them 300–400 percent over normal on their accounts. On 7 November he observed a lunar rainbow.

November 8th. O'Donnell arrived from E[ntre] Ríos by 'Velóz', bringing letter from Crichlow asking me to recall him. Huascar arrived with O'D[onnell] and smiled at me with big left erection. Butterfly, very hot afternoon.... Spent a lazy day. Walked to hills in evg. By stream and at six Aredomi came with a plume-head dress quite well arranged for me as a present, poor boy. He had been home for it, far off all day to show his gratitude.

The 9th was another lazy day, spent waiting for the *Liberal*, observing the arrival of miserable rubber carriers. Even the mules were mistreated. The launch arrived at last at 5.45 p.m., bringing John Brown, a "useless brute." There was much mail from home. "Nothing interesting in these surroundings," Casement writes, bored and tired of his endless chores. There was nothing in the papers, he found, about the Putumayo.

On 10 November he remarks the penniless Peruvian soldiers brought by the *Liberal*; they are bound for Encanto but have no passage. He was busy all day writing his reports and negotiating on behalf of the Barbadians. "Tizón," he adds, "says that Colombia is going to invade the Putumayo and is making a road from Pasto. Peru getting ready.... Also Lima 'Comercio' has articles about the forthcoming enquiry into the crimes here." He also learned of the revolution in Portugal and the flight of King Manuel and his mother to Gibraltar on the Brazilian Dreadnought the *S. Pello*. On 11 November he spent a long day over accounts documenting the indebtedness of the Barbadians but his hands were tied and he had no authority to rectify these obvious wrongs. On the 12th he was preparing to hand out the accounts to the men, arranging with Tizón for the Company to pay them off. By now Tizón was with Casement wholeheartedly and considered himself "a member of the Commission." He went up the hill and bathed with Aredomi in the upper river, glad to get away from it all with his beautiful Indian boy. The 13th was very hot. He glanced at papers. He announced that he could not allow Aredomi's wife to come along and arranged to have her escorted home. On the 14th there were confrontations about the accounts.

November 14th. A very hot day—river falling fast. Some Entre Ríos Indians also came here now.... I am thinking all evening of possible trouble in Iquitos on arr. there with all these Barbados men. Their evidence constitutes the case against Peru more really than against the P[eruvian] A[mazon] Co.

The 15th was a very anxious day, his last in La Chorrera. He arranged tickets for the Barbadians for Iquitos "or intermediate parts" if Brazilian authorities would allow it. On consulting with the Brazilian Customs Officer on the *Liberal* (Mathias) he found there would be no objection at all. Thus Casement could go to Iquitos and get their money while they waited at Javari, to be picked up on his return and duly paid off.

November 16th. My last hours in La Chorrera. Poor Donald Francis came and cried and cried in my room—wanting to go home with me to his old mother in Barbados. Poor boy—I was very sorry for him. A scene with Dyall and his 9th or 10th wife—she refusing to be parted from him and trying to get on board the 'Liberal', but turned back at the gangway.... off at 9.45.... Passed Port Tarma at 11.30, naked Indian women, the last I shall see probably. Eclipse of the moon—just as it rose at 6 and half curved and covered. Became a total eclipse at 8. Lovely night.

November 17th. Very handsome Cholo sailors on board. One is young half Indian moço of 18 or 19, beautiful face and figure. A perfect dusky Antinous and would make a fine type for H[erbert] W[ard]'s statue of the Upper Amazon. Steaming down Igaraparaná and at 10.45 saw Putumayo and entered it at about 10.50. It is very low and a huge sandbank blocks much of it. Called Aredomi to see it and explain thro' Bishop. He calls it Harmia and Igaraparaná is Cottue. He came to my room and I showed him many pictures in Bates' Book and others, to his great delight. It got up I think—was thick anyhow. [Casement goes on to refer to the illustrations for *The Naturalist on the River Amazons* by Joseph Wood Whymper, including amusing anecdotal scenes, and by E. W. Robinson who drew smaller subjects such as fishes, insects and reptiles, chiefly from Bates's specimens and rough sketches.]

On the Putumayo on the 18th, he notes the palms again and questions the Barbadians about their wishes for the future. "Aredomi at 7.30," he also adds, "nude torso beautiful bronze, for medicine against sandflies. Gave it to him. And rubbed it over his lovely body, poor boy. Young pilot apprentice again on deck, forward. Arranged (I think) for the men [to get off] at Javari." On the 19th they reached the first Brazilian post where they spent two hours in customs and bought fuel. On the 20th he had a bad night with a skin eruption "like heat lumps."

November 20th. Captain's steward, an Indian boy of 19, broad face, thin huge soft one, also engineer's steward, big too, steaming up Amazon all day, very slow and tired.

November 21st. We stayed a long time at Boa Vista getting firewood from about 3 a.m. to near 6 a.m. this morning, in a drizzle, deck hands washing deck, then lovely Cholo types, three big ones. Cholo steward too (young 18), enormous in new bags. To decide now if the men for Javari or Iquitos.

They stopped at Palmeras, passed Belém, traveling slowly up the river. The men decided to stop at Javari, which meant that Casement had to make arrangements to land 14 men, four women and four children. He bought a lot of food for them from Captain Reigado.

On the 22nd they got to Javari at 1 a.m. and landed the men. "Young Brazilian Customs officer very kind and pleasant-faced too, he embraced me.... River rushing down, Brazilian troops and young five-striped Sergeant on board, off at once. At Leticia delayed for 2 hours by the lazy Peruvian brutes there." [The Peruvians wanted to seize the *Liberal* and use it to go to Brazil in pursuit of runaway soldiers.]

November 23rd. A hot day steaming past Peruvian chacras all day.... After dinner spoke to steward Indian Cholo about frejot and he got some for me and then another thing. It was huge and he wanted awfully. He stood for hours till bed time and turned in under table—also small pantry engineer's youth and pilot's apprentice too—all up—till midnight and then at Yaguras and saw two Yaguras Indians in their strange garb.... Steward's Cholo very nice, smiled and fingered and hitched up to show.

November 24th. Due at Iquitos today, will it be peace or war? Gave small boy Victor Tizón 25/P. Very rainy morning. Cleaning brasswork. Cholo steward did mine and Captain's and showed it again, huge and stiff and laughed. Smiled lovingly. All hands cleaning up. Engineer says we shall be in Iquitos by nightfall. I doubt it greatly.... Very hot. Nice Indians at Marupa [where they stopped for wood]. Steward showed enormous exposure after dinner—stiff down left thigh; then he went below and came up at St. Teresa where 'Eliza' launch was and leant on gunwale with huge erection about 8". Guerrido watching. I wanted awfully.

November 25th. Gave engineers small boy 2$, and steward. Cluma $1. Asked my engineer his name, Ignacio Torres he said, and I asked him to come to Cazes' house. Arr. Iquitos at 7 a.m. On shore to Cazes' and then to barbers with Aredomi and Omarino.... Visited Booth's and then down to 'Atahualpa', Dr. of her, an Italian, gave me medicine. Saw Reigado and his Cholo sailors—all had been drunk and he put them in the hold, the brute, 'to sweat it out.' Saw Ignacio Torres on the beach looking at me.

He now is waiting to get on board the *Atahualpa*, cruising Iquitos—observing boys longingly, admiringly. He is feeling tired of Iquitos, however, and tired of Cazes, with whom he is forced to socialize. The heavy rains continued.

November 26th. On board 'Atahualpa' again and saw young Customs officer from Manaos—great and well indeed—only a boy, almost pure Indian too. Also fair-haired pilot boy, tall and nice, from Pará. Took my room No. 1. 'Atahualpa' leaves only on 4 Dec Sunday next.

November 27th. Off on 'Manati' picnic to Tamshiako 20–30 miles upriver. Prefect and Lt. Bravo and all. Pleasant day. Saw Indian cook boy on 'Inca' enormous, lying down and pulled often. Huge and thick, lad 17. Also Ignacio Torres told him come 8 a.m. tomorrow. Told Pinteiro come too.

November 28th. Heavy rain all night and this morning pouring. 9.30: no Bishop—no Ignacio, no Pinteiro and no Lewis! What is up? Ignacio Torres came at 10 clean and nice. Gave him £1 and a portfolio for Captain Reigado—asked him to return the cover. He has not been to Brazil—Many from Iquitos in bare feet. Gets $3 per month…. Saw Ignacio Torres below [after meeting with Bishop, Brown and Lewis] at 2.30 looking for me with my portfolio. J. Clark with him. Door shut so he went on to the office, poor boy. I should like to take him too. Saw him later when Cazes and he said he was coming at 8 a.m. tomorrow and then saw him at band. Also saw Viacarra who smiled at me again and again and looked very nice. He was talking to Bishop. Manuel Lomas the pilot stood me a drink of ginger ale and begged me to visit Punchana to see him.

November 29th. Expect Ignacio this morning—on the lookout for him. He came at 8.10 with my portfolio and I sent him for cigarettes. He brought wrong kind and I gave him 28/- and patted him on back…. He left at 8.30. [Later Casement talked with Vatan who told him that if it hadn't been for his official position Casement would have been assassinated in the bush; the company was still out to get him.] Walked after dinner to Booth's house and then with Harrison to Square. Walked round it. Many beautiful types Indian and Cholo. Saw Ignacio at merry-go-round and pulled. He smiled and approached. Anther Cholo with him. Waited till 10 p.m. and then home to bed.

On 30 November he caught sigh of the Cholo sailors from the *Liberal* going home at 5.30; they all smiled at him, which gave his heart a tug. He had now written to arrange the repatriation of the Barbados men and had lunched on the *Atahualpa*, afterwards walking home in "atrocious heat." The rains did not let up, spoiling his attempt to go the cinematograph at the Alhambra. He played dummy bridge during what he called a stupid party at the Cazes'.

December 1st. I fear the 'Atahualpa' will not sail until Monday 5th., certainly not till Sunday 4th. Huge erection Indian boy at C. Hernandez came at 3 to 4, a whole hour. Up at 4.30 and out for coffee. All closed at 7. Fingered and pulled…. Walked to 'Morona Cocha' with "Wags". Very muddy indeed. [In spite of the weather he did go to the movies at the Alhambra with Brown.] Pablo Martinez came in and lots of Indians and peons, splendid chaps, and Cholo soldiers. Back at 11.30 in rain…. No sign of Ignacio Torres since Tuesday night, not a glimpse. Fear he has gone in launch. Saw Julio in white pants and shirt at Alhambra, splendid stern.

December 2ⁿᵈ. Heavy rain in night and all y'day afternoon and it will quite spoil the discharge of 'Atahualpa'. Saw Julio at Pinto Hers., gave cigarettes. He said 'Muchas Gracias.' Enormous limbs and it stiff on right side feeling it and holding it down in his pocket. Saw huge on Malecón. Looked everywhere for Ignacio. No sign anywhere. Very sad…. saw 'Julio' again at store and asked him to come to Punchana. He said 'Vamos' but did not follow far. He asked when I was going to Manaos. Saw some great big stiff ones today on Cholos. Two huge erections, and then from boys at 5 on seat in front, and then lovely type in pink shirt and blue trousers and green hat, and later in Square with 'Wags' the same who looked and longed and got huge on left. To Alhambra with Cazes at 9.30 seeing many types and 'Julio' in white again in a box. Met outside and asked him to come to Punchana tomorrow. He said 'Vamos' and asked where to meet, I said at 10 a.m. but he probably did not understand.

December 3ʳᵈ. Went out at 9.30 to look for 'Julio' but no sign of him, took John Brown's statement up to 9.30. [Judge] Valcárcel is going down to Manaos on a launch, good riddance! Altho' I liked the rascal's bright face and Indian skin and splendid teeth. Went on 'Atahualpa' at 10 and talked to skipper and Brown and then lo! Ignacio on the mole shoveling potatoes into a sack! so I asked him to come to see me today at 6 p.m. He said where, I told him at C.'s house. Reigado called on me at 3 and told me he leaves for Putumayo on 7ᵗʰ. Dec. Waited till 6.40; no Ignacio, or sign of him! Alack! to Booth's to dinner after turn round Square, saw Beauty of last night first in work clothes and then again in pink shirt, at 5.30 in front of Cazes'. After dinner around Square many times till near midnight and saw some types especially [from] Cazes' office and shop. 'Paraense' and feeling left pocket. Took photo of young Booth, Customs clerk, Antonio Cruz Pérez.

December 4ᵗʰ. Very hot morning. Looking out of window saw Ignacio waiting, joy. Off with him to Tirotero and camera. Bathed and photo'd and talked and back at 11. To meet tomorrow. Gave 4/-. At 5.30 Cajamarca policeman till 7 at Bella Vista and again at 10.30 paseando and at 8 long talk, shook hands and offered. Tall Inca type and brown.

December 5th. Ignacio at 6.30 and off together to Tirotero and bathed. Gave
£1, 'tanto ufano' (so much contented) but no more! On to hospital and to Itaia
river by Telegraph—pretty and sat down by 'Azul.' He comes from
Taraporto—is 19 ½—and left the soldiers in Aug., when with 72 Tarapor-
tanos he had volunteered for 8 months—poor lad—some day will go to Brazil
for caucho, what fate! ... At length the parting and at Factoría Calle said
'Adios'—dash for ever. He nearly cried I think. I gave him 2/- and I think he
was wretched. He said 'Hasta luego.' I turned back and found him still standing at corner looking straight in front. I go to Fotografia and he crossed street
last time saw him was then standing and looking. Poor Ignacio! Never to see
again. Wrote a little and out to Booth's to get tickets (£37.10/-), an awful
fraud. After dinner out to Square and saw several types, one young and lovely
and a soldier from Minea, also the huge Cholo policeman with his sweetheart.
Drank beer, looked for Ignacio, but no sign anywhere, turned in at 11.45.
Very hot.

December 6th. Packed up early.... At stage Zumaeta and Reigado and others
came to bid me goodbye—including the Prefect's ass of an A.D.C.—a young
ruffian that....'Atahualpa' off at 11, a crowd on pier, but no sign of Ignacio. I
thought he wd. have come but he has not, poor boy. Said farewell to Iquitos
with every joy but regrets for Ignacio and the Indians all. God bless them.
Steamed down river, lots of people on board and had to shift cabin.... Some
fine Cholos going to Manaos to go up to Areia for caucho, one tall 6 ft. lad
told me for three years, poor boy. Gave many cigarettes and sat up till 10 p.m.
lower deck. Some of them willing and soft.

On 7 December they reached Leticia and Tabatinga. The Barbadians had
gone down to Manaos already. Casement talked to "Seringualo lad from Iquitos, José González, born there 1885 and going up Areia for 3 years. A fine
young chap." He turned in about 10, after a chat with the engineer. On the
blotter side of the diary appears this note: "Left Iquitos, good-bye Ignacio,
never to see again!" On the 8th he was preparing for Manaos, a quiet day of
steaming past pretty Seringualos on the banks and pretty little plantations.
    On 10 December they reached Manaos. On shore he arranged to pay off
the Barbadians. He notes "On board at 5 p.m. and off in 'Atahualpa' to Pará.
Poor wee Ricudo is sick, temperature is 104 degrees in hospital in Manaos.
[This is the other boy that he was taking with him to England, along with
Omarino, having decided that it was unwise to take Aredomi.] Saw the results

of the bombardment of 2 months ago. Quite disgraceful the whole thing. All our Iquitos Cholos left at Manaos, poor boys, they go to that hell, the Areia." Meanwhile he makes plans to stay at the old Hotel in Pará and "have a good time of it, at least."

December 11th. Steaming well down river, splendid breeze. Ricudo sick and in hospital, poor wee chap. New pilot from Manaos, a fine chap indeed and huge Pará Caboclo …

December 12th. [I]t is very doubtful if we shall get to Pará tomorrow in time for the visit. I hope so as I want much to go on shore and find João. Have a lot to do in Pará, and will certainly see him this time—poor old José is dead and gone. I think of Ignacio all the time…. Saw the great flood of the Amazon going n.e. as we turned into the Gurupa entrance. Adios. Talked to the pilot who told me lots of stories of Minga Indians and others, and at 9 entered the Narrows, turned in at 9 and read till 11 and slept all night.

December 13th. Off Pará at 5.15. On shore and to Hotel de Comercio, where got room. Out and out to Marco by tram for a cool ride. O. 14$. A. 10$, and beer etc., 5$ = 29$. Olympo first at Big Square, then Pólvora and followed and pulled it out and to Marco where in deep.

December 14th. Nice day—out for a walk and at Cemetery after going round Baptista Campos etc., met João at 9 a.m. and he gave me a big bunch of flowers, very nice indeed. To meet [at] B[aptista] Campos. [Then he mentions calls, lunch, getting his boys on shore and to the Hotel, letters from home and the General Elections which were nearly over.] After light dinner out to B[aptista] Campos till 8.10 and then to Valda Peso and back home at 10.30. Theatre and ground lit up finely, sorry I did not meet João this evening as I wanted to give him something. [On blotter: "Last time of seeing João Anselmo de Lima at Cemetery corner at 8 a.m."]

December 15th. Not feeling well. In Hotel all day nearly writing and getting ready to go home by 'Ambrose'. [H]ad Kup to dinner and talked to him and Frenchman till 8.30. Then out for a stroll, to Square by Palace and then to B[aptista] Campos, none; and on to Nazareth, and to Valda Peso where soldiers wanted to enter the show; back to B[aptista] Campos and down to Palace Square, two, one same as November 1908, grown bigger and well dressed, this at 10.35 or so p.m.; back to Nazareth at 11.20 and down to Paz for beer, and thro' gardens; home on foot to Hotel at 12. 'Sereno' [the nightwatchman] in hammock at door, enormous, only 18, huge.

On 16 December had a conversation with Boyd, who told him that all the Brazilian rivers for rubber were worked by slavery pure and simple and that the rule of the rifle began at Pará. This was an exaggeration, perhaps. He dined and afterwards Pickerell called, then he went aboard the "Anderson" and stayed until 10.30; "then to Theatre and met Alves, after another type, and to Independencia, 'soldiers' he said 10$ and back at midnight. Into Alves backdoor."

On 17 December he left Pará aboard the *Bulrush* (Bishop, Ricudo and the others were to follow in the *Ambrose*). It was a sorry voyage, with trade winds blowing into their teeth, the ship rolling and pitching (it had about 400 tons of rubber in the hold). The passengers were mostly seasick and an elderly Portuguese in first class suddenly died. He read and played bridge and was execrably bored. Mons. Fabre he learned had been approached in Iquitos by Zumaeta who offered to arrange to sell him at a bargain price the shares held by Julio César Arana in the Putumayo Amazon Company, a sleazy move indeed. He was frightened that they might be quarantined at Lisbon due to the deaths aboard (another passenger, young Boyd, had died of yellow fever at Pará). If they were not quarantined, he hoped "to get on shore and see Agostinho and Antonio too!" By Christmas Eve it was growing markedly colder and they were still over a thousand miles from Lisbon. He played bridge, as usual, on Christmas Day. They passed Madeira of fond memory at about 1:30 a.m. on the 26th. On the 27th the ghastly tub arrived at Lisbon where, in fact, several passengers were quarantined for five days, but not Casement.

December 28th. On shore at Lisbon at 10 a.m. and to Avenida where long-legged sailor and boy type. Then to Largo Camoens. Barnes to lunch and then in Largo again and young soldier lad (18 or 20) in grey twill—splendid—followed to O'Neill's house and down to Largo near Consulate, where arranged things and on to Arsenal and Necessidades Palace and several types and back to Avenida and then by Banco di Portugal an enormous offer—about 9"—lying on one like Agostinho; but too late and so to Lonne Somero and off again at 4 on board "Ambrose' and sailed for Oporto.

December 29th. Oporto and Vigo. Lovely day, sea like glass and bright sun—altho' cold. At Lexos at 7 a.m. glorious sunrise and everything beautiful.

Left at 10 a.m. for Vigo by Spanish coastline, exquisite. Winter day, very cold, but delicious sunshine. Arr. Vigo at 3 p.m. Wrote to Ramón.

They left at 5 and on the 30th were enjoying a "Lovely day over Bay of Biscay." He wrote Tyrell saying he was going to Paris from Cherbourg, hoping to get to Paris by 6 or 7 p.m. on the 31st.

December 31. Arr. Cherbourg early on shore and to Station and at 12.56 after rotten lunch to Paris we were: Laurenson, Van der Est, Fabre, and the train very slow due 6.58 but arrived only at 8.25 Gare St. Lazare. To dinner and 32 Artillery, Denis Hilaire there and to Grande Armée. Later in Champs Elysées, soldier, and then in B[oulevard] des Capucines green hat and small, two last no copper, but Denis 10/-. Mild evening, great crowds. Boulevards and Capucines and everywhere and silly songs being sung, and pretended gaiety, without heart in it.... and so to bed at end of year. Already in 1911.

Here the diary for 1910 ends. Fortunately, this diary and those for 1903 and 1911 were left in his Ebury Street lodgings in London where, while ransacking the place, Scotland Yard found and confiscated them. If these diaries had, like the others, been left at the home of his friend J. F. Biggar in Belfast they would have been tossed on the bonfire.
If we lose the diaries we lose Casement.

Casement has not been fortunate in his biographers. Rene MacColl complains that Casement never went to concerts and was not interested in the arts; that he read little and mostly trash; that fairs such as the Earls Court Exhibit were more to his liking than the opera. "On the whole he seems to have been a man of narrow intellectual horizons. He had an obsessive and bafflingly trivial preoccupation with money and how he spent it. He rarely had time to see or at least recall anything of beauty in the world around him. His own accounts of his life show only an embarrassingly pedestrian interest in what he had to eat and drink, where he dined, what were his creature comforts and discomforts. There was nothing exciting in what he wrote, nothing to uplift or fire the imagination." He believes Casement to be vain and egocentric. "I do not believe that Casement would ever have turned to Irish Nationalism, let alone Treason, unless he had been hurt by Whitehall and was furious, seeking some way of 'getting back' at them."

Concerning culture, Casement never claimed to be an intellectual, in spite of his yearnings to write poetry and his plans for a novel. He was not a scholar, belonged to no "elite" group of thinkers or artists. His diaries are merely a private *aide mémoire*—unlike the creative writer's (to be mined afterward) or the scientist's (recorded data). His Berlin Diaries, on the other hand, were a political document, intended to be read by the Germans. His writings from prison were written for posterity, with an eye on himself as an Irish martyr. The "black" diaries, and his cash ledger, were particular ways of not forgetting; for otherwise, as we all know, we do forget. The 1903, 1910 and 1911 diaries are Casement as he was, scribbled quickly, sometimes illegible, always intense.

Concerning the Irish Nationalist cause, the position of Casement is curious. He had been an Irish nationalist since childhood. He grew up surrounded by violent Home Rule controversy. Certainly he did not catch the Irish Disease late in life. In Alice Green's circle he fit in because he knew by heart the modalities and the phrases. He was always Irish to the bone. In 1905 he developed contacts with the leaders of the Irish Party through his friend Lord ffrench. In Dublin he was introduced to John Redmond—whom he later came to abhor—and other leaders, unwilling to commit themselves to a movement outside the normal constitutional channels. Casement impressed ffrench's wife, who was quite honest about her reactions to a romantic personality, "there was noting ugly or ordinary about him He had.... an ideality of mind which was expressed in the type of looks at once Spanish and Irish. He was the strangest person imaginable to come out of Ulster." Others certainly shared her opinion. Casement was more wildly Irish at the end of the century. He helped Arthur Griffith, the founder of the *United Irishman*, and agreed with Michael Davitt of the Land League who believed the Irish were enslaved and would never be set free until they recovered their land. To Gee, he expressed support for passive resistance on a national scale—no taxes, no recruits for the British army, "it would be a shameful thing that a whole race should be slowly and relentlessly starved to death," he wrote—but the US would surely bring pressure on Britain and she would be forced to grant Ireland self-government. Guess again.

Concerning the rabidly anti-British remarks that he expressed publicly, before he actually retired from Government service—these were not unusually vehement if one takes in the political climate of the times. The British, of all classes and times, especially the educated Englishmen, often made outrageously Anti-Government remarks (compare Livingstone in this regard) to all and sundry. During the conference of the Aborigines Protection Society, reported by the *Times* on 8 June 1904, while its members were considering his report on the Congo, Casement expressed frank views about his employers. "It is the dirty, cowardly, knock-kneed game the Foreign Office has played that puts me out of action.... They are not worth serving—and what sickens me is that I must go back to them, hat in hand, despising them as I do—simply to be able to live." "His Fenian hatred of Britain was as dark a mystery as the furtive little errands of self-gratification upon which he slid off under cover of night into the streets of any town in which he found himself." This is the view of Rene MacColl, again, who also speaks of "sexual eccentricities." Stephen Gwynn, Casement's friend, was horrified by what he considered Casement's dishonesty: while Casement branded Irishmen as traitors if they served the Crown, he himself was a servant of the Crown. Not fair. On the other hand, Casement was useful to John Devoy in New York, who had early tried to "seduce men from allegiance to the Crown."

Concerning Sinn Fein, Casement's stance was clearly sympathetic. The expression Sinn Fein ("ourselves") had been used as a slogan for years by Irish speakers, now it was the name of one of the major organizations fighting for independence. Casement, as an official of the British Foreign Office, could not and would not join—but he did supply unsigned articles on Sinn Fein topics. He did not read, or had forgotten, George Moore's call to forget all Irish memories, Ireland being "a fatal disease, fatal to Englishmen and doubly fatal to Irishmen."

Concerning the C.M.G., Bulmer Hobson clearly stated the situation: "[Casement] simply didn't want it ... if he refused it, that would be tantamount to sending in his papers and resigning from the foreign service." Casement thought he had done wrong by accepting; so he begged off attending the formal ceremony of investiture with Edward VII, claiming ill health. Actually he had just had an operation for piles.

Concerning the Lisbon post, which had been dropped into his lap, unwanted, he made no bones. Although the Lisbon consulship was considered a kind of "honor" or reward for exceptional service to the State, he it considered it a dreaded bore. Tyrell exclaimed how happy he was that Casement was "actively one of us again" when he accepted the posting. When he threw it up in exasperation, giving the excuse of ill health, it seemed an affront to the Foreign Office.

Thus Santos and Pará. And Rio.

On 11 January 1911 Casement was back in London reporting to Sir Edward Grey, fulminating against America. "I think the Monroe Doctrine is at the root of these horrors on the Amazon—it excludes Europe (the Mother of Western civilization), with 500,000,000 people, as against USA (with less than 80,000,000 whites) from her proper correcting and educating place in the whole of South America. That vast continent of 7 million square miles, has only 40 million inhabitants—and this after close on 400 years of Iberian civilization...." Obviously he still considered himself part of the British Establishment, an official—if minor, at least well known—of an Empire that, despite showing signs of advancing decay, was pushing to expand its moral hegemony. The Monroe Doctrine, which had saved South America from exploitation by European nations on the scale of Africa, remained, for Casement, an evil that prevented Britain from reforming the corrupt Latin American republics.

The first task at hand was to prepare the Putumayo Report. This was easier than the Congo Report in many ways, since there would be no major camouflage of names and places. The Foreign Office intended the report to force the Peruvians to reform. Yet the Peruvian government was incapable of policing the vastness of the Putumayo region, and the Amazon region itself was deeply infected with similar abuses. If it was hoped that "criminals" could be brought to justice, the sheer complexity of the case was daunting. Important politicians were involved, and the Peruvian economy.

A short preliminary report submitted to the Foreign Office in January had had the effect of awakening the Peruvian government to British meddling, and Julio Arana to the necessity of dealing with his critics. Arana even wrote to Casement, suggesting a meeting in order to "get suggestions for better development of the country's affairs." This Casement found insulting.

The Peruvian Ambassador was informed about the Putumayo report and its impending publication. Publication of the report would be withheld, Sir Edward Grey told him politely, so that the Peruvian authorities could bring the criminals to justice. In Lima, the British Consul Lucien Jerome, acting for the British Foreign Minister, absent on leave, also reminded the Peruvian Government that the report would be published shortly if they did not put their house in order.

The Peruvians refused to be intimidated. The Peruvian Government organ, *El Diario*, published a honeyed eulogy of Arana as their reply and announced that he would be the official Peruvian representative at the International Rubber Exhibition to be held in London that year under the patronage of the Prince of Wales. Louis Mallet was outraged. (*Everybody* involved in the incidents in the Putumayo was constantly being outraged.) He asked if Arana could be arrested if he set foot in England. No, Sir Edward Grey said, but Arana could be made *persona non grata*—and was duly informed that he would not be welcome in England.

The confrontation seemed now to be on a different level—government against government; the Putumayo Indians were distanced. Ironically the report seemed to concentrate more on the wrongs actually committed *by* British subjects—the Barbadians hired as sentries by the Peruvian Amazon Company—than on the wrongs committed by the company *on* the British subjects. The report did seem strongly biased, even with Casement's asides struck out ("What lying there has been! And those scoundrels accuse Whiffen and Hardenburg of lying and 'blackmailing', forsooth!"). At any rate, "There always seems to be something to prevent them from taking action," said Sir Edward, feebly. Then the rainy season began in Iquitos, fouling communications. So Mallet forwarded copies of the report to Peru directly. It had already been five months, he noted, since Sir Edward had threatened publication if reforms were not set in motion.

What more could be done? Casement's determined efforts—often when ill—in taking statements from witnesses, in interviewing agents of the Peruvian Amazon Company, taking responsibility for hundreds of minor details of the investigation, even measuring the stocks (the infamous *cepo*), weighing the Indians' rubber loads and attempting to carry a load himself, getting photographs and data on weight and size of the victims, spending hours on muleback: were these efforts to be ignored? He had cross-checked information, confronted individuals who could have done him harm, even audited—as a *pro forma* member of the board of directors—the company accounts. Not to mention his unending letters and telegrams. Now the Peruvian government mumbled and shuffled, did not pursue the criminals—allowed them to escape; appointed, and then withdrew, judicial appointments.

Meanwhile, the Indian boys brought back by Casement, Ricudo and Omarino, were shown off at the Anti-Slavery Society and taken to William Rothenstein to have their portrait done. They were very attractive kids—not obviously "victims of oppression" at all—and charmed Casement's landlady and everyone who met them. It seemed questionable, however, whether they would adjust to school in England.

Casement poked around for a way to finance a program of reform in the Putumayo. He even considered soliciting aid from Andrew Carnegie, sending him a copy of the Putumayo Report with the hope that the American millionaire might put a morally transformed firm on its feet. This when the rubber industry in South America was entering a period of alarming decline.

On 15 June, Casement was informed of his knighthood. Writing from the Savoy in Denham, on 19 June to Sir Edward Grey, he used his most ironic tone: "I find it very hard to choose the words in which to make acknowledgment of the honor done me by the King.... I am much moved at the proof of confidence and appreciation of my service on the Putumayo, conveyed to me by your letter, wherein you tell me that the King had been graciously pleased upon your recommendation to confer upon m the honor of knighthood.... I am indeed grateful to you for this signal assurance of your personal esteem and support and very deeply sensible of the honor done me by His Majesty.... I would beg that my humble duty might be presented to His Majesty, when you may do me the honor to convey to him my deep appreciation of the honor he has been so graciously pleased to confer upon me."

To Alice Green he wrote that her "congratulations have been the best, for you alone have seen that there was an Irish side to it all.... [A]lthough few will believe it ... I have not worked for this—for a 'distinction' and 'honor'—or whatever they call it.... [T]here are many in Ireland will think of me as a traitor—and when I think of that country, and of them, I feel I am."

The Foreign Office was disturbed now by similar accusations about other British companies in the Amazon region. An article in *La Prensa* bared the inhumane practices of the Inambari Rubber Company, operating in the Carabaya Regions—and Travers Buxton of the Anti-Slavery Society wrote letters to the *Times* in this respect. Two weeks later the Tambopata Rubber Syndicate was accused by missionaries of even worse abuses against the Indians. Two other US companies were also mentioned.

Sir Edward Grey decided at this point that it would be a good idea for Casement to make a second journey to Iquitos. The case was at a standstill, the Anti-Slavery Society and Aborigines Protection Association were making loathsome noises. Matters were becoming more confused each day.

Casement agreed. He expressed himself "quite willing to go out at once, if it is thought I could be of service in this direction. I think I might be." It would cost no more than his ship passage, since he was still on salary as Consul-General at Rio. He had more than political reasons for making the trip. It would save him from boredom, get him on the move. He sailed on 16 August 1911. His mission was ostensibly to keep an eye on the Peruvian Amazon Company, now in liquidation.

On 28 August he was in Barbados where he found the black Irishman O'Donnell wallowing in luxury after his crimes in Peru. The other Barbadians had dispersed. Sailing from Barbados on 5 September, he was back at Iquitos on 16 October. He met with Cazes. Nothing had been done. Rómulo Paredes, whose dossier had confirmed Casement's reports, in spite of the anti-Arana position of his journal *Oriente*, was being accused of trying to blackmail Arana. This was not helpful. The criminal charges were moribund. Judge Valcárcel had been dismissed. Lima was mute.

October 16th. Monday. Arrived Iquitos 9 a.m. Delayed landing by funeral of John Lilley's son Lionel—died yesterday of yellow fever. Yellow fever outbreak in Iquitos very bad. Prolonged dry weather. Fearful heat. On shore. Breakfast Cazes. No sign of Ignacio Torres or Antonio Cruz Pérez. Went Brown's house. Cazes took two rooms for me ($90 per month) but they are useless—and as I am let in for that! A nice waste of money! Met Vatan and Brown. Called Guy's to console with John Lilley. No news from Cazes. Letters from Nina and others (Gee and Lizzie). Fearful heat—atrocious. Nearly fainted. Sent boys dine Bella Vista. Dinner 2 soles = 4/-. Stayed in and talked with Brown and captain of *Napo*.

October 17th. Tuesday. Slept well. John Brown came. Sent boys to breakfast with him. He lives Punchana. The restaurant wants 12/-a day! for two meals for these two boys. Outrageous! I shall be ruined here.

On board *Hilda* and *Napo*. Got telegram F.O. saying Mitchell sailed 12 October (to come on by *Manca*, she left Lisbon 11 October). Letter from Mitchell [Casement was arranging for him to take over the consulate at Iquitos]—a very stupid one it seems. Very bad cold and sore throat but after dinner to Malecón and met Caja Marco for one—and then a lovely boy on seat—talked to [three words deleted]. He had been in Putumayo. Then in Square and beautiful Peruvian of Chota. Splendid type and big one too. Asked where I came from. Gave him cigarettes.

October 18th. Wednesday. Saw the young Peruvian negro soldier leaving barracks with erection under white knickers—it was halfway to knee! *fully 1 foot long*.

Cold is worse. Went to John Brown's house at Punchana and his Carizo wee boy kissed and hugged me.

Called on Prefect who said the Putumayo mystery had been solved by me—the honor was mine. It had been a 'mystery' even here in Iquitos! Don Pablo [Zumaeta] was hidden here in Iquitos the Prefect says, waiting the result of his appeal against the Judge Dr. Valcárcel's order of imprisonment.

Dr. Paredes's report covers 80 pages and goes to Lima 'next mail'! Just the same as mine. Got the order for Montt and Fonsesca to go down by *Anastasia* with J. Lilley tomorrow. Called on Mrs. Prefect and at Mrs. Cazes, and then talked with Harding and home to dinner and turned in at once with *fearful cold*. Sneezing and blowing my nose terribly, and in real pain. Visited two empty houses today. A *great* eulogy of me in today's *Oriente*!!

Met young pilot [word illegible] at 4 of *Liberal*, the boy with the big exposure. *Lovely* face and huge. Shook hands and begged him to come at 9 a.m.

October 19th. Thursday. Cold and awfully bad. Took lots of quinine and stayed in bed. Send Ricudo to Putumayo today by *Beatrice*. Young pilot came at 9 a.m. Very well dressed. Sat down and I stroked his knee and gave 10/- and cigarettes and photos. Would like it I am sure. Caressed hand too. He has a big one I know. To come on Saturday to *paseāo* with me and get his photo taken. He is beautiful. Tells me Ignacio Torres is on S.S. *Ucayali* as steward. She is now 'on voyage'. Will tell Ignacio to come to me on return. Cold got much worse so to bed and Doctor of *Napo* came to me. Great pain and trouble. Got quinine and to bed. Saw some splendid ones too again today and such lovely faces. Very heavy rain—began at 8.30 p.m. and till 11 in deluge, then stopped and then began again at 5 or 6 a.m.

October 20th. Friday. Ricudo left for Putumayo on *Beatrice*. Prefect's A.D.C. called for him to take him to Captain Zubiad. In bed all day. Saw from my window splendid type, one young lovely Indian thick limbs and standing with big one—found him to be steward on *Rinoc*. Then to quay as *Javari* arrived at 4 p.m. and saw a glorious type. Young tall (about 18 ½) with big limbs and a huge one. Pensive Inca face and long Indian soft hair. Also green-eyed boy who looked at me. Back and turned in after doctor called at 8. Jansen dined with me. [One word illegible] to Cazes. Captain Barnett's story of the Manaos

Caboclo 15 years ago who stowed cargo and had one below knees he could kiss. Did it for fun for a plug of tobacco.

October 21. Saturday. Expect José González at 9 a.m. but am too seedy to go out with him today. Will give him a present and ask him to return on Monday early to go out to stream with me. He came at 9. New pants, showing much and bowed from the street and then up to my room. I shut door and took his hat and almost at once I saw him getting stiff and bulging out sideways his pants. We sat down side by side and looked at Enoch's book and I caressed and held hand and thigh and sometimes back. He blushed and hand hot and wanted *awfully*, leaning close to me and hand against my thigh. Bad cold. Told come 3 p.m.

3 o'clock. Waiting for José, my fly open. Have just seen young Cholo boy 17 [two words illegible] splendid legs and huge erection down left thigh opposite window. Will José's be up too? He fully expects it I am convinced and is coming expreso. Had hair cut too!

José came and stayed till near 5. Got stiff and fingered it. I [one word illegible] often and tried get it mine up and I pulled it out and he got redder and his very big.

After dinner to band and saw lovely boy. Tuesday 17 going home.

October 22nd. Sunday. José González to come at 8 a.m. and take me out to stream. Will show him mine.

Went 8.30 no stream. Dried up to Morona Cocha, embracing hand, shoulder and waist often, in [three words illegible]. Lunch and in together to Plaza. To go tomorrow Itaya. Afterwards to Cazes and then evening Malecón and Square. Some fine types and meet again. Beautiful of 17. Asked to *paseão* on Malecón 9.30 p.m. Cazes former shopboy *paseando* splendid limbs and grown. It *huge*. Was with a gentleman!

Young municipal chap, blue uniform with huge one—splendid and several Indian boys—very big exposure.

October 23rd. Monday. Up at 6 and out to meet José González at Hospital. He there first, ill poor boy with fever. To Itaya River together where we swam, but he kept his *calconcillo* on. However it got up after and was stiff and if not for his illness would have come off. Gave milk and money.

To *Napo* at 5 and then to see House on Malecón on Morey's which will take probably. After dinner out to Bella Vista and round Plaza. Some splendid Indian lads with huge ones and beautiful sterns, and tried with several and then a lovely Lima boy of 19 with glorious face, a gentleman. Finally coming home a young soldier, thick-set Inca Indian and gave him cigarettes and 3s. and he accompanied me. Mine up and he looked and would have done it. 'Manuel'—is going to Caquetá—very sturdy. He was quite ready I could see.

October 24th. Tuesday. Very tired. Writing for *Napo* mail—due to leave tomorrow. Lovely young Indian boy about 16 gone past window, bandy legs like Cazes' shopboy and huge long one on *right* side of dungaree knickers. Saw Manuel (the corporal) twice this morning outside barracks. He is splendid type of sturdy young Indian, grand calves and thighs, and thick set upright body. It must be a good one! Last night he was quite ready for it!

Played snooker pool after dinner, and then out stroll to Plaza and Malecón, latter quite deserted. Saw fine big one [one word illegible] small boy listening to piano on right side and also in afternoon outside Mrs. Cazes' as a sturdy fine moço of 18 bare feet. In evening several soldiers but not Manuel. Follow. One white one, young and tall, and sat beside me in blue a minute.

October 25th. Wednesday. Saw the nice boy of 17 of Sunday last at 6.25 a.m. returning from [one word illegible] with boy to House of Despachante opposite. Probably cook there. Wrote many letters (F.O. and others to go by *Napo* today). She catches *Lanfranc* and will reach England 23 November probably. Saw one Inca soldier from Brown's window with *huge one* all down left knicker, also young guard of day constantly feeling, slim limbs and lovely face. Then one came from Malecón feeling it and making signs to others as if *entering*! Then young white soldier (same as I walked partly with last night from Square) talking to others in shirt (open bosom) and knickers and one put hand on his and he showed enormous extension—as long as palm and big testaminhos. They all gathered round and looked and it was lying down all time, thick and about 7" or 8" long lying! Saw three bathing lovely color and limbs and one big one. In afternoon a huge soft long one. I saw it plainly on left side loose pants. Smiled at him. To Harding's whose store boy has a beautiful too and smiles shyly. Sat in Square with young boy splendid limbs 6.30–7 till darkness came and home to dinner and turned in after.

October 26th. Thursday. Up at 6.30. Heavy rain all night. Took quinine. Soldiers out and 'palm' of yesterday in his knickers and other one embracing young thick set soldier of 18—a beauty.

The lovely boy of 20 came to Reuss store at 7 this morning and two others to shift whisky, etc. He smiled and bowed. I love him. Also one of the carters, a big Inca (white) peon with blue shirt and pants and a perfect monster. It swings and shows a head about 3" in diameter! He has enormous shoulders and curved strong back about 27, and as strong as a stallion. Saw it at 9 a.m. swinging and I'll swear it is 3" across. Lovely boy looked up and smiled and his a big long soft one, or his pants are loose and yet it and his bags hang down a lot. He has a lovely gentle face about 19 ½.

I expect lose some time today. River 63' 8".

5.45 Manuel and the young guard of yesterday (and today) went past. Manuel splendid, both lovely. I saw from window Thom. Cazes' old shopboy well dressed and splendid legs went past and hugged bigger boy. Out after and met and shook hands. Said he was sick, brought him in and gave him quinine. He said 'I have grown much, haven't I?' His name is Alcibiades Ruiz—works John Lilley—and him on *Napo*. After dinner to Malecón and Lima soldier. Gave cigarettes. Met Antonio Cruz Pérez, much grown too.

October 27th. Friday. Lovely morning and very bright sun all day. In house nearly all day. Saw 'Manuel' in morning in guard with bayonet at side in blue and in afternoon at 3.30 several times on guard. Running and straight splendid legs and twirled round once and clasped a man round waist, holding him lovingly thus. It looked pretty big even at distance. Thinking of Manuel often and hope to meet soon now. Saw him often, in afternoon from [word illegible] saw Antonio Cruz twice—very stout strong young man now. Promised yesterday to photo him again. Stayed in house all day till near 6.30 p.m. when out to Plaza for a bit and after dinner and a game of billiards with Brown about 9–10 to Plaza and Malecón seeing none, and no sign of Manuel, although some soldiers to be seen. 'Vaseline' at [word illegible] 2 years ago. *In sua bode!*

October 28th. Saturday. Lovely morning, but my cold is worse and has turned into a steady, dry 'hacking cough'. Will not move today to new house now. No news of Mitchell and fear now for over a month. Saw Manuel several times during day and at 9 p.m. with two well dressed boys under umbrella going uptown. Also saw beautiful green eyed Reuss Store. After and at 5 p.m. when going home he smiled at me. Also saw Antonio Cruz Pérez twice. Round Square at 6 p.m. (none at all) and then out at 9 to Malecón and Square. Some soldiers and one brown one of 9th gave cigarettes to, a big strapping Indian from hills. A [word illegible] moved in at 10 with port wine.

October 29th. Sunday. River 65' at 10 a.m. 'Javari' smiled. Began breakfast at Continental good and cheap. Walked Plaza with Brown after dinner. Met Reuss' beautiful boy in Sunday best. I love him. Also Alcibiades looking splendid. Also dark eyed lad who said *Buenas noches* as he passed. Some fine soldiers too of 9th Battalion but saw no sign of 'Manuel'. Rain and visit from a Major of 17 Battalion till 9. Then bed and slept well.

"As we have quite failed to secure punishment," Casement wrote in despair, "let us drop it, and go for reform! And let the first step to reform be the publication of what it is we are seeking to have reformed."

Casement was frustrated by the maddening delays of the Peruvian government and exhausted by the double-dealing. He decided to go home by way of the United States. He might just convince the Americans that conditions were so bad down south that they should do something to help.

James Bryce was the British Minister now—Chief Secretary for Ireland before his Washington appointment, a Protestant Ulsterman, and sympathetic toward Casement's efforts on behalf of the Putumayo Indians. He was writing a book himself on the South American situation; it would appear later that year and include material from the Casement Report on the disastrous effects caused by the rubber trade. Working under Bryce was Alfred Mitchell Innes, who became friends with Casement and corresponded with him over the next few months. George Young later wrote that Peru at that moment appealed to Washington, then very pan-American and that Casement's bulging file on the Putumayo would have given the yellow press enough material for a month. He said that at the Ambassador's request a US Navy cruiser had brought Casement north—an obvious exaggeration; but Casement did go back home by way of Washington, although he was not authorized to do so by the Foreign Office. He met with important figures in the capital. As Young describes it, "President Taft was lured to dinner in the embassy and led away to a quiet corner where Casement was let loose on him.... the tall Celt, haggard and livid from the Putumayo swamps, fixing with glittering black eyes the burly rubicund Anglo-Saxon. It was like a black snake fascinating a wombat. But Putumayo gave no further trouble in Washington."

Casement held discreet talks, often in social settings, with various influential US politicians. The Americans were well aware of the complexities of the situation; they had long been familiar with the labyrinth of South American politics.

Bryce wrote that Casement "was able to create a personal interest among the higher authorities, which gives strong grounds for believing that the publication of the report will be welcomed by the United States Government." It might be a good tactic, Bryce thought, for the US and Britain to jointly put pressure on Peru. A few days after this, the Secretary of State informed Casement that a cable was being sent to the US Ambassador in Lima, asking him to bring to the attention of the Peruvian Government the fact that local corruption had led to court actions against the Putumayo criminals being dropped. The Ambassador was instructed to formally state that unless drastic action was taken by the Peruvian Government world opinion might be influenced by the "account of that iniquitous system" into believing that Peru "had shown herself unable to properly exercise sovereign rights over disputed regions." This was a hint that the US might side with Colombia in the boundary dispute with Peru, a nation formerly thought of as unreservedly friendly to the US and her great mainstay in Latin America.

Sir Edward Grey was pleased. He suggested that the timing of the publication of the Putumayo Report be a joint British-US decision.

The Putumayo Report

The report from Consul General Casement to Sir Edward Grey is dated 17 March 1911. It begins with a rather dry description of the Putumayo territory and of the Indian population found there.

The Putumayo, Casement explains, is a region drained by the Caraparaná, the Igaraparaná the Cahuinari rivers and is the territory where the operations of the Peruvian Amazon Company are carried on. It is impossible at present to estimate the Indian population of the Putumayo. The upper and middle courses of these rivers are—or were—the most heavily populated, due in part to the elevation (600 ft above sea level at La Chorrera) and the consequent absence of insect pests. The lower course of the Igaraparaná and the Putumayo itself down to the Amazon flows through thick forest, subject to annual flooding. Mosquitoes and sand flies constitute a plague in the swampy areas but are absent on higher ground. Permanent dwellings and cultivation of the soil can be found throughout the area.

An important description of the area and its people, Casement notes, appears in *En el Putumayo y sus Afluentes,* published in Lima in 1907. This report was prepared by Eugenio Robuchon, a French explorer who was hired by J. C. Arana in the name of the Government to conduct a mission of exploration in the region claimed by the firm of Arana Brothers. M. Robuchon lost his life near the mouth of the Cahuinari in 1906 and the work was edited from his notes and diaries by Carlos Rey de Castro, Peruvian Consul-General for Northern Brazil, based in Manaos. The Indian population at that time was given as 50,000. In a prospectus of the Peruvian Amazon Rubber Company (formerly J. C. Arana Brothers), issued in 1908, it is claimed that 40,000 "laborers" live in the company's area of operations. Thus, it can be seen that the Putumayo has been fairly heavily populated, making it an attractive field during the early eighteenth century for slave raids. There were no civilized settlements, however, and the Indian tribes continued to live in their primitive state "subject only to visits from slave-searching white or half-breed bands" until a quite recent period.

There are four major tribes, the Huitotos (or Witotos), the Boras, the Andokes and the Ocainas. Other smaller tribes exist, but they are all "kindred in origin and identical in habit and customs, although differing in language and to some extent in features, complexion, and stature." The Huitotos are the most numerous, with a population of about 30,000, but they are the least sturdy. The word "Hutitoto" itself is said to mean "mosquito"—referring, no doubt, to their typically scrawny arms and legs. The Boras are physically finer and are usually lighter than the Huitotos whose color ranges from dark bronze to chocolate brown. The Boras are sometimes as light as Japanese or Chinese; they have a Mongolian aspect, as well, and are like Asiatics in general, even to their manner of walking. A picture of a Sea Dyak of Borneo using his "sumpitan" or blowpipe is similar to the Boras Indian with his "cerbatana," which is identical in shape and use.

There is some bickering between tribes. The Huitotos carry on a hereditary feud with the Boras, Andokes and Ocainas, but also fight among themselves. Robuchon notes 33 sub-tribes or families among the Huitotos; possibly there are more. Intermarriage is common among the Huitotos, who have a shared sense of origin, kinship and language and a mistrust of outsiders.

The frequent "wars" among the tribes commonly involving kidnapping, thefts of women, family grievances and misuse of mystical powers (witchcraft and sorcery are common). Casement notes that the Indian wars were not bloody: "[T]he Amazon Indian is averse to bloodshed, and is thoughtless rather than cruel." The weapons of the natives are the blowpipe and poison darts, plus small spears with wooden tips. Prisoners of war may have been eaten by the victors, or partially eaten, but Amazon cannibals have not been observed to kill in order to eat, instead eating only those who have been killed. Curiously, the victims of cannibals are reported not to have been terrified of being eaten, regarding it as an honorable end. Lieutenant Henry Lister Maw, of the British Navy, an early traveler, mentions the case of a native girl in the Brazilian Amazon in 1827 refusing to escape to become the slave of a Portuguese trader, preferring to be eaten by her own kind.

Each clan or family has a great central dwelling house for up to 200 individuals. The region around the house is often scattered with smaller dwellings. [Photos taken by Robuchon showing the enormous size of these communal houses are truly impressive.] The Indians are—or were—excellent hunters and the forests were formerly full of game, supplying them an abundant source of meat. They also cultivated cassava, maize, fruits and edible greens, and were skilled fishermen.

The Indians have not yet been Christianized, due to their isolation. Contact with whites was uncommon but not unknown, and usually in the form of slaving forays. When in the early nineteenth century, Lieutenant Maw crossed from the Pacific to the Atlantic via the Amazon he did take note of the Putumayo Indians in rather vague terms. In 1851 Lieutenant Herndon of the US Navy went down the Amazon in a canoe, but his narrative throws no light on the Indians. The region was practically untouched until arrival of Colombian "caucheros" or rubber traders in the early 1880s. Then, around 1886, came the first "conquistadores"—Crisóstomo Hernández and Benjamín Larranaga—who came searching for an inferior type of rubber, "sernambi" or "jebe débil" (weak fine). They found the area of the Putumayo thickly covered with rubber trees, and exploitation began.

The method of gathering rubber was simple. The Indians gashed the rubber tree with his machete or knife, and collected the milk in little baskets made of leaves. The coagulated milk, or latex, was washed in a stream and then pounded into "chorizos"—sausages—which were then gathered together. The rubber trade gave the Indians precious goods such as machetes, guns, powder and caps, beads, mirrors, bowls, fish-hooks, canned sardines and meat. It seemed, at first, quite advantageous. But they were soon disappointed: the rubber traders came as speculators, not as civilizers, and they were controlled neither by the law nor by law officers. The Putumayo territory was a no-man's land claimed by three republics.

The caucheros planned to get rich quick. The rubber trees in themselves were unimportant, of no value, "it was the Indians who could be made ... to tap them and to bring in the rubber on the white man's terms that all the invading 'conquistadores' were in search of." In the Congo there had been a hierarchy of Government officers, and regulations which the natives knew existed. In the Putumayo there was nothing, only ignorance.

As "infieles" or unchristianized savages, the Putumayo Indians were fair game for the small armies of caucheros that went in search of rubber. These miniature armies consisted of a lead man and his partners and a gang of hired peones (or "racionales"—half-breeds who could read and write). The men went into the forest, hunting out tribes of wild Indians who could be subdued and made to work the wild rubber trees in their territory. They had enticements besides force: the Indians would promise anything for a gun or other goods, which they were to pay for with rubber. Once "hooked" the Indians lost their liberty and were reduced to unending demands for more and more rubber. A Cacique or "capitán" might be brought in to guarantee that his clan would work for the traders, with promises of reward never fulfilled. The Indians of the area had a natural docility which made them easy to manipulate. There was little opposition, even from the ferocious Boras.

Casement again cites Lieutenant Maw who in 1827 observed that even inferior firearms terrorized the Indians. "So great is the dread of white men among these Indians, who are said to fight desperately if opposed to each other, that if, as is sometimes the case, a hundred or more of them are seen dancing at night around a fire, seven or eight 'blancos' (whites) by taking different stations and firing a few shots may seize as many as they can get hold of, the others only thinking of escape." The Indians sometimes fought back. "If the Indians get information of 'blancos' being on any of these hunting expeditions they dig holes in the paths in different parts of the woods, and fix strong poisoned spears in them, after which rotten sticks are placed across and covered with leaves, earth, etc., and it requires much caution and some experience to avoid them."

The Colombians, after much killing, finally managed to establish numerous rubber stations on the Caraparaná and Igaraparaná rivers. Barter goods were generally brought from Iquitos, conveniently accessible by boat.

About 1896 Arana began trading with the Colombian caucheros. This trade ended by the acquisition of almost all the Colombian rubber stations by the firm of Arana Brothers. The rubber trade was, at that time, in a fluid state. Men ascended or descended the hitherto unsettled rivers, established themselves on the banks and induced the neighboring tribes to work on their terms. Each private sphere became a closed preserve, jealously guarded by the first to arrive there. Any attempt by another to move in on the territory was seen as an act of piracy. To enter into friendly relations with the Indians was a capital offense. "Rubber pirates" were shot on sight. An Indian tribe, once "conquered" was the exclusive property of the rubber agent. None of this had any basis in law; it was simply a custom sanctioned by tradition. That the Indian had no rights was an accepted fact. There were even examples of magistrates (in regions more effectively administered than the Putumayo) intervening to capture or compel runaway Indians to return to their bondage.

Soon the Indian realized his own weakness against the whites, the impossibility of opposing those he dreaded, and the loss of freedom brought about by surrendering to the control of the rubber traders. One answer seemed to be to surprise and kill the rubber traders in the forest; but when this happened there were terrible reprisals, fresh barbarities.

A popular excuse for massacring and torturing Indians was that they had killed a blanco. One agent of the Putumayo Amazon Company told Casement how, some years previously, the Andoke Indians had killed a large party of Colombian, Peruvian and Brazilians coming upriver to establish rubber stations. (The informant was a Peruvian trader responsible for a large section of the Putumayo Amazon Company territory.) In 1903, just before the man's arrival, a party led by a man called Gutiérrez, and comprising some sixty armed men, went up the Japurá, carrying a large amount of trading goods. The party was received by friendly natives, so friendly, indeed, that the party went to bed that night without placing a guard. While they slept, surrounded by the natives, they were attacked and slaughtered. The Indians killed them with machetes, cut their heads and limbs off—preserving the bodies as long as possible in water, to show the neighboring tribes.

Casement's informant later buried a dozen bodies. He also spoke of many such incidents that had taken place. One detail: the Indians did not eat the whites, finding them repugnant. "Terrible reprisals were carried out for these crimes" committed by the Indians.

The Andokes were induced by the Colombians to raid the Arana Brothers station at Matanzas, where Ramón Sánchez was in charge. The situation in the Matanzas area was extremely uncertain during 1903–4. The company got its first contingent of Barbados men, originally recruited as laborers by Abel Alarco in Barbados in October 1904. About thirty-six men arrived, along with five wives. They were brought to the Putumayo by a Peruvian or Bolivian by the name of Armando Normand who acted as interpreter. When they showed up at the La Chorrera station, where Larranaga had died in 1903, they were immediately assigned to Ramón Sánchez to accompany him on a mission of vengeance and rubber gathering in the Andoke country.

When Casement visited La Chorrera in October 1910, Normand was still in charge and more than one of the original contingent of Barbadians were still there—one man had never left Matanzas since first being brought there in November or December of 1904. Casement received depositions from these men; these were attached to his original Report. The men accused Normand and Sánchez of atrocities and crimes which were later excused by claiming they were justifiable reprisals for Indian massacres of whites.

Clifford Quintin saw many Indians killed by Sánchez and by Normand.

Quintin:	They were tied up and chains put around their necks; and they were hung up, and he, Sánchez, would take a 'sword,' or machete, and stick it right through them. I saw Ramón Sánchez do this to plenty of Indians.... One day Sánchez killed twenty-five men—he shot some, others he cut their heads off—and some he hanged slowly with a chain.
Casement:	Did the Indians not resist?
Quintin:	They were tied up and killed.
Casement:	You saw them killed?
Quintin:	Yes! I saw several shot, chiefly those that had run away.

The whites were anxious to keep firearms out of the hands of Indians. They made continual raids of confiscation if they learned that Indians had come into possession of rifles. Possessors of arms were severely punished. Only the young native "cholos" or "muchachos" were allowed to carry rifles. These muchachos were trained to oppress their fellow Indians in the interests of the caucheros. They brutally terrorized even their own kinsmen and were often ruthless in extreme.

Some muchachos were assigned to serve the white men in their houses. "Cholitos" were from an early age trained to do the trader's bidding, no matter how extreme. Some even married and lived at the rubber stations with their wives and children. Every station Casement visited had an "Indian house" (built by forced labor) where the muchachos lived. These men were as bad as their bosses, obeyed any orders, committed the most atrocious crimes. The worst crimes were done by order of the whites. The muchachos had to obey, Casement was told, or they might be killed. Casement certainly saw many "thoroughly demoralized" muchachos on his journeys in the jungles; some were murderous, others were simply amiable lads (as he says). Becoming a muchacho represented a promotion. Boys were selected on approval, easily recruited since the job included possession of a rifle and cartridges. Once they became muchachos boys could indulge their predatory instincts on unarmed and defenseless countrymen—bullying, robbing and terrorizing at will. Theft of everything—food, ornaments, spears—was allowed, except for wives and daughters. The muchachos were however constantly under threat of reprisal themselves; Casement heard of muchachos who had been killed by and who also had killed their employers. He adds one such report from a statement by Clifford Quintin:

A man called Bucelli, a Colombian, came to work at Matanzas when the operation began under the direction of Ramón Sanchez, in 1904. Bucelli worked for the Putumayo Amazon Company until 1909, when he was murdered along with three other whites by four muchachos during a raid into the Republic of Colombia in pursuit of runaway Indians. The muchachos had taken the dead men's rifles and escaped into the selva. Strange to say, at one of the settlements, Casement had inquired about the parents of two little half-breed girls; they said that their father had died on the Caquetá river. This turned out to be the same Bucelli who had been killed during the mutiny of the muchachos who wanted the white men's rifles. Bucelli's native wife, who had accompanied the party, knew about the plot to kill him and his companions, but did not warn him, obviously sympathizing with the murderers. Later the four muchachos had a falling out and two were killed. The survivors gave themselves up at the station of Entre Rios. Here they were repeatedly flogged and confined in chains at neighboring Matanzas. This was not long before Casement arrived on the scene. The muchachos had then managed—still in chains—to escape into the forest where, since they were Huitotos in the Andoke country, it would not be long before they were massacred by Indians whom they had maltreated.

Flogging of Indians was frequent. The Barbardians as well as the peones or racionales (who were salaried staff) were often compelled to flog Indians who "defaulted" on rubber gathering. A Chief of Section was responsible for assigning this duty and some, like the Colombian Negro, Simón Angulo, actually enjoyed flogging Indians. Some men were chosen for their skill in wielding the lash, drawing blood or cutting flesh at every blow. The Chief himself often took over the job from a racional.

The Indians were terrified of being flogged. "The Indian dread of the lash was early recognized by the followers of Pizarro," says Casement in a learned aside (straight out of Cunninghame Graham), "in their first dealings with the population of the Andes, for we read in the records of the Spanish rule that the Viceroy, Don Francisco de Toledo, who came to Peru in 1569 and left it in 1581, among other laws for civilizing the remnant of the Inca people prescribed that, 'Any Indian who makes friendship with an Indian woman who is an infidel is to receive 100 lashes for the first offense, that being the punishment that they dislike most.'"

Evidence of flogging was noted by Casement everywhere he stopped. From the time he arrived at La Chorrera until he left to return to Iquitos he met more than 1,600 natives, including native staff at the various rubber stations. Most were forest Indians (the "laborers" of the company). The women went entirely naked. The men and boys wore only a strip of beaten bark "cloth" tightly wound around their loins. The first "wild" Indians he saw with the marks of flogging were Boras from the Abisinia district, brought to the station as carriers by Miguel Flores who came from Abisinia for supplies. Of the seven nude carriers, five were scarred across the buttocks and thighs from the lash.

From then on, Casement paid particularly attention to buttocks and thighs. The great majority he inspected showed visible marks of flogging. Young, old, women and children were also scarred. Even caciques and their wives had not escaped. Some were slightly marked, others had terrible scars; some were quite recent. From time to time young men came to him begging for a healing lotion. On 19 October Casement spent the night in a deserted Indian house in the forest with over a hundred Andoke and Boras Indians on a march to carry heavy loads of rubber from the station at Matanzas down to the Igaraparaná, for shipment to La Chorrera. (A trip of about 40 miles.) Casement applied healing medicines to a dozen or so young men and boys. Since only one or two muchachos were accompanying the party, he had a chance, while they were resting, to inspect their bodies closely. Many wounds had not healed. Boys of ten or twelve years of age were scarred the worst.

A white agent, resident in the region for about six years, admitted to Casement that he regularly flogged Indians and that 99 percent of the entire population bore traces of flogging. One of the men who admitted flogging Indians said that six weeks before Casement's arrival in September, a native chief had been flogged to death, dying in the infamous *cepo* (or stocks) where he was confined between his wife and one of his children.

Flogging without doubt was the most universal and indiscriminate torture, as it had been in many places throughout the world, including Europe, until relatively recent times.

At one station the principal flogger, for some reason, was the cook. Casement ate the food prepared by this man with some misgiving. Casement's personal porters also showed terrible scars and some told him they had been flogged while in the stocks. Usually the bare buttocks were flogged while the victim was lying on the ground, or pegged out. It was not possible to witness flogging, of course; and the Chief of section got rid of the evidence of the worst cases on Casement's arrival. This was not always possible, and he saw some horribly scarred victims who were brought forth as evidence. Before the end of his visit, one Peruvian agent admitted that he regularly flogged Indians and said that other agents not only did the same but were guilty of even greater crimes.

"In many cases the Indian rubber collector—who knew roughly what quantity of rubber was expected of him by the agent—when he brought his load to be weighed and saw that the needle of the balance did not touch the required spot, would throw himself face downwards on the ground, and in that posture await the inevitable blow." Then "the Chief or a subordinate advances, bends down, takes the Indian by his hair, strikes him, raises his head, drops it face downwards on the ground, and after the face is beaten and kicked and covered with blood the Indian is scourged." One man who often took part in flogging admitted two murders of Indians and left a record of the manner of flogging at stations where he worked. His testimony was confirmed by a Barbadian who admitted to Casement being guilty himself of having flogged an Indian girl and then shot her when her wounds had putrefied and become full of maggots. "Indians were flogged not only for shortage in rubber, but still more grievously if they dared to run away from their houses, and, by flight to a distant region, to escape altogether from the tasks laid upon them. Such flight as this was counted a capital offense, and the fugitives, if captured, were as often tortured and put to death as brutally flogged."

Indians were often rounded up during raids in Colombian territory north of the Caquetá (or Japurá). The main agent of the Putumayo Amazon Company at La Chorrera, Victor Macedo, sent out an expedition in March 1910 which returned not only with Indians but with three white captives. (One of the latter went to work at the Arenas station where Casement met him on 26 October; the other two were sent downstream by Macedo.) This expedition was led by Augusto Jiménez, chief of Último Retiro, and two Barbadians, Edward Crichlow and Reuben Phillips. A Peruvian, Eusebio Pinedo, also a member of the group, gave Casement a statement describing the excursion. He claimed that two Indians, a young man and a woman, had been shot by another member of the party, Aquileo Torres. This was borne out by the testimony of the two Barbadians. The Barbadians also claimed a bonus (or "*gratificación*") from the company for their share in the expedition, citing an order issued by Macedo that "employees who conduct themselves well on the Expedition to the Caquetá, and who present a certificate on their return from the leader of the Expedition, Sr. Augusto Jiménez, will receive a reward."

Crichlow and Phillips both got fifty soles. Later, other raids of this nature were carried out by Armando Normand in which two British subjects, James Lane and Westerman Leavine, took part, according to testimony given to Casement on 18 October at Matanzas.

Casement presented copies of these declarations to the representative of the Peruvian Amazon Company, Sr. Tizón, who was accompanying the Commission of Inquiry. The men claimed that Normand had for many years hunted down fugitive Indians. The reason was not hard to find. Normand received a "reward" of 20 percent on the gross output of rubber in this section. This was clearly spelled out in the Planilla de Sueldos, or pay sheet, of the section.

Normand represented a low point on the scale of humans working for the company. His crimes dated from the end of 1904 to October 1910, when Casement visited the area. They included numerous murders and torture. He poured kerosene over Indians and set them afire, burned men at the stake, dashed out the brains of children, cut off arms and legs and left the victims to die. The Barbadians, racionales and others confirmed these charges. Westerman Leavine said he had frequently witnessed Normand's crimes and "had seen Indians burned alive more than once, and often their limbs eaten by the dogs kept by Normand at Matanzas."

It was alleged that over his six years of service, Normand had killed "hundreds" of Indians outright and had caused the death of many more due to starvation, floggings, exposure and hardship of various kinds during the collection of rubber and its transfer from the Andoke territories down to La Chorrera. It was estimated that upwards of a thousand Indians had died from the forced carriage of rubber from distant regions to company stations. On these marches, which took place two or three times a year, no food was given to the carriers.

Casement himself witnessed one of these marches. He accompanied a caravan of some two hundred Andokes and Boras Indians, including men, women and children, leaving Matanzas on 19 October. The Indians carried the rubber collected over four or five months down to Puerto Peruana on the banks of the Igaraparaná for trans-shipment to La Chorrera. This was a journey of about sixty miles, following a path through the forest, not easy even for someone not carrying a heavy load. Casement marched for two days with the caravan. The men carried loads of about seventy kilograms (150 lbs), women less; the children brought a small supply of cassava bread to feed them on the way. Muchachos armed with Winchesters accompanied the caravan; one of the racionales, Adán Negrete, brought up the rear, beating the stragglers. Normand himself and a few racionales followed the trail a day later to check if no one had fallen out, slipped away home or dropped a load. On the second day the caravan reached Entre Ríos. Most of the Indians, after sleeping in the forest, had begun the march at five in the morning By five in the afternoon they reached Entre Ríos in an exhausted state. There was a company rest house at the station, and supplies of food available, but the Indians were driven by Negrete into the forest to spend the night under guard. This was obviously so that Walter Fox, a member of the Commission of Inquiry, should not see at too close quarters the condition of these people or ascertain the weight of the loads they were forced to carry. Casement took numerous photographs and made extensive notes at the time, however. He mentions that several women had fallen out sick on the way. He had left them with food in a deserted Indian hut, watched over by a Barbadian until Sr. Tizón, the company representative, following a day later, could reach them.

One straggler reached Entre Ríos about noon, staggering under his load, just as Casement and Fox were sitting down to lunch. The man fell at the foot of the ladder leading to the veranda where they were sitting. They had the man carried up, revived him with whiskey, and later fed him soup and food from their table. He was a young man, slight, with skinny arms and legs. His load, weighing only fifty kilograms, was still too much for him; he had had no food since starting out. (Casement arranged for him to be allowed to go to Puerto Peruano empty handed the next day with Normand.) The other Indians returned home the following day, footsore and exhausted. No food was given them at Entre Ríos. Casement stopped many, examined their little string bags, and found not a scrap of food. They had been subsisting on roots, leaves and berries; the path they had followed was blocked with branches and creepers they had pulled down for food, looking, Casement said, like the work of wild animals.

Indians were flogged to death infrequently; death from flogging usually came later when the wounds putrefied. Some victims were shot at this stage on order of the chief of section, as a rule by one of the racionales. At times salt water was applied to the open sores. Often there were "maggots on the flesh." Hopeless cases were set adrift in the forest to die. One of the Barbadians at Abisinia (a confessed flogger of Indians) said that occasionally the mother of a little boy who did not bring in enough rubber would be flogged in his stead, being too young to punish in this way. Seeing the mother given a few strokes of the lash, the terrified child would cry and promise to do better.

Men and women were suspended by their arms, twisted behind their back and tied together at the wrist. Their feet would hang just above the ground. Then their back and lower limbs would be flogged, usually with an implement made of strips of dried tapir hide plaited together, stout enough to cut a body to pieces.

During the later months of 1910, some Indians were punished by strokes of the flat blade of a machete. Blows across the shoulder blades or back did not leave any traces. At Occidente this type of beating began in June 1910 and was varied with other tortures devised by the chief of section, a Peruvian named Fidel Velardo. Indians' arms would be tied behind their backs and then they would be taken down to the river (the Igaraparaná) and held underwater until unconscious and half drowned.

At the end of October, Casement returned to La Chorrera. Having been unable to reach all of the rubber stations, he had the Barbadians working in isolated locales called in for questioning. One of these men admitted to him on 2 November that on 20 June 1910, only a few hours after Sr. Tizón had left Occidente on his way upriver to Último Retiro on his expedition of inspection, Fidel Velardo ordered four Indian boys, their arms tied together, taken to the river and held under water—until, as James Mapp put it, "their bowels filled with water." Mapp, ordered to do the job, had refused, so a racional, one Eugenio Acosto, took over. One of the young men kicked free and sank in the swift current. Unable to struggle since his hands were bound, he sank out of sight. Casement, who had swum at this same spot, knew quite well how the banks fell off into deep water. The boy's body was recovered on 24 June. When Mapp recounted this story, Sr. Tizón was present and was convinced that the man was telling the truth. Since Velardo was still at La Chorrera, it would be easy to prove the charges. Mapp was willing to accuse the man to his face, especially as there had been other eyewitnesses there at the time. There was no attempt to bring this crime to light, however; since it was well known that the criminal had hundreds of other similar charges against him. The guilty men would simply be discharged, Sr. Tizón said.

Casement uncovered innumerable cases of flogging—and evidence of it abounded wherever he went. Floggings seemed wholly illogical, even when Indians admitted to doing wrong. It was perhaps admissible to administer a flogging for a proven offense, but not when no offense was committed. Agents admitted using flogging to torture and terrorize the Indians, in order to induce them to bring in more rubber. The men ordering floggings of this kind were generally agents, like Normand, who received a commission on the amount of rubber collected.

Flogging and tortures such as near-drownings, stopping just short of death, were common in all stations. They inspired terror and physical agony. Defaulters or fugitives would be strung up by chains fastened round their neck to roofbeams of houses or stores, their feet scarcely touching the ground. The chains were hauled taut until the victims, unable support themselves, finally fell to the ground when released, their tongues protruding. Sometimes a victim's arms were chained and he was hoisted up to the ceiling or into the branches of a tree; when the chain was suddenly loosed the victim would crash to the ground. Casement saw one case of a boy who was tortured in this way. When the boy fell he struck his head and had bitten clean through his tongue—his mouth was filled with blood.

Starvation was used to frighten and kill. Prisoners were often kept in the *cepo* until they died of hunger. This happened, according to witnesses, not by simple neglect but by design. No one was permitted to give the victim food except the chief of the station. The starving could be seen "scraping up the dirt with their fingers and eating it" or even picking the maggots out of their wounds and eating them.

Casement reminds us that he had no proof of some of these allegations, nor did he have any rights to interrogate anyone but the British subjects—the Barbadians. However, he could bring charges against those men still working for the company who admitted to crimes. Sr. Tizón for his part considered it necessary to make a fuller investigation; charges were often made unwillingly or, in the case of some Barbadians, by men not wanting to be involved themselves. One of the men openly admitted his guilt when he saw that Casement had received information from another quarter. Yet convictions would be hard to come by, due to the nature of the investigation, in spite of abundant confirmation at every stage of the journey.

Even before Casement had reached the Putumayo, Frederick Bishop—who would accompany him as interpreter and guide—described the many horrors he had witnessed during his five and half years of service with Arana Brothers and the Putumayo Amazon Company. One of the crimes he mentioned involved an Indian girl who had been flogged at the orders of Elias Martinengui. (Martinengui had recently left the employ of the company and had gone to Lima). In a declaration by Bishop—attached to the report—he states that he knew this girl well and had flogged her at Martinengui's orders. Casement discovered the same girl at a company sub-station not long after, and wanted her shown to Sr. Tizón and the Commission of Inquiry in case they doubted Bishop's charges. Tizón declined the pleasure, saying that Bishop's testimony was obviously genuine but that this represented a crime of personal malice and had nothing to do with rubber gathering.

Such crimes against women came from the "prevailing immorality" of the agents, who had their pick of the Indian girls.

Casement emphasizes that the Indians were citizens of the Republic of Peru and thus entitled to all their rights. But who was to ensure that they got their rights? Casement at no time during his travels met any Peruvian authorities, only agents of the Putumayo Amazon Company, who were in absolute control of the land and of persons' lives, as well as of the movements of people into and out of the territory. The letter carried by Casement was addressed to shadows: "His Britannic Majesty's Consul General of the Republic of Brazil goes to the Putumayo and its affluents sent by his Government, and with the assent of ours, to investigate and evaluate the condition in which the subjects of His Britannic Majesty may be found in that region.... I hereby order all the Authorities of the district to afford him every kind of facility, and to furnish him such data and information as the Consul may be in need of for the better discharge of his mission, and to lend him all the support he may require." It would have been simple for Arana to have had him killed, as he perhaps had ordered Robuchon done away with; but there was the matter of the Commission of Inquiry and Sr. Tizón. The Barbadians were in real danger, too, as witnesses and actual perpetrators of crimes. The Putumayo was basically lawless. The only Peruvian Government representatives the Commission met with were a contingent of soldiers and their officer who arrived shortly before Casement left for El Encanto on the Caraparaná. A magistrate was said to reside on the river, but no one had ever seen him.

One curious aspect of the investigation was that when particularly atrocious crimes were brought to light, admitted to, and deplored, the culprit might be sitting at table with Casement, who was warned to avoid expressing disgust lest the man do "worse things" to the Indians or "provoke an impossible situation" with the armed outlaws under his command. The reason given for this was that there was "no authority, no administration, no one near to whom any appeal could be made"—and Iquitos was 1,200 miles away. Each Chief of Section was a law unto himself, and many of these Chiefs were murderers, pirates or bandits.

The *cepo*, or stocks, figured as a popular type of punishment or to terrorize the Indians. Every station had stocks, either on the upper verandah of the residence of the Chief of Section or in the area below the house. The victims were thus under the eyes of the Chief and his subordinates at all times. In El Retiro the stocks were in the middle of the house near the cellar (the Black Hole referred to by some Barbadians). All houses were on raised beams, about 12–15 ft above ground. The lower space was open or palisaded for storing rubber; usually the stocks were in this store. There was such an open space at Matanzas and two days before Casement's arrival the stocks had been removed and hidden under a pile of palm fronds and rubbish, so that when questioned the agents could claim that they were no longer in use. The Chief swore to Sr. Tizón and the members of the Commission of Inquiry that they had no stocks. But one of the Barbadians led them to where the stocks had been concealed. The same Barbarian told them how a few weeks before an Indian chief had been flogged and had died in these stocks. At the same time as he was reporting this, Armando Normand was in the neighboring room declaring to the commission that *no* Indian had been flogged at the station for two years. Normand claimed that the only implement permitted was a flat board with holes (called a "placatory" in Africa) applied to the palms of hands in "light" chastisement of those who had done wrong.

The idea of the stocks was associated, in Western European cultures, with the obsolete institution of *exposure*—a pillory—where wrongdoers were subjected to the gaze of the curious and their insults. Sodomites were commonly put in stocks in England, a fate worse than hanging—since the populace, especially the whores, had the right to pelt them with garbage and more solid objects. The stocks often meant a horrible death. In Peru the so-called *cepo* was a recognized method of detention up to modern times. Lieutenant Herndon refers to the stocks as well as to floggings as common in 1851; he does not, however, mention their misuse. The missionary fathers, responsible for the control of large territories, often employed both the stocks and flogging as part of their "machinery of government." In Iquitos and in the village of Punchana, on the outskirts, the stocks were still in use when Casement was there. In Punchana the local schoolmistress was in charge of the *cepo*. Once when an Indian got drunk and beat his wife the schoolmistress had him thrown into the stocks. The next day, the man's wife and his friends were out, building a shelter against the sun and comforting the repentant evildoer, receiving his heartfelt apologies. Casement notes this as an example of the naturally kind and affectionate nature of the Indians. In the Putumayo, on the other hand, the stocks were used for torture and Indians might be confined in them for months, only being freed under guard to answer the calls of nature. The overlapping beam might press so tightly on the confined ankle, Casement says, that the flesh would be cut, "but even without this added torment the long confinement in this cramped position … must have become well-nigh unendurable." With starvation at the same time, "death when it came may well have been a happy release." The Indians were afraid of the *cepo* but not as afraid as they were of flogging.

At Occidente the stocks had twenty-eight leg holes, at Entre Ríos twenty-four, with large neck holes in the center. There was also a special kind of "flogging *cepo*" with moveable extremities, devised by Aurelio Rodríguez at Santa Catalina (and carpentered by Crichlow). Awful offenses were sometimes committed on those held in the stocks, as attested by James Chase and Stanley Lewis in an attached statement. Racionales often had sexual intercourse with women held in the stocks. Legs were often fastened several holes apart. The Último Retiro stocks had very small leg holes (about 2 ½ inches) and the beams would have to be forced down, cutting the flesh. The holes were about five inches apart. Many Indians were confined with their legs five holes apart—about a yard—and after a few hours were in acute pain. Whole families might be put in the stocks, with the children watching while their parents slowly died.

Once Fonseca had threatened to kill an Indian, but the man had protested, saying he had not killed a Blanco or tried to run away. James Chase, who describe the event, says that Fonseca first had the man hung by the neck, the chain choking him, then had him taken down and one of his legs placed in the stocks. He then held the man's free leg with one foot, tore the man's loincloth off, and—with a heavy club—smashed the man's genitals. The Indian died. Another time, James Chase himself beat an Indian to death in the same way, with Normand holding the man's legs apart. It was claimed that Agüero and Jiménez, two station managers, had competed to see who could shoot off an Indian prisoner's penis.

An apparatus similar to the *cepo* was also hastily constructed to hold Indians captured after a raid. Usually, however, captives were tied up or put in chains at the various stations, sometimes for months at a time. At Indostán, where the steamer stopped for firewood on 21 September, Casement found an Indian boy with a chain eight feet long around his neck and waist and fastened with a padlock at his ankle. His crime was having tried to flee to Brazil downriver by stealing a canoe. Casement had the boy released and took him along with the Commission of Inquiry.

White men could also be maltreated. When Colombian poachers were caught and not killed, they were sometimes marched from station to station in chains, insulted, kicked and beaten. For example, Aquileo Torres was taken prisoner with a party of Colombians who had been sent out by the firm of Urbano Gutiérrez in 1906 to build a rubber station in Andoke territory. There were eleven men and two women in the group, led by a Colombian, Felipe Cabrera, with Torres and another man, José de la Paz Gutiérrez, second in command. While the Colombians were building their house, they were surprised by Normand and a band of men including two Barbadians. Most of the Indians escaped but those captured along with the whites were tied up and taken to Matanzas. Here the Indians were clubbed to death. All the Colombians but three were set adrift on the river near the Brazilian border. The three leaders were kept prisoners—separated and confined at different stations where they were beaten and tortured. Cabrera and Gutiérrez managed to escape in 1908 from Abisinia (helped by Stanley Sealy, one of the Barbadians who was escorting Casement.) Special treatment was reserved for Torres who, as "corregidor" in Colombia had once captured and imprisoned Elías Martinengui (who had just recently left the employ of the Putumayo Amazon Company when Casement arrived). While Martinengui was working at Atenas he laid waste the whole region, reducing the Indians to starvation. The forty Indians, men and boys, acting as carriers for the Commission of Inquiry from Atenas to Puerto Peruano in October were examples of the results of Martinengui's labors—living skeletons, pitiably weak. Forced to bring in rubber, they were unable to cultivate their own clearings, and as a consequence had nothing to eat.

Martinengui gave Torres the grand tour, passing him from station to station, chained by the neck, waist and ankles. He was held prisoner for a long time at Port Tarme and Oriente, spat on, slapped, kicked. Then he was finally released if he agreed to sign on with the company. He was given the job of flogging the Indian workers. In May 1908 he was assigned to Abisinia to aid Agüero and Jiménez against the recalcitrant Boras. They committed murders, cut ears off the living, helped by another man who was still working for the company.

Although Torres had been badly treated, his crimes were "wanton acts of savagery" without any purpose. He was subsequently dismissed by Sr. Jiménez. Later Casement learned that he had been rehired at Abisinia—one of the stations on the "Black List" of the worst offenders.

All these men had led "degraded and debased" lives; some were proven, or confessed, murderers. Whole tribes had been handed over to them by the company; they had been supplied with arms to be used in "subduing" the natives. As agents they were also an integral part of the "business"—for example, the Rodríguez brothers, Aurelio and Arístides, got 50 percent of the profits of the Santa Catalina and Sabana districts, in the Boras country, where they had murdered hundreds Aurelio had recently retired with a "small fortune"; his brother had died. It seemed illogical that these men would kill the very persons who brought in rubber—it was like killing the goose that laid the golden egg; but there were always more Indians, they said, and they would last as long as the rubber lasted. Crime leads to crime, Casement comments, a lesson taught by major criminals throughout history.

Sexual immorality and heavy drinking were common at the stations. The agents kept a harem of young Indian girls, their "wives," and even the peones might have more than one girl. There was heavy competition for sex. Jealousy was sometimes given for the massacres of fugitives. Sometimes it was revenge. Sometimes it was for pleasure. Filomeno Vásquez boasted on his return after a series of beheadings (witnessed by James Chase) that "he had left the road pretty." These men delighted in bloodshed.

It gradually became clear that in spite of all their efforts, the agents were in debt to the company, and the exploitation of the districts were being conducted at a loss, sometimes in the thousands of pounds. Only the notorious Normand had a credit on the company ledgers, soon to be augmented by his share of the eight tons of rubber carried by caravan down to Puerto Peruano.

The social system of the Indians worked against them: they were fragmented and disorganized. The white, on the other hand, worked together, were organized and well armed. None of the Indians now had even the traditional blowpipe or spears, and what guns they possessed were almost worthless. Any dangerous Indians had been killed. In fact, most of the older Indians were gone, and Casement met only a few Indians beyond middle age. The Barbadians said that in 1905 there had been many old people, vigorous and respected, but all had disappeared.

Casement heard exceptional tales at Entre Ríos.

An influential Chief, Chingamui, had shot and wounded the head of the Atenas station. He had subsequently been executed. One of the crimes of the Chief was giving "bad advice"—that is, advocating revolt.

The most famous opponent of all was a Boras cacique or "capitán" named Katenere from the upper Pama, a small stream emptying into the Cahuinari.

Bishop had seen the chief in 1907 when Normand went to talk him into gathering rubber. The chief consented—but later fled. Captured later, he had been put into the stocks. While he was held there, his wife was publicly violated by the head of the Abisinia district, a Peruvian who later escaped prosecution for crimes that included numerous murders and rape.

When Katenere escaped from the stocks he got Winchesters from the muchachos working in Abisinia, armed his clan and waged war against the whites and their rubber workers. He finally tracked down the Peruvian agent, and shot him dead. After that, many expeditions were sent out to capture the chief. Finally his wife was taken and brought back as a decoy. At the end of August 1910, Katenere was finally killed trying to rescue his woman. His brother, meanwhile, had also been captured and was being held in the *cepo*; soon after this he was murdered by Juan Zellada, a racional.

Of the many girls in service at the stations carrying water, planting sugar cane and cassava, washing clothes, doing light work, none were paid. At La Chorrera they were put to sewing strips of cloth to make pantaloons, with which Indian men were paid for their rubber. Scores of these pantaloons were stored at La Chorrera. Women doing household chores were not always sexually abused.

Casement mentions the family arrangements of chiefs of section and their subordinates. One man had four native women and three children by separate mothers, all living under one roof. Agents and racionales were always followed closely by their girls, and were invariably accompanied by them even when they went to the river to wash. Even the half-breed cook traveling with the Commission of Inquiry had his girl. A chief of section traveled in state with a troop of young females dressed in long chemises of bright cotton prints, well fed, gleaming with health. Some girls were ordered to shoot prisoners, and thus became murderers of their own people.

"Little or no regard to decency existed where lust impelled," Casement comments, describing the great furor of crying and grief when the steam launch of the company left La Chorrera. Agüero had "taken a fancy to one of the humble Indian women workers of La Chorrera"—an Indian girl who daily swept out the dining room and the verandah past the door of the rooms where the commissioners and Casement were accommodated. "We had often noticed her at this task, and had been struck by her gentle, pensive face." The women of the station were lamenting the loss of the young girl. Agüero already had a harem of eleven girls, but had forced her on board nevertheless to make up his round dozen.

It was well known that the agents never stole Indians' wives because, "Sir, if they takes an Indian's wife, that Indian don't work rubber." "The Indians love their wives and if she is taken they won't work rubber. They can kill them, do anything they like to them, but the Indians won't work rubber."

Once Fonseca had fancied the wife of an Indian. He took her. The Indian protested. Fonseca said that he would return her if the Indian brought in a certain amount of rubber. The Indian brought this in. Fonseca repeated his demand for rubber. At last, he offered the Indian another girl from his harem in place of his wife. The Indian refused her. He also refused to work rubber any longer. Fonseca ordered one of the muchachos to kill him.

The Indians were not only faithful loving husbands, they would not betray the hiding place of their people. Normand once cut off the arms and legs of a captured chief who refused to tell him the whereabouts of his people.

Then Casement gives a rather shocking comment: "The tribes of the Putumayo in the hands of good men could be made into good men and women, useful and intelligent workers under an honest administration."

"Under the actual regime," Casement remarked to a Peruvian who had spent some time in England, "I fear the entire Indian population will be gone in ten years." The Peruvian answered, "I give it six years—not ten."

Sr. Tizón turned out to be very helpful throughout the journey. He pledged sweeping reforms, and promised to get rid of criminals in the employ of the company. The worst stations, those of Matanzas and Abisinia, would be abolished. Reforms would be put in place to help the Indians and also to improve the company's prospects in the region. However, the economic resources of the area had already been affected and the financial prospects of the enterprise were not good. Rubber output was already down to about 400 tons per annum and wholesale abuses ensured that it would fall even further.

"That every detail of this testimony is equally trustworthy, I do not assert," Casement wrote. "It is evident that men of this class, some of them illiterate, all of humble calling, many demoralized by long years of savage indulgence, would sometimes be untruthful from fear or unworthy motives."

Joshua Dyall, Frederick Bishop, Stanley Lewis all admitted to grave crimes. Casement was prepared to give them legal assistance if they were tried. Sr. Tizón accepted the evidence of the British witnesses. However, "in the absence of a Peruvian authority upon the Putumayo" the wrongdoers could not be arrested or submitted to any form of trial there. Sr. Tizón actually thought it better to get rid of them quickly. As for the Barbadians, they had, after all, been *ordered* to commit the crimes.

At Iquitos Casement impressed personally upon the Prefect of the Department of Loreto the urgent need for prompt action by the Peruvian Government. If nothing were done, he assured him, "a deplorable impression would be created." Not a particularly strong statement, but what could he say? "Not only should the Indians be protected, but those found guilty of the many crimes alleged should be adequately dealt with."

A Government Judicial Commission would be sent out to the Putumayo with large powers—or so the Peruvian Prefect said, hopefully.

Casement may have agreed with Hardenburg, that "With all that it has given to the Amazon Valley of prosperity, of flourishing steamship communications, of port works, of growing towns and centers of civilization, with electric light and tramways, of well-kept hospitals and drainage schemes, it may well be asked whether the rubber-tree has not, perhaps, taken more away."

On his return to Iquitos in 1911 Casement had found that of the hundreds of accused criminals, only nine had been arrested—and all of these had been let off free. The Barbadians by then were scattered. One of the worse criminals, a Peruvian, was now running a hotel in Barbados, bought with his "earnings" from the Putumayo.

More forceful measures, if not actual threats, to force reform might have to come from the United States. He decided that would be the salvation of the situation, if salvation there was.

He left for on the *Atahualpa*, heading for the US.

The Cash Ledger 1911

The Cash Ledger that Casement kept for 1911 contains to the minutest detail his daily expenditures, including tips, gifts to beggars, food and drink, transportation, occasional loans—for example to his brother Charlie in Melbourne—and "presents" to the boys he had sex with. There are familiar names here from the diaries, as well as occasional additions. It will be recalled that at the end of 1910 he had returned to Europe via Cherbourg and Paris, where he saw the New Year in:

> January 1st, 1911. Sunday.
>
> In Paris with Denis first. To prefecture and
>
> Quai d'Orleans and Montparnasse and back to
>
> Place de l'Opéra and Pierre. "Bien servi" Fcs 40.
>
>
> January 3rd. Tuesday.
>
> Monday lunch with Berry at Embassy. Tuesday
>
> Ernest Lift of Philadelphia.
>
>
> January 4th. Wednesday.
>
> *Ernest.*

January 5th. Thursday.

Dinner 4/6. 6 Cigarettes 7d.

Enormous   Ernest 6/-. Cab 2/-. Ernest 10/-. Fred 15/-.

On 10 January he noted receiving, and paying for, the typed copy of the Hardenburg manuscript from the Anti Slavery Society. He also paid for a dress coat
which he didn't really need but had bought to wear to a fête at Herbert
Ward's. On the margin is the notation F.O. X. On 11 January he was at the
Foreign Office and the next few days began working diligently with his
"typer," noting expenditures for lunch for his secretary as well as stationery and
transport. On Friday, 20 January he notes "Fanti" 1.0. and the next day, Fanti
(did not come up to 6.20). [Margin: *X*] He was seeing Mrs. Green, visiting
the turkish baths, having a whiskey or two and dinner with the Blüchers. His
list of expenditures seems perhaps niggling but they were considerable, forming a sort of checklist of common outlays for the middle class government servant.

January 28th. Saturday.

Postage on parcel to Iquitos, say 1.3.

Beautiful at 12.30 at T[ottenham] Court Road

January 29th. Sunday.

Abdullah cigarettes. 1.7

X.   Poor Jew 7/6 Piccadilly

January 30th. Monday.

6 to Harrow, Jew X. Enormous and liked greatly. 1.14.10

February 3rd. Friday.

To Mrk Lane and W.I. Docks.

Young Japanese Sailor and then back. Nil.

February 7th. Tuesday.

"*Welsh*" 4/6 Splendid in Park

3 times and also outside several

and to Buckingham Palace at 11.45.

7 Grenadier. Huge.

Consider this list of expenses on the 8th: lunch, envelopes, paper, postage, train to Richmond, train back, tea, Beecham's Pills, Port wine and coffee, programmes, buses, cigarettes, whiskey, beggar, Sundries.

February 9th. Thursday.

X.   Welsh Rarebit at Sloane 3d

February 10th. Friday.

Heavy rain at Windsor and cold stream

chilliness at Hyde Park Corner. Dark eyes and beautiful.

February 11th. Saturday.

X.   Laurens at W.I. Docks 4/6.

February 12. Sunday.

Went to Poplar, Laurens *out*.

Lovely Italian Clerkenwell Rd. on tram, off at Bridge. *Huge*.

February 13th. Monday.

X.   Clarence Gate 3/6. Soldier X.

Scots at Victoria 6.30 and Irish after dark.

February 14th. Tuesday.

Welsh Rarebit 10/-. Lost at Gate X.

Victoria Station 11 p.m. 2/6 X

Walked Paddington to Park, Wales lost at Gate.

February 15th. Wednesday.

Parry not in—so to Mrs. Green till 7

(lovely type at Westminster, tailor)

February 18th. Saturday.

X.   Buses after all over 1/-. "Scotsman"

To Aldgate and on to W.I. docks.

Only Chinese and none, thin long type about 16,

small sturdy and firm. Later Scot in Sl[oane] Sq[uare] till 8.

February 19th. Sunday.

X.   Scot 12/6

On 21 February he left for Dublin, where the day after arriving he heard
from Ramón. He was sick from the 24th to the 26th. On 1 March he visited
the Turkish baths. A few days later he had obviously recovered. His expenses

expand to include an oculist (he continued to suffer from eye trouble) and spectacles, medicine, books, postage, tea and beggars (as usual).

March 5th. Sunday.

Enormous X   Trams 1/-. "How"? 2/6 X.

19 about

7" and 4"

thick X.   Enormous Dublin under 19 very fair

                     thin legs legs, knickers and coat white,

                     say, blue eyes and *huge, huge* stiff

                     long and thick one.

On 6 March he left Ireland for England. On 7 March he notes postage expenses for letters to Ramón and B.A. Bernardine and Rio. On 9 March he began writing the Putumayo Report, to continue through mid-month. On 11 March he heard from Millar. He was at the Foreign Office on the eighteenth [Margin: *X*] and on 27 March entered a tip given to Reggie Parminter, his godson [Margin: *X*]. Obviously not all of the *X*s are related to sex.

April 1st. Saturday.

To Zoo with Nina at Gloucester Road Station

Waiting for E[arls] Court train saw lovely fair hair,

20 or 19, big, fingering and stiff, wanted. Nice respectable,

looked often and often.

April 3rd. Monday.

X.   Beautiful fair hair type at Oxford Circus and Regent St.

Young country

On the 3rd he mentions expenses for trains, buses, whiskey, lunch, coffee, stamps and papers, a sandwich, dinner, lavatory, cigarettes, odds and ends. On 4 April, Tuesday, there is a single X in the margin.

April 6th. Thursday.

Taxi 2/6. *Karl* 12/-. (*Baden*)

"Fat" 2/6 X.

(Saw many types Ritz's Karl.) *Karl* 12/-. (*Baden*)

X.   Saw Welsh rarebit M[arble] Arch 11.25. 17/-.

April 8th. Saturday.

X.   Pasto 5/-. (South American 21.)

April 14th Friday. Good Friday.

Arr. Belfast. Motor to Dunegore Mrs. Green …

and then to "News Letter" Office and then round town

and one splendid strong type. Clean and offered again and again.

X.   Beautiful Irish young man in Belfast.

April 19th. Wednesday.

(Lovely boy in Ormean Park, legs.)

Heard from Millar

April 20th. Thursday.

Gloriously beautiful type. Loveliest ever saw in life,

soft and auburn and rose.

Love all evg.

April 22nd. Saturday.

In Belfast all day. Small friend Ormean Rd. 4/6

Duggan Boy (Dungammon) 8/-. Like it rightly.

April 25th. Tuesday.

At Cushendria walked to Nina and then on to Park.

Fine types.

Letter from darling Bernardine at Rio. Also card from Millar.

April 26th. Wednesday.

Lovely morning in Belfast, to sleep with Millar tonight.

At Carnstroam with Millar and Mrs. G.

X.　Entry at 12.50 a.m.

April 27th. Thursday.

At Carnstroam. Trams in with Millar 5d

Wrote long dispatch to F.A. on Putumayo.

To Miss O.R. and to dinner and late to Millar,

both tired so turned in alone.

April 28th. Friday.

Left Carnstroam with Millar on trams together.

A large number of small expenses continue to be noted, which add up to a considerable daily budget; entries for one day include trams, postage and many telegrams, postal orders, a subscription to *Irish Freedom*, telephone, cigarettes, collars, car to boat, porter, luggage, London ticket, Mrs. Thomas's bill for rooms, carriage for baggage, food and drink, whiskey, tea and sundries.

April 29th. Saturday.

Boy 2/6.

On 30 April he was in London for the testimonial to Morel; on 4 May he was back in Ireland. He was not well. He remained at home, "cold and wretched," thinking of Ignacio and Bernardine.

May 8th. Monday.

Heard from Millar suggesting he should call

tomorrow evg. at 7. Replied yes.

Saw glorious type at Co. Down Ry Stn,

huge one and stern too young in knickers.

May 9th. Tuesday.

Saw fair hair force and all July 1906

and 1907 last time at Carlyle Circus. Met him at corner of Done-gall St waiting for me and got on it and up. I longed. Long limbs as of old.

X.   Joe McCullagh. Splendid

Touched   Millar came to tea but altho' clean and strong did not go room.

May 10th. Wednesday.

Very hot indeed. To old Turnpool by Braid and Devieux Burns of Nov 1897. Rippling in brown and swift, and there too

when I plunged across in Mch 1887.

Glorious boys of Erin, big and fair. Back at 5 train very tired.

Harry at Fort William 10/-.

May 11th. Thursday.

Saw *the* man, a glorious type get in Belfast. Fair hair

and blue eyes and tall, strong, well dressed at "Junction".

He looked and smiled and felt again and again.

To swimming bath and *four beauties.*

Harry 10/-X

May 12th. Friday.

Letter from Millar agreeing to Newcastle.

Met Millar in street.

May 13th. Saturday.

Lovely day go to Newcastle with Millar.

"Grand" 5 times I hope.

Gratten and Co. Hair and Vaseline. 2/6.

Train with Millar to Newcastle. 13/-. Papers for Millar 9d.

Arr. Newcastle. Huge! *In Bath.*

Splendid. Millar into me.

May 14th. Sunday.

At Newcastle with M. Into Millar!

and then he came too.

Imagine! Bath. Hard luck.

May 15th. Monday.

Lovely one in Post Office and then

John McG. In Ormean Park.

May 16th. Tuesday.

To leave Ireland again today!

Lovely one in Post Office and then John McG in Ormean Park.

On the 16th he was off to London again and on the 17th notes taxi expenses from St. Pancras to Earls Court. He went to the Crystal Palace at once for an outing. In the evening he was at Piccadilly Circus.

May 20th. Saturday.

To E[arls] Court [Exhibition] Niggers, then to Crystal Palace,

French type splendid and soldier C.G. big. To E[arls] Court.

Egyptian and then White City

All through Exhibition but see nothing.

May 22nd. Monday.

Friend 4/-. Do. 10/-. Algerian 1/-.

May 29th. Monday.

6/-small chap Euston Square.

"Fanny".

On the 30th he wrapped up the month with an overall list of expenses, including nine Exhibitions. The Summary for January to June of 1911 amounted to a total of £441.3.4.

May 31st. Wednesday.

Somali 6d

Unusual expenses for June include £25 for a motorbike, a gift to "dear Millar," and shipping costs to Ireland. He is staying at the Savoy, but there is not much action there. He continues with occasional Asian connections.

June 11th. Sunday.

Buses in London on return (some

types and stout Japanese in Oxford Street.) (Wanted!)

[O]ut for 2 hours walk in London. Very crowded.

Seamen at P[iccadilly] Circus.

June 14th. Wednesday.

X. X.   Present to Charlie.

June 15th. Thursday.

Letter from Sir E. Grey telling me of Knighthood. Alack!

to Uxbridge, lovely boy scout and Chaney's baker boy.

June 16th. Friday.

Japanese youth 25. G. Miyagawa, Kingsway W.C.

June 17th. Saturday.

Was to have met Miyagawa at 4 at Gr[eat] W[estern]

at Paddington but did not go.

On Coronation Day, 22 June, he is still staying at the Savoy, busily putting
together the Putumayo Report; he often works all day.

June 24th. Saturday.

(Splendid Japan Wrestlers.)

June 25th. Sunday.

To go Southhampton for Ricudo and

Hammurummy [Omarino].

Lovely French lad or Italian 20 dark,

dark cap, fair, very tall, strong.

Sailor in Ship Street and then thick

young German or Italian sailor, round Gardners.

Boys.   Lovely Italian Ice boy, 18. Tall, splendid

loved, also young dark boy, *huge*, wanted awfully.

To Best Station and there darkie by Watt's Grove.

Lovely boy wanted too.

June 27th. Tuesday.

At Southhampton. To leave today with Ricudo.

Donald Ross. £ of Egypt.

He notes from this time on numerous expenses and assorted purchases of personal articles for his Indian boys. During the period when the two young-sters are with him, Casement seems to curtail his cruising somewhat. Omar-ino and Ricudo are a significant drain on his finances: he is generous and caring, buying them clothes, keeping them well fed, showing them off and entertaining them. Charlie is hard up in Melbourne. He also gets his share of money. On the 13th Casement sends him £80, a considerable sum.

July 19th. Wednesday.

X.   *Mexicano.* 12/6

20. (Freid) T[ottenham] Court Road.

July 21st. Friday.

Huge one all day!

July 22nd. Saturday.

Bus 2d. (Notting Hill—Huge!)

Dinner Marguerite. (Lovely Italian.)

Many types. One showed big head.

Hard stiff wagging H[yde] Park Corner.

July 25th. Tuesday.

X. "Jean" of Algiers. 20, enormous.

Jean Oui monsieur, il est très grand, mais il est joli aussi. Que j'aimais ça. Promised £2 tomorrow 9.

July 23rd. Sunday.

Dinner Café Marguerite.

(Dear Free again!) Dinner 3/-.

Waiter 6d. Dear Free 1/-. Looked in eyes 1/-.

July 24th. Monday.

Dinner Marguerite. (Fear Free gone.)

July 26th. Wednesday.

Saw beautiful type. Oxford Circus and some huge ones.

In city with Horner, Laidlaw and there Van Oppel.

No go! To meet my Algerian at 9 p.m. to Harrow. Friends.

Went there already beautiful. To H[arrow] 9.15 and 10 mins. After in. Huge split and clasp.

Back 10.41. Supper and Piccadilly. Young.

July 27th. Thursday.

X.   Friend German Jew. 16/-.

July 28th. Friday.

French from Paris.

On 29 July he met with Gerald Spicer at the Foreign Office. He offered to go out to Iquitos again if they insisted on it.

July 30th. Sunday.

At Warlies. Lovely youth there 18.

Coal black. Alexander Scot, Son of Master

of Polwarth. *Magnificent one.* Huge. Bathed together in pond.

July 31st. Monday.

Back from Buxton's after early bath with Alex.

Perfectly *huge* head and circumcised, splendid.—He is lovely.

On 2 August he received his orders from the Foreign Office to return to Iquitos. This would be an opportunity to wind up unfinished business, both personal and professional.

August 3rd. Thursday.

X.

Soldier 5/-. 3rd Bat. G. Guards.

Buses into M[arble] Arch 10d.

Many types Park and H[yde] P[ark] Corner.

Beauties.

Marching orders to Putumayo again today from F. O.

August 5th. Saturday.

Good on for Tuesday. Hurrah! Expecting!

Out after dinner with J. Nelson and family in Gresham.

Lovely evg., to Harcourt St. and one *huge* exposure, *red head and all*, and then Wicklow lad, knickers. "His alright" *stiff.*

To Burlington Road 3/-.

August 6th. Sunday.

In Dublin.

Out at 9.30. Lovely evening to Harcourt St. and

Hatch Street, and several, and then all at once

Huge thick

as wrist

the lad of the 5th. March. "How". To Burlington Rd.

pulled it out. Huge 2/6. 8d.

August 7th. Monday.

In Dublin. Baronstown.

I to meet enormous at 9.

Will suck and take too.

He was not there! I waited till 9.30.

No sign. To H.O. wait and Park.

About 11 p.m.   August 8th. Tuesday.

I thrust and shall   Leaving for Belfast.

Thrust too! My   To sleep with Millar

Last night with

Millar was 12th

May at Newcastle

Slept with Millar.

In at once. Turned

And pushed onto it.

August 13th. Sunday.

1st Jan.   Arr. Dublin. 5.20 a.m. To Gresham.

4th Aug.

X.

August 14th. Monday.

Arr. London.

Friend "8 *inches*".

Brass worker 5/-

August 15th. Tuesday.

In London, packing up. My passage to

Barbados £21.12/-. Ricudo and Omarino £36.

Donald Ross (of Kingsfield) 23

On 12 August he had picked up a copy of Agassiz's *A Journey in Brazil*, published in 1868, as recreational reading on his way out. On the On 15 August he was packing up for the return to Iquitos, taking his Indian boys back with him. He left England on the *Magdalena* on 16 August, bound for Barbados, which he reached on the 28th. On the trip out he spent a great deal on wine, beer, stout, cocktails and whiskeys. In Barbados he stayed at the Sea View Hotel, obviously a good choice.

August 29th. Tuesday.

X. 6d   Boy to bathe

2 boys to swim today. Expect Teddy at 4.

At 4 he has not come, so I fear he is away in St. Vincent.

Teddy came on bicycle and back to room

and dinner. After dinner to room and he looked and looked.

I saw his big huge and felt mine and he looking all the time and back on bicycle.

Teddy to come tomorrow at 5 to bathe.

Then will see and feel.

August 30th. Wednesday.

To Hasting's Bath 7 .50 and several

and then light fair haired boy, blue pants

and thick and stiff. To bathe together at 11.30. Bath.

He then glorious form and limbs and *it*.

Teddy and "Budda" at 5.30. Latter lovely and *huge* one too.

Only 11 years old on 17th. July. Bath. "Budda" present 5/6.

Seen today. (1). Oldish man, huge one. (2). Clergyman, small. (3). Lovely youth, thick fine one. (4). Big youth, nice clean one. (5). Lover, only top stiff and lovely. (6). Budda beauty.

August 31st. Thursday.

To Hasting's Bath 5d. Clergyman there

told me he was father of beauty

returned 11 and beauty came, glorious limbs,

but did not show it. Alas. I love him.

September 1, 1911. Friday.

Begins Barbados in Sea View Hotel.

My 47th birthday!

To Bath at Hasting's to meet Bath beauty

for the last time. His name is Hughes.

X.   Born 16th March. (Did not come.)

                   Then shortly Metsize boy 16 or 17 in blue

Coleridge King   at Church Square. Longed for and talked to

                   and asked to come to bath Sunday, was most willing.

                   The Biddys' at 6. Teddy looking often.

September 2nd. Saturday.

Passage to Pará by Bomfrey. X.

St. John's poor white boys. X.

Coleridge King.

September 3rd. Sunday

Bathed at Lighthouse, fine big darkie. 1/-

Saw several beauties.

September 4th. Monday.

Stanley Weeks   Out to Lighthouse and saw a nice boy.

XX   Asked him to bath and he came along.

Stanley Weeks 20 stripped huge one circumcised.

Swelled and hung 9 *quite* and wanted awfully

asked come at 11.30. [O]ut at 12

and Stanley Weeks wanted it fearfully.

His stiff and mine stiff. Then had to leave.

Farewell to Stanley!

Coleridge King 5/-, who left his address with Mrs. Senn.

I want Stanley Weeks.

Casement and the Indian boys left Barbados on the 4th on the *Boniface*, a "filthy tub" (as he describes it) with legal accommodation at New York for five passengers but now carrying 161. The ship is scheduled to arrive in Pará in five days.

September 10th. Sunday.

To arrive in Pará today.

Hope to meet João tomorrow.

Arrived at 5. To Hotel de Comercio.

Sereno gone! Out after dinner and Baptista Campos and Nazareth. None. Huge exposure. B. Campos with girl and in Nazareth

Nice Paraense. Young 16 big soft.

September 11th. Monday.

In Pará. Out at 7 saw João Anselmo

at Carcaby Cemetery, but did not speak.

He busy but I am sure saw me.

September 13th. Wednesday.

Lovely day. Out to Una and Val du Caens and Back

and then to dinner with Andrews and McH.

Huge tram Inspector after 9.10 p.m. at Palace Square.

Stiff as sword and thick and long. Big tram Inspector.

He is obviously having a high time, and again he lists gin, stout, vermouth, whiskey, beer and wine among his expenses.

September 14th. Thursday.

To Zoo. Met João Anselmo and talked.

Friend X. Entered strong at Cemetery.

September 15th. Friday.

Huge exposure 8". Kiosque at Palace Square at 8 p.m.

September 16th. Saturday.

War between France and Germany!

Augusto to Pavanes dos Santos. Met him at 8 Cemetery

and in at once. "Gusto" Police. There Spaniard

theater and a small thing at corner of fund. X.

Friend 17$ = £1.2.0

September 17th. Sunday.

To Sacramento and bathed. To Zoo twice and huge ones.

In at 5 p.m. and beer and lay down till 7 p.m. and

out to Palace etc. at once huge and furious.

"Rio" To him 17$ X

September 18th. Monday.

£24.14.4 to Augusto of Tavares for his X.X.X.

Refused to accept. Did not meet Rio.

He has cocktails, vermouth and whiskey on the 19th, and drew £40 at the bank. On 22 September he left Pará on the *Hilda*

September 22nd. Friday.

Left Pará about 2.30 a.m. on Saturday after being

11 hours on this detestable craft there. God!

How hopeless this people is!

September 23. Saturday.

Nil on board.

September 30th. Saturday.

Boots. (Italian boy.) (Big one.)

Caboclo followed. X X Indian of Madeira-Mamoré.

"Não me falta". 4.000

Cafuzo in square. 18,000

October 1st. Sunday.

In Manaos. 1. *Raymundo Aprendíz Marinero.*   12,000

X.X.X.   2. Sailor. Negro.   15.000

3. Agostinho de Souza   40,000

3 lovers had and two others wanted.

October 2nd. Monday.

X Boots 400

On 16 October he arrived at Iquitos on the *Hilda* at 9 a.m. and was on shore at 11.30.

X.   October 18th. Thursday.

Met José.

October 19th. Thursday.

X. José González. Young Practicante.

October 22nd. Sunday.

At Iquitos, out with José González

to Ignacio Stream at 8 a.m.

To Morona Cocha with José 9/6.

Present to José 4.000

October 23rd. Monday.

Out with José González to swim.

Soldier Manuel 3$ No. 7 Regt.

October 30th. Monday.

José González came but nothing arranged.

October 31st. Tuesday.

To José 2.60 Present after swim.

Then he gives a rundown of his expenditures for 1911. The journal is coming to an end, with another strangely heartbreaking list of those he wanted or expected to see, those he had seen, and those he would never see again:

To see (D.V.) in Iquitos in Oct. 1911 Ignacio. Simon Pisango (Seen). "Caza Marco" seen. Beautiful legs—young big eyes—huge one—police. Office boy Cazes gone. Shop boy—gone—Antonio Cruz Pérez—seen. Huge one plain clothes.

Julio—no sign of. Brown legs—woodcutter—no sign of. Soldier boy, no sign of. Do. of *Photo*—gone I fear. Pink stout beauty, no sign of. Pilots boy, José González—came 18th and 19th Oct. et seq.

Headlong into Chaos

1

On 29 January 1912, Casement was back at his Philbeach Gardens digs with the nice landlady, Miss Cox. The Foreign Office immediately asked him to work on the final draft of the Putumayo Report. He holed up in the Green Bank Hotel, Falmouth, to complete the assignment. At the same time he also began to organize a committee to work at raising money for the Putumayo Mission; £15,000 was needed, to match a pledge from the Vatican. But money trickled in. Meanwhile, in Peru, the government dawdled; officials mouthed phrases, appointed judges and dismissed them, ignored ultimatums. There were troubles in Ireland, distasteful demonstrations by Suffragettes, rumblings of war from Europe, all distracting the public's attention from the Putumayo. The Blue Book on Infamies in the Putumayo at last appeared on 17 June 1912, price 1s 5d at the Stationery Office. Sales were sluggish.

There had been the expected international outrage. Roger Casement became the hero of the hour, as he had been in 1904. But this time it was different.

The noise died at once. The Putumayo Mission Fund raised only £1,557 by the end of June. Protestants claimed to be reluctant to give money for a mission to be run by the "corrupt" Catholic fathers in Peru.

Casement was also called on to help his brother Tom in South Africa. Tom, "not a waster, but an extraordinarily reckless, amusing and unconventional person" had become the owner of a mountain resort hotel, the "Mont aux Sources," and needed money. Casement tried drumming up investment funds from several sources including Herbert Ward and Tom's father-in-law, a Mr. Ackerman.

In the late summer and early autumn Casement was in Ireland, resting, ill.

The Select Committee hearing on the Putumayo question began in November 1912. Casement was to attend, along with Arana, who would soon see the Putumayo Amazon Company through final liquidation. Whiffen, Hardenburg and others would attend.

2

Casement was so disturbed by his ailments that he wished to retire—or perhaps was terminally fed up with the Foreign Office. Or both. He felt he had come to an end of his career—the pinnacle, or the final point—when the Putumayo Report appeared. History was repeating itself. He was getting older. Almost fifty, and the boys were so beautiful. In November he went to London for the Select Committee. His performance during the inquiry was superb.

The South American rubber boom was petering out. The Putumayo Amazon Company was bankrupt. In the Amazon the human and ecological atrocities had been numbing and unreal, and now the destruction of the rubber industry meant that ruin would continue.

Although of enormous value in calling world attention to the plight of the Putumayo Indians, Casement's report had little effect on reforms. Economic reality was simply crushing the wrongdoers; in a few years they would vanish, like a nightmare.

Casement had been actively preparing for his retirement, getting medical assessment of his physical condition. However, the examination he had in London made it seem that his condition was generally good. Sir Lauder Brinton, an eminent physician, gave him a thorough check-up and made the following Medical Report: Age: 48. Heart: Normal. Liver: Full and very tender. Spleen: Full. Lung: Curious creaks on respiration, as if from an old adhesion. Bowels: Constipated. Tongue: furred and turns slightly to the left. Appetite: Very bad. Flatulence: A little. Nausea: None. Piles: Operated on for obstruction. Nervous System: Sleeps well. Headaches: Slight.

Casement was annoyed. He *knew* he was sick. His intermittent fever did not just disappear, nor his intestinal ills. Abdominal pains led him to believe that he had appendicitis. He was off to the Canaries, he wrote Mrs. Green, and South Africa for a much needed rest cure. Sick leave had been granted by a grateful Sir Edward Grey, aware that Casement was planning to retire.

At the end of January, Casement wrote to Sir Edward from Tenerife that a local doctor—one more easily alarmed than Sir Lauder Brinton—had agreed about the seriousness of his condition. He would be unable, physically unable, to return to the Consul-Generalship of Rio without grave risk of "this disease becoming permanent." Gerald Spicer advised him that his salary cut had been corrected and that he was now back to full salary. This was good news, and alleviated one worry; but Casement still held back. The job of consul was just not interesting enough. Nor did it offer anything more than a familiar situation in a familiar niche, surrounded by familiar—and ultimately grotesque—colleagues. There had to be a change.

Heading for Cape Town, where he was to meet his charming but financially troubled brother Tom, he decided to sound out the Foreign Office about his prospects for early retirement. In London they discussed the matter. Lord Duferin wrote to him in South Africa: if he were to retire, he said, still being far short of sixty, he would be allowed only £400 per annum. The Foreign Office would be sorry to lose him. A suitable medical certificate would be required, if Casement decided on early retirement for health reasons, in order to satisfy the Treasury that he was indeed in poor condition. Casement thought about this as he visited bungling brother Tom's Mont aux Sources Hotel, a diversion that did him good, emotionally if not financially.

Casement came home via Germany, where he visited various cities and mingled with the people. He admired the excellent conditions of the country and the efficient organization of the government. He was not the only Irish Germanophile. Many looked to Germany for support in their struggle for Home Rule.

In mid May he was back in London. There would be no more Rio. He received another plea from Tom, but did not wish to go back to South Africa, either on holiday or to live. The future was open. Ireland looked like a Cause. His Irish friends encouraged him. He would—being a famous man and influential—be good for the Independent Movement that was gathering strength.

In September 1912 Casement was still working for the Foreign Office when he published, under a pseudonym, "Ireland and the German Menace" in the *Irish Review*. In July 1913, "Germany, Ireland and the Next War" came out in *Irish Freedom*, a paper edited by Bulmer Hobson. He was convinced that war between Germany and Britain was inevitable. He lobbied furiously to have liners of the Hamburg-Amerika Line call at Irish ports—but the Germans were playing it cool at this time and they avoided any confrontation with England and English interests. Casement had always liked the Germans and believed in them. In Lourenço Marques he had developed a lasting friendship with Count Blücher; he was also friends with a German merchant, Fritz Pincus.

He was feeling his age. He was tired of the Foreign Office and its machinations, depressed by the Great Nations who were interested only in trade. He accepted early retirement with relief. "I'm finally finished with the Foreign Office for good and all," he wrote. He had hoped for the maximum pension, considering his enormous efforts on behalf of the Government. In fact he was granted only a little over four hundred pounds per annum, hardly enough to maintain a dignified life style.

But any life style was preferable to working as British Consul. He mused on his earlier assignments: "At Delagoa Bay I could not afford a secretary or clerk. I had to sit in my office for two years and open the door to everyone who came in. I was bottle washer and everything else.... You have no means of keeping yourself apart from any drunken individual who would come in. I have known ladies to come in and ask me for their cab fare. I have been asked to pronounce a divorce and have been upbraided for not doing it. Once a woman came into my office in Delagoa Bay and fainted on the sofa, and that woman remained in the house for a week." Granted, the post of Consul-General had been different; but it was, basically, more of the same. The social whirl at Petrópolis left much to be desired.

By giving up the Foreign Service he could throw himself into Irish Nationalism. Ireland needed him, or he thought she did. As an Irishman he was "well equipped" for understanding suffering elsewhere. The Irish poor were debased and degraded. In the Dublin slums there were 6000 families living seven or more to a room. The filth and the misery were unbelievable compared with the wealth of the British Empire.

3

The Irish question had been corrosive in Britain. Margot Asquith, wife of the Prime Minister, knew quite well what Home Rule implied in British politics. "When Mr. Gladstone went in for Home Rule," she writes in her autobiography, "society was rent from top to bottom, and even the most devoted friends quarreled over it. Our family was as much divided as any other." In 1914, "Now that we have discovered what the consequences are of withholding from Ireland the self-government which for generations she has asked for, can we doubt that Gladstone should have been vigorously backed [in 1886] in his attempt to still the controversy? As it is, our follies in Ireland have cursed the political life of this country for years." "All the brains of all the landlords in Ireland, backed by half the brains of half the landlords in England, had ranged themselves behind Sir Edward Carson, his army and his Covenant. Earnest Irish patriots had turned their fields into camps and their houses into hospitals; aristocratic females had been making bandages for months, when von Kuhlmann, Secretary of the German Embassy in London, went over to pay his first visit to Ireland. On his return he told me with conviction that, from all he had heard and seen out there during a long tour, nothing but a miracle could avert civil war...."

Margot's husband Herbert had become Prime Minister after Campbell-Bannerman's resignation in 1908. He had formed a new government pledged to Home Rule. Fortunately, the cabinet of this milquetoast included Winston Churchill and Lloyd George who were willing to take risks. Asquith—in his usual dithering way—brought his intelligence, such as it was, to bear on the matter. With his assent, King George opened consultations with party leaders, moving toward compromise—the most attractive one, for British interests and those of many Ulstermen, being partitionment, leaving the North part of Britain. The House of Commons might pass the Home Rule Bill, but the House of Lords could stop it dead, however. It was, Asquith decided, necessary that the King load the Lords with favorable nobles. The House of Lords had to be beaten back.

John Redmond had eighty-two votes of Irish Nationalists against forty for labor; it was a good time to act. He met with Asquith on 14 April 1911 (meanwhile Casement was "hard at it again" with a beautiful young Irish lad in Belfast). On the same day Churchill announced to the House that the Home Rule Bill would soon be introduced. After much debate, and furious charges by the Lords, in August 1911 the Parliamentary Bill limiting the Lords' power to veto bills became law. It looked like Home Rule was to be achieved at last. (Casement was getting screwed at Warrenpoint by Millar at about this time—so much for *his* Irish question.)

But Sir Edmund Carson and his Ulster Unionists were determined to keep northern Ireland British. They would, if worse came to worse, go to war—the wherewithal, the arms and the men were ready. Carson and his Ulstermen claimed to be the "descendants of the men who had been deliberately sent to Ireland with the commission of the first sovereign of a United Britain to uphold British interests, British honor and the reformed faith across the narrow sea." They were also terrified of being swamped by the Catholics in the south, feeling richer and superior to them. "Home Rule would be Rome

Rule," was their slogan. Carson upheld the Ulster Cause in the House, and his was a powerful voice; the most famous lawyer at the English bar, he had joined with James Craig, an Ulster MP, in attacking Churchill's announcement. An immense demonstration was held before Craig's house on 23 September 1911, at which over a hundred thousand people gathered in solidarity. "We must be prepared in the event of a Home Rule Bill passing, with such measures as will carry on for ourselves the government of those districts of which we have control," Carson declared. But could one tenth of the Irish population stop Home Rule? Carson and Craig believed so.

Padraic Pearse stated on 31 March, sensibly, "We have no wish to destroy the British, we only want our freedom."

Millions in Ireland—and in the United States and other countries abroad—agreed with him. A great slice of the US population had roots in Ireland. Since the first major immigration in 1728, when 4,200 Ulster Scots came over to escape religious and economic persecution, the stream had continued. During the 1850s over a million came; from 1860–90 more then two million. The Irish typically settled on the east coast, in cities like Boston, New York and Philadelphia. There were many Irish clubs and associations—the Ancient Order of Hibernians was especially active. And the Irish were above all *political* creatures. Many US presidents had Irish blood, including President Wilson who came of Ulster Protestant stock. The recent formation of the Friends of Irish Freedom group had as its goal the support of the Irish Volunteers. T. St. John Gaffney, the American Consul in Munich (who would later support Casement's German mission) expressed the general sentiment: "to encourage and assist any movement that will tend to bring about the national independence of Ireland." As Home Rule rose to international attention, the Irish in America launched a Victory Fund.

The Ulster Protestants remained a stone wall. In Ireland, when John Redmond and Joseph Devlin, MP for Belfast, arranged with Churchill to speak at a meeting in Ulster Hall, they found that it had been booked solid by the Ulster Volunteers. Churchill had to make his speech on the Celtic Football field; Unionist dockers pelted him with rotten fish on the quay. Two days later the Prime Minister brought the Home Rule Bill to Parliament and committee work began in serious, in spite of the continued signs of violent reaction from the Unionists.

A major strike was called in Dublin during August, led by James Larkin. The police broke up one meeting, killing two men and a woman. Larkin was arrested for using "seditious language." As Casement would remark, "These people have no rights, much less civil rights." When sympathetic strikes were called they failed. Larkin was now convinced that the only way to insure fair treatment and respect was to organize a citizen army. When he got out of prison in October he addressed a Dublin gathering to announce the organization of a military force. The Citizen Army began training in Croyden Park, Dublin, under an Ulsterman, J. R. White, who had served with the British army in South Africa.

4

Casement returned to an Ireland much changed. Ulster was gearing up for rebellion—"a country of marching, armed men, a lawless and illegal body." Gunrunners had brought in shiploads of rifles and ammunition for the Ulster Volunteers, under the noses of the authorities. In the south, the activists and intellectuals were trying to energize the masses. Casement, undergoing a crisis of personal identity, found the tension in Ireland did not help. In his discursive letters and in his conversation he showed himself increasingly bitter toward Britain, but not clear as to his role.

Singleton-Gates, author of *The Black Diaries*, writes, "As the months and the years go by, his writings and diaries betray a growing weakness of character and an indulgence in self-pity which are difficult to associate with the unrestrained personality of earlier years.... No doubt his great fatigue may partly explain this change. But it would be more reasonably accounted for by the feeling of loneliness, persecution and singularity which must have assumed increasing importance for him." However, it is difficult to find much weakness of character in Casement's diaries, or bitterness. His letters, written to fellow Irish Nationalists, invariably carry invective against Britain and the English in general—but there is no loneliness, no real sense of being persecuted, except perhaps in his resentment about retirement benefits.

Casement was sick and tired of the Foreign Office, of the Liberals—but so were many. He was generally apolitical though with definite political *sentiments*, but Mrs. Green and other friends encouraged him to try his hand at politics. (E. D. Morel had gone from his role as reformer to run successfully for parliament.)

Soon after his arrival in Dublin in October 1913, Casement spoke at a public meeting of Ulster Protestants in Ballymoney. Mrs. Green was also on the platform. He was chosen as Treasurer of the newly formed Irish Volunteers on 25 November. (By now over 4000 young men were enrolled in military training.) He may have had a hand in the Manifesto of the Citizen Army, designed "to drill, to learn the use of arms, to acquire the habit of concerted and disciplined action...." The Citizen Army was a counterpart to the Ulster Volunteers, except that the Ulster Volunteers were well equipped and ready for action.

Confrontation, it seemed, was not far off.

Germany, to Casement, seemed the right model for the Irish Nationalists. The Germans were a growing international force both economically and militarily. Their navy was developing fast, challenging Britain's supremacy on the seas. After Queen Victoria's death in 1901, King Edward VII recognized the threat posed by his egomaniacal cousin, Kaiser Wilhelm II, and joined France and Russia to oppose the growing military threat of Germany.

Casement had been impressed by Germany during his recent visit there on his way back from South Africa. It was possible that the Germans might help in the movement for Irish Independence. He was not sure how.

Ironically, F. E. Smith—who would later prosecute Casement during his treason trial—was also convinced that Germany could help the Ulster Protestants. Carson as well, recuperating in Hamburg and lunching with the Kaiser, received verbal support. "We have the offer of aid," he reported, "from a powerful Continental monarch, who, if Home Rule is forced on the Protestants of Ireland, is prepared to send an army sufficient to release England of any further trouble in Ireland by attaching to his Dominion.... [T]he Protestants of Ireland will welcome this Continental deliverer."

Casement had failed to lobby successfully for ships of the Hamburg-Amerika line to call at Irish ports—"the Germans eluded the whole issue to avoid an untimely diplomatic conflict." However, observers in Germany had been watching the evolution of the Irish Question with interest, amused at the prospect of an "irregular" militia mustering and training under the eyes of British forces. This could never have occurred in the Reich. Then there was the incredible Curragh Mutiny. In April 1914, the British Army officers based at their main camp in Curragh, Co. Kildare, refused to move against their fellow Irish in Ulster. This "mutiny" by fifty-eight senior officers would normally have brought about their instant court-martial or dismissal, but the times were special. "The significance of the Curragh *coup d'état* will not be mistaken by any European Government or people," Casement warned, "or by the Government and people of the United States."

The Orangemen had 3,000 rifles and 3,000,000 rounds of ammunition, which the British had allowed in. The Irish Volunteers, in contrast, were practically unarmed—until July 1914 when 1,500 Mauser rifles and 49,000 rounds of ammunition were unloaded at Howth.

Erskine Childers and Darrell Figgis were responsible for bringing arms to the south. They had gone to Hamburg to make their purchases. They brought the shipment back by private yacht. Childers, sailing the *Asgard*, carried 900 rifles and 29,000 rounds of ammunition. He landed these at Howth Harbor on 26 July. Sir Thomas Myles, in his boat, the *Chota*, landed the rest at Kilcoole. The Howth shipment was unloaded openly and distributed to the thousand Volunteers sent out from Dublin under Cathal Bragha. Telephone wires had been cut beforehand, but word soon reached the military that something was afoot. A detachment of the King's Own Scottish Borderers was dispatched, along with constables. At Clontarf the Volunteers met a hedgerow of bayonets. No armed confrontation took place by miracle; the Volunteers had been ordered not to shoot. Instead, the officers began discussions, a few rifles were grabbed—but a number of police constables refused to be involved. After a while the main body of the Irish Volunteers simply faded away. They carried their rifles off to places where they could be hidden until the time came to be used.

City crowds in Dublin were ecstatic, and incensed by the arrogance of the British military. In Bachelor's Walk they hooted and threw stones at a contingent of Scottish Borderers who, provoked, fired into the crowds. Two men and one woman were killed. Thirty-two were wounded. The next day there was a great Irish funeral, unforgettable in its grandeur. The British were beginning to create a long list of Irish martyrs.

5

At this point, Casement decided on his own to travel to America, to seek aid for the Nationalist cause. In early July of 1914 he sailed from Glasgow on the S/S *Cassandra*. He reached Montreal on the fourteenth, traveling incognito.

From Montreal he took the train to New York, passing through scenery that brought to mind the native Indians whose lands had been confiscated by the whites. "You had life," he wrote, "—your white destroyers only possess things." In New York he went to see John Devoy immediately, and met with other leaders of the Clan na Gael, including the distinguished lawyer John Quinn, Judge John W. Goff of the New York Supreme Court, Judge Daniel F. Cohalan, Bourke Cockran, Patrick Egan and Joseph McGarrity of the Ancient Order of Hibernians, the publisher of *The Irish Press* in Philadelphia.

The prospect of war had splintered Irish sentiments. Since the assassination of Archduke Ferdinand in Sarajevo on 28 June, Europe was on the brink of a great conflict, which many Americas dreaded being drawn into. The solid unity of Irish sympathy in America was no longer assured. The fight for Irish independence, in the light of universal conflagration, seemed of little urgency to many, given the chaos of death and destruction into which the world was sinking.

At the end of July a mass rally was organized in Philadelphia to protest the recent shootings in Dublin. Casement—well known to the public—was scheduled to speak. "I was interviewed by some of the Philadelphia papers," he writes, "and photographed, and the interview appeared in full in the evening papers, particularly the *Bulletin*. In this conversation I spoke very strongly of the lawless action of the British authorities in Ireland, culminating in the murder of women and children … and I put the blame fair and square on the shoulders of Mr. Asquith."

When war was declared he wrote his loving sister Gee: "Here I am, marooned on a desert island, Manhattan!" Well, Manhattan was not exactly a desert.

Casement had decided to give up his anonymity early on in America. What was the use, after all? "I was now in for it," he admitted, "up to my neck." The public had been wildly pleased by the speech-making of the famous Sir Roger Casement in Philadelphia. "I avoided political references, and to some extent I eulogized the Ulstermen, in the evident content of the great majority. It was a shirtsleeve and fan audience."

History was catching up with him.

On 20 July, George V had called a party conference to discuss Home Rule at Buckingham Palace. The Prime Minister and Lloyd George represented the Government. Lord Lansdowne and Bonar Law represented the Opposition (and the landlords of Ireland who were against Home Rule at any cost). Carson and Craig represented the Ulster Unionists with Redmond and Dillon for the Irish Nationalists. As might have been expected, the conference ended in deadlock. On 24 July, the same day that Asquith announced the outcome of the conference to the cabinet, Sir Edward Grey revealed that Austria had sent an ultimatum to Serbia.

On 3 August, in London, the Home Rule Bill was to be submitted to a final vote. Then the matter was roughly shunted aside. More spectacular historical questions than Irish Independence were confronting the nation. This was the fatal August of 1914. War was coming and there seemed no way to avoid it.

Sir Edward Grey rose to announce to the packed House that Great Britain would stand by Belgium in the present conflict. The peace of Europe, he said, could not now be preserved. The French Fleet was in the Mediterranean, which meant that the northern and western coasts of France were now undefended. If an enemy (that is, the German) fleet came down the channel and bombarded the French coast, Britain could not stand by and watch "with folded arms."

After much analysis of the French situation, Sir Edward went on to assert, "Nobody can say that in the course of the next few weeks there is any particular trade route the keeping open of which may not be vital to this country." Could France count on Britain's support in protecting her coasts?

Belgium was being raped and destroyed and had appealed to Britain for support. It was clear that war with Germany and her allies was inevitable. Britain would "suffer terribly in any case"—foreign trade was bound to stop, not because the routes would be closed, but because there was no trade at the other end. Continental nations with all their populations, energies, and wealth, engaged in a desperate struggle for survival, would be unable to carry on the trade with Britain that they carried on in times of peace. Britain must "prevent the whole of the West of Europe falling under the domination of a single Power," Sir Edward declared. Britain could not remain neutral.

In retrospect this speech sounds like a statement of intent to keep trade flowing, to maintain the balance of economic power on Britain's side, rather than a brave decision to go to war to protect Britain's beleaguered allies.

On 4 August 1914, Asquith made the formal declaration of war.

Redmond immediately rose and offered the support of "his" Irish Volunteer Movement in the cause of the British Empire. He did this without consulting with any other members of the party, without considering the wishes of the Volunteer leaders and without the thought of consequences for Home Rule. He simply rode the crest of emotion. The British Empire—British trade, primarily—thrown into jeopardy by events in Europe suddenly became the only political reality of the moment. If Redmond wanted to become a hero he did so—for a day and at the expense of the Irish.

Later, James Stephens would write, "On the day of the declaration of war between England and Germany, [Redmond] took the Irish case, weighty with centuries of history and tradition, and he threw it out of the window. How could Ireland be disloyal to Britain, he asked, if she had never been loyal in the first place?" Carson, for his part, had stated that "If required … a large body of Ulster Volunteers will be … willing to serve anywhere they are required." In Ireland, the Nationalists were furious, but the populace had caught fire with the very idea of war.

In London Margot Asquith noted the wild excitement of the crowds, the crush of delirious spectators who seemed—she thought as she made her way home after witnessing her husband's speech—to actually welcome war. (The Prime Minister's son, Raymond Asquith, who had played an important part in the Select Committee on the Putumayo question, would be killed early on in the war.) Many throughout Europe, with or without a declaration of war, seemed enthralled with Death. Pacifists were looked on with contempt and isolated. ("No one converses with me beside myself," Nietzsche had written some time before, "and my voice reaches me as the voice of one dying.")

Home Rule now needed only the Royal Assent to become law. On 18 September, the King pronounced "le Roi veult," with Home Rule to become effective only after one year or in any case at the end of the war. The Amending Bill, however, would have to be decided upon—and this would cause some trouble, deciding what counties would be left out of the Union.

America's Long Hot Summer

1

Washington was hot. But New York was hotter. The home of aberrants of all types—Atheists, Deists, Freemasons, Naturalists, Swedenborgians, Gymnosophists, Anarchists—America had also established a new sexual morality, or so it seemed. Timothy Dwight, President of Yale University, felt, along with others, the "growing immorality" of Americans, equated with sexual activity. "[E]very social influence including art, literature and business," was working to stimulate the latent (but easily) reached passions of the people. Some intellectuals blamed the French and American Revolutions for having destroyed the values of aristocrats, replacing them by the dubious values and more dubious morals of workers and peasants.

The greatest good for the greatest number of men seemed to be outright depravity.

The Transcendentalists in America had not been helpful. Thoreau, Emerson, Louisa May Alcott, Margaret Fuller, had advocated releasing social restraints. The Brook Farm experiment and the New Harmony group sought to strip away inhibitions, elevating woman into something unrecognizable and repulsive. Lust was sanctified by marriage, in which the female kept male desires in check. Meanwhile, in the cities sub-cultures of promiscuity were developing, with the influx of Southern European immigrants who, it was said, enjoyed much grander sex lives than others. There was an emphasis on the body, clothed and unclothed, "artistic" exhibitions everywhere you turned—along with a social philosophy that considered the body and its needs at the same time as "immoral." No one in America was as batty as the well-known English aesthete Ruskin, the pundit of the Beautiful, who found it impossible to consummate his marriage because his wife was found to have pubic hair—though he would fix this later by falling in love with a ten-year-old. Sensuality in American cities was rife and unashamed and raunchy.

Painted boys propositioned passersby in New York. Certain restaurants, saloons, clubs were notorious haunts of homosexuals—even the paperboys knew the "signs" such as a red tie, and would suck their fingers and giggle at men wearing one. In the United States, delayed marriage was encouraged, which only resulted in increased prostitution, pornography and homosexuality.

All this was a heyday for the medical eccentrics and pseudo-sexologists. Many American doctors had studied in Britain and knew what they knew, but there was a widespread revulsion against "unhealthy" acts. Benjamin Rush, who had trained in Edinburgh—like so many famous physicians—declared that sexual indulgence could lead to "seminal weakness, impotence, dysury, tabes dorsalis, pulmonary consumptions, dyspepsia, dimness of sight, vertigo, epilepsy, hypochondriasis, loss of memory, manalgia, fatuity and death." Sylvester Graham (who invented graham crackers and pushed wheat germ) was in agreement. Sex had to be curtailed or controlled. Claude-Francois Lallemand had confronted the problem of spermatorrhea, and recommended—along with many American doctors—quick sex and infrequent, to maintain health; no masturbation of course. John Harvey Kellogg's Battle Creek sanatorium was successful in curing innumerable cases of sexual mismanagement caused by "modern civilization" and its stresses. Medical experts such as Victoria Woodhull who advocated *greater* sexuality were looked upon as quacks dangerous to the public at large, and were ostracized professionally.

Not many Americans were willing to give up sex, or the quick in-and-out philosophy, least of all the homosexuals who were in evidence in all big cities, in frontier towns, in the military and throughout society. Washington DC was notorious for its Black Queens, its almost institutionalized gay scene, and this would continue for decades, the "Erotopaths" carrying on with "drag dances" and public immorality. Blacks and whites were even prone to mix, especially in St. Louis, where widespread "miscegenation" was reported. It was hard to tell lovers from friends: most gays were often simply unrecognizable. There may have been no name for them, or a reluctance to admit what they did in private, but there they were, no doubt about it.

Pornography was popular, as it always had been. Strange to say, a popular type of pornographic book dealt with male homosexuality. English writers were particularly prone to compose crypto-homosexual stories and verse—and in America there was the infamous example of Walt Whitman, a little more open, but there were others. Why so much emphasis on sodomy? You had to admit that if women were on a pedestal—Females pure and good—males could hardly clamber up and reach them. The answer was simple, that men, who were by nature impure, when left to their own devices would simply do it with each other.

The camera obscura proved a powerful adjunct, as did other types of reproductive media, in the production of pornography. In the theater, too, there were broad hints of doubtful morals, and in popular publications—not only the yellow press—news of widespread unredeeming activities was available for a nickel.

Science was also increasingly interested in homosexuality. The decade from 1898 to 1908 saw the publication of hundreds of titles on the topic. The terms "invert" and the unfortunate "urning" were gradually dropped, or less used, replaced by "homosexual" (favored by Havelock Ellis). The term "pederast" was also popular, especially in France, where F. Carlier reported 6242 pederasts who had come to the attention of the police in Paris. Of these, 3709 came from the provinces; 484 were foreigners. He also mentioned male prostitution, quite common in the capital.

Not only in Paris. Male whorehouses were known in London, too. New York was not far behind. In 1879 a St. Louis newspaper reported matter-of-factly that a house of ill fame had been raided. Eight prostitutes were arrested, half of them male. In New York, Reverend Charles Parkhurst found male brothels popular: The Golden Rule Pleasure Club, Manila Hall, The Black Rabbit, The Palm, and Paresis Hall.

Philadelphia (where Casement spoke) was also sizzling hot. So was Chicago (the windy city's vice commissioner in 1909 found gays "rampant" and calculated their numbers at over 10,000)—and New Orleans, of course—and San Francisco. Even some occupations were known to be full of homosexuals. "Counter jumpers" or clerks in the dry goods trade were typically gay. The authorities, even if they want to "root out" the evil were often stumped. Whole colonies of gays never fell into the hands of the police, or even vaguely *looked* effeminate. Large numbers of "sex perverts" simply were never known in their true character even to the medical profession because their immoral habits produced no sign of bodily disease.

It was recognized that there was "in every community of any size a colony of male sexual perverts; they are usually known to each other, and are likely to congregate together. At times they operate in accordance with some definite and concerted plan in quest of subjects wherewith to gratify their abnormal sexual impulses." Homosexuality was more of a "city" disease, and its urban practitioners were often classed as "criminally insane."

During the Civil War there were a number of curious incidents concerning the "third sex." Several women impersonated men in order to go to war. Magnus Hirschfeld, the famous sexologist, said—although he himself couldn't find much evidence of it—that homosexuality was *"Kolosal viel los"* or widespread. Homosexuals found each other easily (as Casement, and everyone else, knew quite well) and there was no need to advertise, though a little exposure was to the good. The immigrant groups had a high percentage of sexual deviants: many well-known homosexuals migrated to the US. A German visitor said that in America "the unnatural vice in question is more ordinary.... [T]he Americans' tastes in this matter resemble my own; and I discovered in the United States, that I was always immediately recognized as a member of the confraternity."

In 1870 George Napheys reported that "every unnatural vice recorded in Juvenal, Martial and Petronius was practiced in America. Not just rarely and accidentally but deliberately and habitually and there were even restaurants frequented by men in women's dress."

Havelock Ellis believed that homosexuality was widespread in American cities, as shown by the wide recognition of its existence. Ninety-nine out of a hundred normal men had been accosted on the streets by inverts, or had been, unwittingly, "cruised" by them. Most had friends whom they knew to be sexually inverted. The public attitude was simply indifference, amusement or contempt. Ellis believed that every fifth man was an invert. In major American cities there existed a wide range of gay cafes, dance halls, clubs, salons, restaurants. James Huneker reported being propositioned by a young homosexual while out walking with Stephen Crane in 1894; Crane was concerned with helping the boy "with painted purple eyes." Italian immigrant kids especially had taken to the streets: it was claimed that Southern Europeans were responsible for a rise in pederasty in the US. There were also certain segments of society, however, where pederasty was endemic. Hobos, for example—always a plague in America—were familiar with the usage. Every hobo knew what "unnatural intercourse" was, according to Joseah Flynt, a rail rider, and it was talked about freely. He thought one hobo in ten practiced sodomy, usually with boys called "prushuns." The boy's protector was known as a "jocker" and usually fucked the boy face down. Tramps were considered by non-tramps, Flynt said, as fair game. Tramps would fuck for a handout or a dime.

2

When Casement went to America he entered a familiar world. It was natural that he would want to return to the US, if for a short time, as he had been drawn—apart from the Indian question—back to Iquitos for the usual reasons, the well-equipped boys and the active cruising.

It is debatable whether the "Victorian Era" in the US was really prim or proper. Hard evidence concerning the gay scene is difficult to come by. The "Gay Scene" itself was probably less prevalent than the undifferentiated—unlabelled—sexual relations that occurred everywhere between males.

The records are exceedingly meager. Such documents as the Black Diaries throw a wonderfully revealing light on the times. As Peter Gay notes, "[I]n an individualistic, introspective, and reticent century like the nineteenth, the diary and journal ... became almost obligatory companions to a class endowed with a modicum of leisure." The keeping of a diary was essential to the bourgeois, an organizational method of ordering one's thoughts, and also "providing space for freedom and individuality." Accidental revelations could come about through the publication of such diaries, even when the writer was poignantly anxious to "hide" the full truth under evasions or secret codes. Walt Whitman is generally safe on this score—except for moments of self-chastisement and guilt or when he mentions casually picking boys off the street and taking them home to sleep with him. "To sleep" is perhaps harmless, and not necessarily indicating sex; but it was still rather odd to bring young men home and go to bed with them.

Outright *confession* of deviant tastes was to be avoided at any cost, even if made to a "friend" who shared those tastes. (Whitman, for example, in reply to John Addington Symonds.) The late nineteenth century preferred ignorance to honesty. It was symptomatic that the public reacted with vindictive glee when Oscar Wilde was put on trial in the spring of 1895; the principal reason was that his "sordid sexual adventures" were indiscreet. But at any rate the subject was out in the open. Even in England the law, though not as liberal as the Napoleonic code, adopted by France, the Netherlands, and Italy during the 1880s, was less rigid or was rarely enforced in the case of sodomy. In 1885 the Labouchere Amendment to the Criminal Law Amendment Act made sodomy a felony. Sodomy was defined as the carnal knowledge (*per anum*) of any man or of any woman by a male person, and punishable with penal servitude for life as a maximum. Any attempt to commit sodomy was punishable with up to ten years penal servitude, while the commission in public or in private of any act of gross indecency [such as mutual masturbation] between males was punishable with two years imprisonment at hard labor. However, convictions were hard to come by, especially since witnesses were needed, and "culprits" would rarely implicate themselves. Throughout the 1890s there was a growing debate about sodomy—or buggery—and "science" came into the picture, tending to make any homosexual offense more a symptom of disease than anything criminal. Then again, as was frequently pointed out, some of the greatest princes, statesmen, poets, playwrights, painters and scientists had been homosexual. What a disastrous effect their imprisonment or execution would have been to world culture!

We are faced with the homosexual—but what of his partners? As Ellis said, society cannot be expected to tolerate the invert "who flaunts his perversion in its face and who claims to be of a finer clay than the vulgar herd" because he likes to "take his pleasure with a soldier or a policeman." What then of the police force or the military? What if all the members of these organizations who had homosexual relations were convicted? Society would fall apart. Obviously something is wrong here.

The widespread habits—customs, usage, tradition, acts—of homosexuality in the US meant that a considerable segment of the American population, some of the tenderest age, were guilty of outright felonies. But sodomites were guilty only if the acts were committed "at home" (and duly *proved*) but not in a foreign country. Everyone knew that "furriners" were nasty folk. Thus the charm of world travel, the Wild West, the frontier towns, South America—and beyond, in Africa, the Orient, the Ottoman Empire (see Stanley's early travels). Or even unsuspecting Europe where American adventurers—tourists and traders and renegades—were roaming like wild animals.

3

Casement was obsessed by sex as well as by Irish matters. His private life—as usual—was a stimulus to his public acts. He wrote letters, carried on discussions, responded to Irish propaganda with enthusiasm. He was beginning to redefine the Enemy. The act of distinguishing the enemy was basic, from King Leopold to J.C. Arana, from the Belgian agents in the Congo to the sadistic agents of the Putumayo Amazon Company in Peru. "The entire life of a human being is a struggle," as Carl Schmitt has written, "and every human being symbolically a combatant." Conflict was life: this assumption was not about political conflict but about human nature and, as such, "reveals the true lessons of history."

Casement was now increasingly and openly anti-British, ever more vociferously an Irish Nationalist. Of course he had been "for" Irish Independence since the beginning, even while pursuing his career—the Consular Service was always involved with British commercial interests, as was the Foreign Service itself: a major reason for the Great War. Now, at the end of it all, he saw himself redefining his goals in terms of the Enemy. There may not have been any *absolute* enemies, of course, but Britain as the Enemy was well-defined, with its political raison d'être based on the conquest of land and trade, on the subjection of weaker peoples in an Empire that was slowly falling apart.

The arrogance of the English vis-a-vis the Irish was notorious, even in time of national crisis. Kitchener even scorned the idea of an Irish Unit at first; soon, however, two Irish divisions were fighting bravely, and dying, on the French battlefields. The Irish suffered significant losses in Flanders and also in the Dardanelles, in combat alongside Carson's Ulster Division. Over a quarter million Irish would take part in the Great War; there would be 27,405 dead. So much suffering and all for a nation that had kept Ireland, in Casement's words, enslaved for centuries. The British Liberal Party, having been sworn to give self-rule to Ireland for twenty-eight years, had failed. As Singleton-Gates points out, "[Britain] now offers to sell, at a very high price, a wholly hypothetical and indefinite form of partial internal control of certain specified Irish services, if, in return for this promissory note (payable after death), the Irish people will contribute their blood, their honor and their manhood in a war that in no wise concerns them."

The Irish Nationalists insisted that England's war with Germany had nothing to do with Ireland and that there was nothing Ireland could get out of it, economically, morally or materially. The Irish were dying on the battlefield in order to assure that fatuously wealthy landlords and British businessmen might grow fatter.

Redmond had destroyed the Irish Volunteers, taking the majority with him. Asquith had promised the Volunteers arms; they never saw them. Redmond decided that the Irish would become British soldiers: "Your duty is twofold, and it would be a disgrace if Irishmen refrained from fighting, wherever the fighting extends, in defense of right, freedom and religion in this war."

Only 12,000 or so Irish Volunteers headed by Eoin MacNeill and Bulmer Hobson remained an organized—if ineffectual—force, to be known later as Sinn Fein Volunteers.

The movement for Irish Independence had not died. A small group of men remained determinedly active—Padraic Pearse, Sean MacDermott, Joseph Plunkett, Eamon Ceannt, led by Tom Clarke—in the Irish Republican Brotherhood, later the I.R.A. These men believed in armed insurrection. Tom Clarke, who spent fifteen years in prison for his beliefs, had returned from America in 1907 to fight for Irish freedom: he would not be turned aside, even by the Great War, or by the wholesale defection brought about by Redmond. Many Irish-Americans were solidly behind the Brotherhood.

In America, in only a few weeks, Casement was able to collect $8,000 for the cause. If the war had not broken out, he would, however, have been able to drum up more support. "God save Germany! I got here," he wrote, "in peace and began a nice campaign for the Irish Volunteers and would have got probably £40,000 or £50,000 for rifles—when this War of Devils broke loose." John Devoy, intense and dour, was still after forty-three years of work in the Irish Movement in the US (he had immigrated soon after being released from British jail in 1871) a vital force. Originally he had written to Bulmer Hobson, when Casement had already left for America, "I regret also to say that under present circumstances, it would be useless for your friend … to come here" but now seemed enthusiastic about using Casement as an envoy. He, along with many in the Movement, now believed it was time to ask Germany to help in their struggle for independence.

Delegates of the Clan met with Count von Bernstorff, the German Ambassador in the US and the military attach, Fritz von Papen, at the German Club in New York. Devoy's hatred of the British was so extreme that he may even have agreed to work for the Germans as a spy—in later German dispatches he is described as "confidential agent." Casement was also his usual impressive self; Theodore Roosevelt, whom he had seen in Washington, assured him, he said, that "Britain was finished." The German Ambassador was pleased to offer the Irish a tentative alliance.

American sentiments were not wholeheartedly on the side of Britain and France in the early stages of the war. Nevertheless outright support for anti-British activities was lacking. "The average American has no ideals," Casement, rather nastily wrote, "no national mind or spirit, and is a gas-bag to a great extent."

Casement on the other hand sympathized with the German working class: "My heart bleeds for those people, beset by a world of hatred; their crime is their efficiency." Addressing the Kaiser, he wrote of his "sympathy and admiration for the heroic people of Germany."

Devoy and the other leaders of the Clan agreed with Casement that he could be of service to the movement by soliciting help from the Germans in Berlin. Talks with German authorities in the US had convinced them that the Kaiser was sympathetic to the Irish cause. In a letter to the Kaiser, signed by the officers of the Clan and delivered to von Bülow in Berlin, plans for an Easter Uprising in Dublin were suggested and the possible formation of an Irish Brigade from Irish prisoners of war. (Major John MacBride, who had led the Irish Brigade during the Boer War and was now living in the US, offered his services.) Casement was enthusiastic about recruiting Irish POWs.

Von Bernstorff cabled the German Foreign Office in Berlin on 25 September, "I recommend falling in with the Irish wishes, provided there are really Irishmen who are prepared to help us. The formation of an Irish legion from Irish prisoners of war would be a great idea if only it could be carried out."

In New York Casement had put up at the Belmont Hotel, a familiar place with an Irish staff, and a hotel which Henry James had often used when he was in the city. Casement was "eager to discover this great city and its people," Singleton-Gates writes, "with whom his own had so many affinities."

4

Singleton-Gates and Rene MacColl believed that Casement and Adler Christensen had met by chance while Casement was out sight-seeing in New York. "Walking down Broadway," Singleton-Gates confidently writes, "he was assailed by a man who told him a tale of woe in broken English; he was Eivind Adler Christensen, twenty-four years of age, a husky blond fellow with a gap in his front teeth; he had run away from his home in Moss, Norway, years ago, and became a sailor. He was now stranded in New York without work, starving...." Christensen's appearance in Casement's life, he went on to remark, was a sign "of an accelerated and non-resisted degradation in [his] character which was, thenceforth, only checked on rare occasions."

Casement was out on Broadway. He picked up Christensen and brought him back to his room at the Belmont. The size of the Norwegian's cock and his criminal personality may have constituted a fatal combination for Sir Roger, but there were other considerations as well: Adler spoke German and knew the Scandinavian countries through which Casement would pass on his way to Germany. That Adler was an "obvious" queen was beside the point. One could overlook the fact that he used makeup, had expensive tastes and was, it would appear, a petty criminal known to the police. Casement ignored the risks in view of the advantages.

The Berlin Panopticon

1

By the time of his departure for Germany, Casement's mission priorities had slightly changed. He now defined three main goals: to get a document from the German Government confirming that they would grant complete Irish freedom in the event of a German victory in the present war, to acquire arms from the Germans for the Irish Volunteers in case of an uprising, and to create a body of Irish troops recruited from Irish POWs.

Casement had recently written—and received a reprimand from Arthur Nicholson, Under-Secretary of State for Foreign Affairs, for having done so—a politically indiscreet letter to the *Irish Independent* recommending that Ireland side with Germany in the war. He had also written that "If Asquith and his ally come to Dublin, they should be shot." He also wrote to Gee that President Wilson would get shot if he tried to get the US into the war on the side of Great Britain. These are uncharacteristically violent statements for Casememt and perhaps symptomatic of emotional instability.

Sir Roger Casement, amateur secret agent, now washes his face in buttermilk to give it a deceiving pallor, and shaves off his beard. He slips out of his hotel, where he is registered as Mr. R. Smythe of London, and heads for the docks. To throw any enemy—British—agents off the scent, he has previously made reservations in Chicago at the La Salle Hotel for Sir Roger Casement who is expected to arrive soon. He has a passport in the name of a Mr. Landy, who has booked passage on the *Oskar II*, a Norwegian ship. He accompanies "Mr. Landy" on board ship to see him off but then remains on board in his stead, traveling (again) incognito. His luggage has already been brought onto the *Oskar II* by Christensen.

All this elaborate subterfuge is observed from afar by the British Foreign Office whose cryptologists early in the war had broken the German code and were able to decipher all messages sent by the German embassy in Washington to Berlin.

On board the *Oskar II* the other passengers (many fleeing, no doubt, from the US for one dark reason or another) considered Casement a British spy. He had a British accent even though he was carrying a US passport and his "off-hand" manners were obviously an attempt to appear Yankee. The reception his fellow passengers gave him was icy, which rankled a little.

His trip is recorded for posterity in a style designed to throw any agents off the track. He writes to his sister Nina as a "young woman" traveling with her girlfriend. "We steered further north, and the dear, kind captain, such a nice Dane, with a beard just like cousin Roger's, told me he hoped to go up by the Faroe Islands, and get past those cruisers." However, on 24 October the *Oskar II* was overtaken by a ship of the British Navy, the H.M.S. *Hibernia*, and taken to Stornoway. The young woman writes, "that dear dear Norwegian helped me stow away all the old hairpins.... Now when I saw *Hibernia* on the caps of the men I nearly kissed them—it took my breath clear away." (Casement, fearing discovery, had immediately dumped all incriminating papers and diaries overboard.) The ship's interception only served to convince the rest of the passengers that Casement was indeed a spy. "They had it going I compiled reports from the other two spies as to all people who were fakes on board and that I sent a wireless to have the *Oskar II* cut off."

For some strange reason, Casement was passed over by the authorities—not recognized or simply ignored—and after several crew members were taken off, the *Oscar II* was allowed to continue its voyage. No convincing reason has been given for this oversight, since the Foreign Office was anxious to have Casement arrested and returned to Britain. This failure to get their man must have especially frustrated two Government officials working on the assignment: Captain Reginald Hall (in charge of Naval Intelligence) and Basil Thomson (Assistant Commissioner at Scotland Yard), both of whom had developed an insane hatred for Casement and would pursue him to the end with a savage intensity unusual in a case of such relatively minor importance.

2

Casement and Christensen arrived at Christiania on 28 October. They stayed at the Grand Hotel. The Foreign Office meanwhile had alerted the British embassy there. The arrival of the two had been observed with obviously malevolent pleasure. Just how malevolent was to come out when British agents accosted Christensen at the Grand and spirited him away for an interview at the British Legation. Here however the records are inconclusive and contradictory.

The Foreign Office files record that on 25 October 1914 a young Norwegian with a strong American accent called at the British Legation at 79 Daamersveien and asked for the Minister. The Minister was out, so a legation officer, Francis Lindley, spoke with Christensen who claimed to have just arrived from the United States with an English nobleman, decorated by the King. "I understand," Lindley wrote, "that his relations with the Englishman were of an improper character." Christensen said he had steamed open letters, found a cipher, and was willing to hand this over—with conditions. The next day, he did see Findlay, the Minister, who describes him as "Age 24, about 6 ft, strongly made, clean shaven, fair hair, blue or gray eyes very small and set close together, gap in front teeth.... Speaks English fluently but with a strong Norwegian-American accent.... Has fleshy, dissipated appearance." Inquiries were sent off to the New York police; their cable in reply stated that Christensen was a dangerous type, a Norwegian-American criminal." The Minister gave him 25 Kroner. Later, when Christensen returned with the cipher and a specimen of Casement's handwriting, he gave him 100 Kroner more, although he had demanded $100.

On the evening of their arrival, Casement, still traveling under an assumed name, took his credentials to Count von Oberndorff, the German Minister, at the German Legation. The letter had to be decoded, which would take time. He was told to return the next morning.

When Casement got back to the hotel he heard a strange story from Adler. While Casement had been at the German Legation, Adler said he had been "lured" to a mysterious house (perhaps the British Embassy) and questioned about a "tall, dark Englishman." He had been given money. There would perhaps be more. He was to return the next day.

After Adler related what had happened, Casement expressed no alarm. He was, on the other hand, intrigued. He agreed that Adler should go back to find out what the British wanted. This is Adler's story: On arriving at the mystery house the next day, he was confronted by a gentleman who claimed to be the British Minister. This man said that he knew the identity of his traveling companion, and showed Adler copies of telegrams sent by Casement to New York that very morning. The Minister then suggested that Christensen "knock Casement on the head" or get rid of him in some other way, in exchange for the protection of the British Government and a substantial reward. Adler said he would think about it and return that evening with his decision.

When Casement heard this, he became concerned and informed Von Oberndorff. The German shrugged the story off. This was, he quipped, typical of how the British operated.

Casement and Adler decided to leave at once for Copenhagen to throw the British off their trail. Adler, however, returned to keep his appointment with the Minister, Findlay. Findlay's offer was now $5,000 in gold if Christensen would lure Casement anywhere on Skagerrack or the North Sea where a British warship could pick him up. Meanwhile, he was to stick by Casement, steal letters, copy them and send them to Herr Sigwald Wiig Thorwald, Meyersgate 782. The news of this offer both enraged and alarmed Casement.

Plans were then devised by the Germans for the movements of Casement and Christensen—a preposterously involved maneuvering simply to reach the German border. On 31 October they went by rail to Copenhagen; during the trip, at the Engelholm Junction, they slipped into another section of the train where an official of the German Foreign Office, Richard Meyer, was expecting them. From Malmö the three crossed the Baltic to Denmark, then traveled by train to Sassnitz on the German border. On the same day they crossed the border they reached Berlin. Here, Casement, continuing his incognito, registered at the Continental Hotel as "Mr. Hammond of New York."

Casement was instructed not to leave his hotel without proper identification. So the first day he spent in his room fuming over the Findlay affair. The following day, a Monday, he was taken by Richard Meyer to the Wilhelmstrasse where he met with Under Secretary of State von Zimmermann. What was most on Casement's mind was Findlay. Von Zimmermann pooh-poohed his concern. "They stick at nothing," he said, echoing von Oberndorff. He sent Casement on to Count Georg von Wedel, Head of the Foreign Office English Department. Von Wedel was instrumental in arranging a *laissez passer* from the secret police. ("Mr. Hammond of New York is not to be molested.") What we know of these movements comes from the Berlin Diaries, which ended, this day, on an uncharacteristic note of success (complete sentences, normal punctuation, hyperbole, the "historical" style):

"No regrets, no fears—well—yes, some regrets, but no fears.... my country can only gain by my treason.... If I win all it is national resurrection—a free Ireland, a world nation after centuries of slavery.... [T]he time has come for me to see the

break-up of the British Empire ... a monstrosity. The world will be the better, the more sincere, the less hypocritical for a British defeat and a German victory."

With von Wedel, "We talked of the Irish soldiers in Germany and the line of action that I hoped to follow there.... I made it plain beyond all misconception to Wedel that my efforts with the soldiers must be strictly defined as an effort to strike a blow for Ireland—not an attempt merely to hit England." He had no doubt that scores, perhaps hundreds, of the Irish prisoners could be talked into following him.

Von Wedel later summed up the meeting to Reichs Chancellor von Bethmann-Hollweg. Roger Casement, he said, proposes 1) The formation of an Irish Legion from British prisoners of war in Germany of Irish nationality and of the Catholic faith; 2) A public declaration that Germany has no intention of bringing Ireland under German domination. He adds that Casement believes the Irish in the United States would give their backing to him, which would be a serious setback for Great Britain at this time. "My personal impression of Sir Roger Casement inclines me to give serious consideration to his proposals."

Casement wrote letters, one to Devoy, expressing his optimism. He also cabled Judge Cohalan, instructing him to tell Biggar *to conceal everything belonging to me.* Biggar was storing at his home in Belfast the trunks containing Casement's large collection of highly incriminating personal diaries and correspondence.

3

The Germans were interested in getting good press in the US. As Fritz von Papen, in Washington, remarked, "American opinion is governed by widespread misconceptions about the war." In this sense, the Irish question might help to straighten them out as to the Reich's true sentiments concerning freedom and democracy.

Casement, inside Germany, also had a special view of the German condition. "The Germans deserve to win," he wrote Gee. "They are making heroic sacrifices.... The [reported] 'atrocities' in Belgium etc. are a horrid lie. I've been there and seen with my own eyes.... Everyone's sorry for France and Belgium; it is only England, he originator and plotter of the war, they loathe, and rightly."

In his diary he wrote, "I regret I am not a German."

He might just as well have been a German, to judge by the British attitudes when the news appeared in the international press that the celebrated Sir Roger Casement was in Berlin. The story appeared on the front page of German newspapers, along with his photograph and a short biographical sketch. His presence represented a propaganda coup for the German Government.

The hero was "flawed" by ill health, however, by frustrations, dreadful psychological depressions and a growing sense of persecution. His close companion was not helpful. The German Secret Service immediately had Adler Christensen checked out. The story was that Adler had a wife in America. He claimed to have once been secretary to a millionaire (unsubstantiated). He told people he was in Germany for "business" reasons. "A talented boy," was von Oberndorff's opinion, "but troublesome." And he had a police record.

It would soon become clear that Adler was also a flamboyant and active homosexual. This did not seem to bother Casement, though it made the Germans uneasy. Meanwhile, Casement was seeing much of Count Blücher (a co-treasurer of the Putumayo fund and an old friend). (Blücher's English wife later claimed that the Irishman's perverted tastes became evident in Berlin and caused a scandal. This was obviously an exaggeration. Berlin was rotten with perversions. "Scandals" only developed among people who really mattered.) Blücher became useful to Casement because he could send out letters with him.

Adler, if not honest, was resourceful. Using the code given him by Findlay, he contacted Herr Sigwald in Christiania. Casement had decided Adler should make a return trip to the capital, carrying two fake letters especially designed to confuse and infuriate Whitehall. Back in Norway, Adler would hand these over to Findlay with the hope that he would forward them to London. The text of the letters included phony data on the sending of arms and men to Ireland, and included potshots at the Foreign Office ("stupid men playing war games").

Casement felt within his rights to be in Germany, and to be negotiating with the Germans for aid to the Irish. Although his friends in Britain had written him off as a traitor, he told himself he was simply an Irish patriot. Herbert Ward, a friend from the Congo days, wrote, "He is a traitor pure and simple, and he will probably be shot when he is taken." Change that to hanged.

Casement now pressed for an official declaration from the German Government stating their attitude on the Irish Question. He wanted the world to know that the Irish had the support of Germany in their struggle for independence, and that Irish sovereignty would be respected if Germany won the war. Scribbling away in his room at the Continental, Casement rarely stopped to reflect on his fragile position. He *was* a traitor. He had come to Germany, Britain's enemy in the Great War, offering friendship and asking for aid. He hated the British and wished them evil. He hoped to organize an Irish Brigade to fight against the British, although he later denied this. The future in any case was a chaos.

He was escorted to Charleville, German Army Headquarters, to meet the General Staff. Plans were discussed for building a special camp at Limburg Lahn for the Irish POWs. Here they would get special treatment. Once the Brigade was formed, they would be trained for the fight to come. When Casement returned from Charleville, he was peeved to find that Christensen after all had not taken his letters to Christiania. The German Government remained silent on the Irish Question.

Then on 20 November he was frontpage news again. There was his picture, the usual eulogy, and the Declaration by the Imperial Chancellor, exactly as Casement himself had composed it. "The German Government repudiates the evil intentions attributed to it ... and takes this opportunity to give a categorical assurance that the German Government desires only the welfare of the Irish people, their country and their institutions.... The Imperial Government formally declares that under no circumstances would Germany invade Ireland with a view to its conquest or the overthrow of any native institutions in that country.... Should the fortune of this great war, that was not of Germany's seeking, ever bring in its course German troops to the shores of Ireland, they would land there, not as an army of invaders to pillage and destroy, but as the force of a government that is inspired by good will towards a country and people for whom Germany desires only national prosperity and national freedom."

This striking piece of propaganda buoyed Casement up enough to send Adler off with the letters again to Christiania, along with "stolen pages of a diary" hinting imminent invasion of Ireland by Roger Casement and his friends (50,000 of them!) by the end of December. Adler left, trailing the scent of a strange and unsavory reputation.

At Frankfurt-am-Main, on his way to the prison camp, Casement writes in his diary: "I was unwell and stayed in my room all day. Professor Schliemann called late at night with disquieting statements about Adler that were unwarranted and malicious. Poor Adler!" "The one-time beggar Casement saved from starvation in New York had metamorphosed into a self-assured personage of an original type," Singleton-Gates, in all innocence, writes, "gaudily dressed and given to the use of feminine cosmetics." The fact was that the Berlin police had monitored the young Norwegian's behavior—for obvious reasons—just as they routinely monitored the behavior of all foreigners in the capital. Without doubt Casement himself, an aging Irish homosexual, was under constant surveillance by the secret police too. It was clear he could no longer count on the arrogance of anonymity. He was warned pointedly by Schiemann to be careful.

All of this added to Casement's sense of persecution. He as well as Adler were now suspect, he thought. He had never doubted Adler's simple-minded tales—such as being handed the key to the back door of the British Legation by the Minister himself, or being given 500 Kroner to pay a copyist to come back to Berlin and record Casement's written plans. He even went so far as to hint that Casement might act as bait to lure the British fleet into a trap set by the German Navy. But the boy was … well, Adler.

After being introduced at last to Reichs Chancellor Bethmann-Hollweg, Casement wrote, "[The Chancellor] agreed that an independent Ireland … would be a good thing for Germany." He does not elaborate on this point. "We discussed, at his request, 'Christiania' and Mr. Findlay and the extraordinary later development with Findlay's present offer of £10,000 for me anywhere—the North Sea or Skaggerrak, and his entrusting the key of the back door of the British Legation to my rascal Adler!" He simply could not get Findlay off his mind. The obsession would continue.

There were now about 1,500 Irish POWs at Sennelager. Here, they got an encouraging speech from a senior officer. "By the command of Kaiser Wilhelm II all Irish soldiers now prisoners of war will be assembled in one distinct camp, be treated better, have more freedom, better food and clothing, and suitable games." But the POWs resented the special treatment, since their colleagues in misfortune would not be getting the same; they wrote a letter to the Camp Commandant, for transmission to the Kaiser in person, that "we regret we must beseech his Imperial Majesty to withdraw these concessions unless they are shared by the remainder of the prisoners, as in addition to being Irish Catholics, we have the honor to be British soldiers." The letter was dated 1 December, the day that Casement presented himself to the first contingent.

Posters had been nailed up in the huts at Limburg, exhorting the POWs to fight for Ireland. "The object of the Irish Brigade will be to fight solely for the cause of Ireland, and under no circumstances shall it be directed to any German end." This may have seemed like double-talk to the prisoners, who had been in battle and many of whom were professional soldiers with unshakeable loyalty to Britain.

Casement fell ill at Limburg. He stayed there until the tenth, keeping to his bed and writing in his "historical diary" which it appears he thought might be read by German agents. On the train back he wrote, "I pass through the best tilled lands I have seen in Europe—not a square yard wasted—the best fed people one can find in the world—and this once quiet medieval town (Eisenach) a large thriving, bustling city—full of life, of industry and smoke! No one would dream this people was at war; the life of the country—as I saw it at Limburg—goes on all the same, and food is as plentiful and as cheap today as when on 2nd August the war devil was loosed against Germany."

The Germans threw up a cold barrier of silence. Bettmann-Hollweg refused to waste time with Casement, who felt insulted and betrayed. His qualms were destroying him slowly, irrevocably, and he needed all the support he could get to keep from sinking into despair. Then a message was forwarded to him from the German Ambassador in Washington:

> For Casement: Confidential agent arrived in Ireland at end of November. The declaration of the German Foreign Office has made an excellent impression.... Judge Cohalan recommends not publishing statement about attempt on Casement's life until actual proofs are secured. Requests for money have been complied with. There have been purchased from India eleven thousand rifles, four million cartridges, two hundred and fifty Mauser pistols, five hundred revolvers with ammunition. Devoy does not think it possible to ship them to Ireland. I am trying to buy rifles from Turkey and South America.

Setting out the conditions for the Irish Brigade now took up his time. Christmas passed; he was alone. Then on 28 December he met with Zimmermann to discuss his work. He was anxious to get back to Limburg. He was at the same time becoming more and more depressed. Physically he was not well. "I have been ill," he writes in the Berlin diary, "and greatly upset at the failure of my hopes." What failure?

For one, the failure to recruit men for the Irish Brigade. Only five had signed up. They were not what one would call "representative" patriots. No professional soldiers would care to join, giving up one war for another, traitorous, one. "Now that I have practically abandoned the idea of the Irish Brigade, there seems little object in remaining in Germany," Casement wrote.

For another, failure to get redress for the insulting way he had been treated by Findlay. Findlay was never far from his mind. Adler had returned to Berlin from Christiania where he had actually been given a letter signed by Findlay himself.

> *On behalf of the British Government I promise that if, through information given by Adler Christensen, Sir Roger Casement be captured either with or without his companions, the said Adler Christensen is to receive from the British Government the sum of £5,000 to be paid as he may desire. Adler Christensen is also to enjoy personal immunity and to be given a passage to the United States should he desire it.*

Adler had handed over the letter to the German Foreign Office, where they could hardly believe that it was genuine; however, on checking the hand-writing against a sample on file, they were convinced of its authenticity. They duly popped it into the Casement Dossier, and that was that. Von Wedel finally agreed to show the letter to Casement, who was incensed not only by the message itself but by the Germans appropriating the document. It was a "state document," in his opinion and he felt he had been robbed of it—especially after an outlay of about £200 on Adler's trip. How could Findlay have been so stupid—unless he was in collusion with Adler. Casement suffered an attack of paranoid rage.

The subject of his pension had also come up in the House of Lords, where Lord Crewe had stated insultingly that "Sir Roger Casement's action merits a sensible punishment." Casement answered with an open letter, addressed to Sir Edward Grey. He begged "to return the insignia of the Most Distinguished Order of St. Michael and St. George, the Coronation medal of His Majesty King George V and any other medal, honor or distinction conferred on me by His Majesty's Government of which it is possible to divest myself."

By now he was sinking beyond pessimism into despair. In his arrogance he believed that the British Government was scheming against him.

He now became adamant that he would return to Norway with Adler for a confrontation with the British Minister there. The plans for this trip were, as usual, bungled. When the two met at Stettinbahnhof on 31 January they found that their train would not in fact arrive in time for the connection with the ferry crossing the Baltic. They scrabbled back to the hotel. Just as well, the Germans informed him, since the packet was due to be intercepted by a British submarine.

He was still determined to go. On 1 February he wrote, "after a hardly spent night—I got up at 5.30 and was got off at 6.50 for Sassnitz. Arrived there about 9 o'clock and to Monopol Hotel to wait for the boat. There I went over the pros and cons with Adler ... and finally, decided to return to Berlin instead of going on."

All this hemming and hawing was not cheap, especially for a man living in fancy hotels and refusing to accept handouts from his German hosts, and with a companion who had expensive, and peculiar, tastes.

Smarting and steaming still, Casement composed a massive letter, setting forth his grievances and recounting the Findlay affair. Copies were dispatched to representatives of countries not yet at war and to the Vatican, with the original shot off through the Hague to London, where he hoped it would do most good. Foreign Ministers looked on the letter with confused amusement; the Portuguese, uninterested, returned it. When the letter was—with malice aforethought—published in newspapers in England, it was commented on with derision. Scandinavia haw-hawed obscenely.

Casement took refuge in a sanatorium at Grünewald, in Bavaria, more deeply disturbed than he had ever been. Over the next twelve months he would suffer from chronic acute depression and was—obviously—mentally unstable, to judge by the letters he wrote during this time.

The last entry in his Berlin Diary is 11 February 1915, and thus the observer is saved a year's tedium. In March of 1916 he will begin again, however, with a vengeance.

4

Casement was down with fever, extreme depression, physical exhaustion, intestinal symptoms—the usual list of complaints, a wide range of ailments physical and psychological which were the legacy of the tropics. Malaria affected both the body and brain, a "maddeningly intermittent dislocation," in Henry Morton Stanley's words.

The number of Irish POWs at Limburg had meanwhile climbed to 2,500. Most of these men had few notions about and little interest in Irish Nationalism. They were in the British Army and they had been fighting a war against the enemy, the German Nation It is reported that when Casement had announced to them that Britain was nearly beaten, he was attacked by several Munster Fusiliers and even struck by a Sergeant Major. Rescued by sentries, he had made his way out followed by boos and hisses. Recruiting was not easy in Germany. But Redmond in Ireland, on the other hand, was doing well in his recruitment efforts. The *Times* had reported that "from the ranks of the

Irish Volunteers alone, 16,000 recruits have come forward since the war broke out." Added to this were tens of thousands of Irish recruited in Britain, Canada, New Zealand and Australia. At least 140,000 Irish were fighting in the Great War by now.

Casement had recruited five rather shifty characters.

He tried to convince himself—and perhaps loyal "readers" of his diaries from the German Secret Service—that he was psychologically and politically sane. From the Berlin Diary, before he clammed up: "I believe Germany will achieve a successful peace as against France and Russia, unless Italy takes the field for the 'Allies' (with Rumania possibly too) … I agree with von Hindenburg that the nation with the best nerves will win. That nation is Germany. Her greatest resource is that her people are one and united and march, fight and die as one man—prince, Herr and peasant. I believe with the Chancellor that 'Germany is unconquerable.'"

But Casement was giving vent to negative feelings, too—especially since the German Foreign Office was trying to dampen his fulminations against the Minister in Christiania, the nefarious Findlay. "I have caught the British Government in *flagrante delicto*," he wrote, "and with all the difficulties put in my way by this stupid, pig-headed German Government and their wretchedly run Foreign Office.… It is almost impossible to have true dealings with them. You never know their minds—save that if there is a wrong way to tackle a problem, they are likely to choose it."

Why not return to America? That was a solution—and one which the Germans seemed to agree with, to get him off their hands. But the problem was to reach America safe and sound. "I told von Wedel last night that were I sure of getting over, I should return to the USA, but the risks are too great. And yet, I know not what to do. To stay in Berlin, or Germany, idle, inactive and with the huge disappointment of the Irish Brigade failure staring me in the face and with no hope for further action by the German Government anent Ireland—is a policy of despair."

Casement certainly received some kind of medical or psychiatric treatment in the sanatorium in Grünewald. The place was not designed simply for a "rest cure." Various methods of treatment for depression and paranoia were known at that time—and had been developed to a state of a fine art in German asylums—but the record is dumb on this score.

When Casement had returned from the abortive trip to Sassnitz, he mentioned burning *secret documents* which the German Foreign Office was anxious to expropriate. The three armed "detectives" that accompanied him he believed to be secret police agents.

The fact of the ongoing war and the terrifying casualties, the convulsions of the civilized world, seemed to escape him. He was the Lone Hero fighting against the Evil Empire. "To go out single-handed to thus challenge the mightiest Government in the world and to charge them publicly with infamous conspiracy through their accredited representative is a desperate act. I have no money—no friends—no support—no Government save that of the One bent on destroying me, to appeal to. They are all-potent and will not sacrifice Findlay without a fight and in that they must win."

Then again, the sanatorium in Grünewald was more than a hospital for the disturbed, it represented a refuge for a person with dwindling resources.

Meanwhile the British were experiencing heavy losses in France and in the Dardanelles where men and ships were being wantonly obliterated. They badly needed recruits for the slaughter—but the whole Ulster Division of the Regular British Army, a force of 20,000, remained in Ireland along with the 80,000 men of Carson's Ulster Volunteers. Ireland, in spite of the catastrophic war, was still considered untrustworthy. Keeping world opinion favorable to Britain—especially in the US—remained of great importance, especially since Britain wanted to receive aid. From Washington, Sir Cecil Spring Rice, the Minister there, urged that "no action should be taken in England which would cause a strong Anti-British sentiment among the Irish here." Not only the Irish-Americans but the German-Americans were against the war and American involvement in what they still saw as a purely European conflict.

Arthur Griffith, Bulmer Hobson and Eoin MacNeill, the "Professor" who was Chief of Staff of the Volunteer forces, were all against an uprising at this time; but from 1914 the members of the Supreme Council of the Irish Republican Brotherhood were preparing for armed rebellion in 1916. They wanted the rebellion to appear a *defensive* action, to avoid accusations of attacking the bleeding lion. The Supreme Council included MacDermott, Pearse, Plunkett, Clarke, all fanatically pro-revolt; they ignored the opposition as they made their plans. Anti-British feelings were growing throughout Ireland with rumors that Irish troops in France were being needlessly sent to slaughter. The numbers of Irish recruits in 1915 fell off sharply. Crises were occurring almost daily. On 7 May the *Lusitania* was sunk. In May Asquith formed a new Coalition Government—marking the death of the Home Rule Bill.

Then in July 1915 Jeremiah O'Donavan Rossa died in the US. Rossa had founded the Phoenix Club in 1856 and had taken part in the rebellion of

1867. His body was to be returned for burial in Ireland, in the Glasnevin Cemetery. The funeral would be another great event for the nation. The I.R.B. and the Clan na Gael wanted a demonstration of solidarity. The British Army, deciding to avoid any clash, withdrew and left Dublin in the hands of the Irish Volunteers, who marched through the city with hordes of supporters. This spectacular event was capped by the funeral oration by Padraic Pearse who called, indirectly, for revolt. "Ireland unfree shall never be at peace!" he intoned.

Soon there was talk of conscription. Suddenly thousands of young Irishmen of draft age fled overseas to escape the draft. There were riots at the Liverpool docks where they embarked. English mobs taunted the Irish "traitors." Then, the emigration wave petered out. However, Irish feelings of resentment against the British, and the "British War" grew. There was incessant, intense, talk of revolt. Everyone expected it. The Irish Women's Council was preparing its members to send semaphore signals and to help out when the troubles began. Countess Markievicz's Irish National Boy Scouts were sworn never to join the British Army. The boys were trained to spy, signal and to carry dispatches in the coming struggle. One month after Rossa's funeral many organizations, having seen the evidence of their own numbers and the reticence of the British, were urging open rebellion.

5

Casement had been ill for a long time. He diagnosed himself as suffering from mental and physical exhaustion, but the strains he had undergone during the past years had undermined not only his physical wellbeing but his will. He stayed on at the Grünewald sanatorium (where he was registered as Mr. Hammond of New York) week after week. The patient himself realized his state of decomposition. Hyam theorizes that "The strain of concealment, especially when everyone regarded him as a person of unimpeachable integrity, was severe enough to produce a gradual disintegration of personality. By his late forties, Casement was probably a manic-depressive and prone to sporadic breakdown." However, here again we are faced with labels.

Casement *was* being threatened during his long stay in Germany. The Findlay case apart, he was attacked in the British press, had been criticized and abandoned by his friends and colleagues, and most certainly was being closely watched by the secret police in Berlin. The self-conscious complete sentences, the sentiments and painful rhetoric of his Berlin Diaries prove that he was unsure of himself in his present situation.

Casement's diary tells us nothing about his medical treatment, about German life in general. He does not describe his environment, the sensory aspects of his life. There are minimal details about constipation or sleep habits, fever, impotence, symptoms of any sort. It is as if he has died, without the shorthand notes on boys, his Xs. There are no real "persons" in his Berlin diaries except himself. The diaries do not include information about Berlin or Munich, a shocking vacuum considering the importance of both cities. Munich especially, where Casement spent so much time, is hardly mentioned. Both Berlin and Munich had been for at least twenty years in a period of unparalleled artistic and intellectual ferment. The plastic arts were revolutionary, showings were exciting cultural happenings; innovative and iconoclastic painters were at work. In Munich there were exciting ideas at work, and magazines and periodicals to publicize them. The sciences were respected modes of transformation, the social sciences as well as physics and applied technology. Rilke, Wedekind and Thomas and Heinrich Mann were fascinated visitors to Munich, which was rebellious both intellectually and artistically. You would never know this from Casement's diaries, or his reported conversations. He never cracks a smile, analyzes life or his part in it; his diaries are dreadful without the sexual asides.

It is tempting, and perhaps unfair, to compare the jottings of other diarists (and there were lots of them) writing at approximately the same time. Kafka in Zurich, for example, lists what he saw (not just well-organized garden plots): after breakfast, the cathedral, the swimming pool (men only), a concert by the Officers' Touring Club, then lunch—pea soup, beans with baked potatoes, dessert, sterilized wine (since the Swiss water is undrinkable). As for the sanatoria—German—Kafka spent time in a natural therapy institution in the Harz Mountains, about the same time that Casement was returning from his second investigative trip to the Putumayo. Nudism, special diet, open-air activities, "waters." Kafka felt nervous with so much nudity—naked sports, naked meals, naked exercises, naked sleeping; naked people approaching silently, naked old men leaping over haystacks. Not particularly delightful. Embarrassed, he kept his swimming trunks on and became known as "the man in the swimming trunks." As for the doctor: "affected, insane, tearful, jovial laughter"—in spite of his grave face. His advice to Kafka is Germanic, "don't eat fruit—but you can ignore this prohibition if you like; do certain erotic exercises (but not masturbation) to make the sexual organ grow; take atmospheric baths at night but avoid moonglow which is injurious." Still, a sanatorium was a good place to meet girls.

Casement was seriously ill and suicidal, However, he recovered somewhat in Munich, where St. John Gaffney, the US Consul-General, looked out for him. Casement says, "I stopped the diary when it became clear that I was being played with, fooled, and used by a most selfish and unscrupulous government for its own sole petty interests." A more logical reason, for this incorrigible record keeper, was that he was psychologically disturbed. When in March 1916 he began to make entries again after this long hiatus, he is feeling better and is now committed to his task of heading off the Irish Rebellion, having "lost all faith in its purpose and hope of success."

"[M]y hope to find the Irish soldiers willing to enroll in an Irish Brigade must be given up," he wrote in disgust. "They are mercenaries pure and simple and even had I the means to bribe them I should not attempt to do so." After months of propagandizing there were still only fifty-one recruits to the Irish Brigade. The Germans refused to publish the treaty signed by Casement and the German representatives until the number of recruits reached two hundred. There remained faint prospects for any additional conscripts. Father Nicholson, obviously a German agent, had antagonized the Irish POWs. When he was saying Mass, they refused to attend. Rations had also been cut for the men at Limburg, after the last German offensive failed: they believed they were being punished for not joining the Brigade. In these perplexing conditions, Joseph Plunkett suddenly arrived in Berlin, announcing that plans were underway for the uprising. The Irish people were ready, he said, but they needed arms and German officers to help them. Would they be ready in time?

Plunkett was enthusiastic, young but obviously in poor health—perhaps dying—and impossibly romantic. The Germans mistrusted such men who were blind to fact. It was risky indeed to entrust a revolt to such people, even while they encouraged that revolt. Casement tried arguing with Plunkett that it was not the time to act, that rebellion—even with the doubtful help of the Germans—was doomed to failure.

"If you do it," he told him, "if you are bent on this act of idiocy, I will come and join you (if the Germans will send me over) and I stand and fall beside you. Only I deprecate it wholly and regard it as the wildest form of boyish folly."

Plunkett, undeterred, carried the treaty with him to Switzerland, hidden in a hollow walking stick. From there he went home.

Casement was part of the general lunacy. "[I]t would be a fight—an act, a deed—and not talk, talk, talk," he wrote. "I, who have always stood for action (but not this action and not in these circumstances) could not stay in safety in this land while those in Ireland who have cherished a manly soul were laying down their lives for an ideal." Another passage for posterity. In other parts of his diary he is more straightforward: "If I learn that neither von Jagow or von Wedel can see me I shall ask for my passport." "In my heart I am sorry I came." Then, the political digs: "England supplies all the necessaries—ships and brains—Germany thinks to do it by ships alone, and without brains."

Smart green uniforms had been issued for the Brigade, meanwhile, and the men were transferred to a section of the camp near the Russian barracks. The Russians, seeing these well-fed men in new uniforms, were incensed. Fights broke out, which did not surprise Casement, who considered many of the Brigade members to be "riffraff and drunks." To avoid any more disruption of camp discipline, the Brigade was then transferred to Wunsdorf near Berlin, then in November to Zossen where they lived in normal military barracks and were no longer classed as prisoners.

Adler remains in the background. Singleton-Gates fantasizes this little speech of Casement to his boyfriend: "You are fearfully wasteful of money, my dear faithful old Adler, much more so than I am—because you buy things you don't need at all—like that raincoat and those gloves. I have no gloves, and you have about six pairs! and your face and complexion bloom! and God knows what! All you need is some healthy good work to keep your mind occupied, and the sooner this damned Findlay scoundrel and his infernal mentor, Grey, are polished off and done with the better."

"I am not sure of Adler!" he writes, mysteriously. "His air and manner have greatly changed since he came back—or rather since he was away ... he sticks at nothing—he would roll these god-damned Germans up!" Adler had been held up by the Germans at Sassnitz, stripped and searched, and his gold coins had been replaced by paper money, infuriating him.

Adler did not mend his ways. Berlin was a superb place for him to be, and he had a source of income. At long last, however, Casement out of desperation got him passage back to the United States, where he would act as an "agent." He thus vanishes—for a moment.

Adler in the United States was given the brush-off when he tried to get work as a German agent. The Irish project was beginning to seem both hopeless and a waste of effort. "It appears doubtful whether the continuation of the propaganda among the Irish prisoners of war is worth while," Captain Nadolny of the German General Headquarters Political Division noted. Finding no takers in Washington, Adler went to New York. He called on John Devoy, at Clan headquarters. The Irishman was taken aback by this creature. Devoy had been enraged and disgusted by the endless letters from Casement in Berlin, and now this "agent" of all things! However, the man—so to speak—might prove useful, in spite of his looks, just as he had proved useful before.

6

It had been decided to send an experienced military man out to Germany to help with the training of the Irish Brigade. Robert Monteith was a natural choice for the job. He had an anti-British record and had been working with the local Volunteers in Limerick. Devoy arranged for Monteith to come to the US, followed by his family. From the US he would have to make his way to Germany, not an easy matter since he was unable to obtain an American passport. One answer would be to stow away on board a ship bound for a neutral country bordering Germany.

That was where Adler came in. He immediately came up with a solution. He would book passage to Copenhagen in his own name, and Monteith would hide under his bunk during the passage. It would, he said, be easy for Monteith to get off the ship without a passport, since the port would be neutral. If there was any trouble, money would fix it.

Monteith and Christensen would leave from Hoboken, New Jersey, on the *SS United States*, bound for Copenhagen and scheduled to stop at only neutral ports. On 7 November Monteith met Adler on the docks and, with the Norwegian carrying his bags, they boarded the ship. Monteith hid under the bunk of the tiny cabin, coming out occasionally to exercise and use the toilet. On the eighth day out they were taken in charge by a British cruiser.

The British put a prize crew on board and they were escorted to Kirkwall in the Orkneys where the passengers and crew were taken off for questioning. Monteith remained in hiding, with Christensen supplying him with food and water. The British detained several passengers, German citizens, considered "spies." Then after five days the ship was allowed to continue. Two days later they entered the port of Christiania. Here it suddenly turned out that passengers would have to show their passports and landing papers. Christensen could be no help—and almost seemed willing to abandon Monteith who managed, by pretending to be drunk, to stumble through the officials and reach shore.

They stayed at the familiar Grand Hotel. Here the suspicious manager immediately went to the police and reported a foreigner, possibly an illegal immigrant, who had "misplaced" his documents and was staying at his hotel. Adler got wind of this somehow—he was out and heard rumors; Christiania was like a small town. He helped Monteith slip away from the hotel. The two men reached Adler's home; his father had tickets for them on the train to Copenhagen the next day.

After maneuvering past police and avoiding any passport check, Adler and Monteith finally reached Copenhagen where they visited the German Legation. The clerk there said they had no passport for Monteith. However, the guards at the German border were expecting them. They left on the packet at ten in the morning, and immediately a British submarine surfaced near them. The passengers were terrified, but the vessel soon submerged and they reached the port of Warnemunde in the afternoon. Here they passed through customs at once, just in time to catch the train for Berlin.

In Berlin, Adler disappeared.

7

In Munich Casement had been trying to get well. He was helped by Dr. Charles Curran, an Irish-American physician living in Munich who had befriended him. Casement made holiday visits to Ammer See with Dr. Curran and his family, even kept rooms at a country inn there for the weekends. Curran got in touch with St. John Gaffney, the American consul in Munich, in an attempt—if need be in a "neutral" American warship—to get Casement to the United States. Casement himself, in a letter to Ed Morel (who was now being attacked himself as a pacifist) expressed his wish to leave while he still had a little money left—about 3000 marks at writing; perhaps he might travel via Sweden. Von Wedel, as usual, was optimistic—but did nothing to help. As his breakdown gradually intensified Casement eventually gave up all plans for escape. The only escape was the sanatorium in Munich and a kind of living death.

In November 1915, while Casement was ticking off the days in silence, Robert Monteith was on his way from New York to take charge of training the Irish Brigade, such as it was.

General von Lowenfeld was horrified of giving Irish drunks and undisciplined soldiers rifles. Casement remarked, in writing, that perhaps after all they could be sent to fight with the Turks in Syria, if Enver Pasha would accept them.

8

Monteith, unlike Casement, was an experienced organizer. He had worked as a clerk in the Ordinance Department in Dublin as well as with the Irish Volunteers. He was enthusiastic about recruiting more men, or perhaps getting officers in through Scandinavia; that he himself had arrived safely was proof it could be done. Christensen, on his way back to New York, was the man to put together such a plan. Monteith was anxious to discuss these matters with Casement, but learned from von Wedel that he was ill in Munich. He took the train as soon as he could.

In Munich Monteith arrived at the Grünewald sanatorium to find Casement in a shocking state, physically and psychologically. "He presented a death-like appearance," Monteith wrote. "His bronzed face had turned ashen color, his features were pinched and haggard and he lay so still that his breathing was scarcely perceptible.... His mood was despondent and, strange for him, almost bitter." Casement had him read some letters that had come from America, to demonstrate what a false position he was in. "His strong, independent methods were evidently disapproved by the writers in the United States [particularly Devoy] and they were at no pains to disguise the fact." There was also the problem of money. The Germans continued to offer. He continued to refuse. There was also the matter of outright enemies abroad. "He knew that his work had been hampered by letters written to the German Foreign Office from apparently authoritative sources in the United States. Some of these letters insinuated that he was not a fitting representative of the Irish people, and these aspersions, he was well aware, had caused the Germans some misgivings."

In Casement's dealings with the Germans he had fooled himself, convinced that they were double-dealers but stupid. They were not stupid, and knew who they were dealing with. They had massive files on him, with information on his past, on his present condition, reports from various sources including the "unreliable" Adler Christensen. His movements had been noted, and his contacts. He lived in a vivid Berlin, in an aggressively liberalized Munich; if he was followed—and most certainly he was—they knew his tastes. Adler himself was enough accusation. In general, Sir Roger Casement was more of an embarrassment than an asset.

Monteith was another type entirely. It was immediately obvious that he was a man who could be trusted.

9

Casement in Germany was living in one of the most sexually liberalized nations in the world, as he no doubt realized. In Bavaria—where he spent a great deal of his time, in and out of the sanatorium—there was a long tradition of sexual freedom. In 1813 the State, influenced by the French Revolution and the supreme practicality of the Napoleonic Code, abolished the laws criminalizing homosexual acts between consenting adults. Although in 1871, with the unification of Germany, the old criminal law, the infamous Paragraph 175, came into effect for the whole nation, there was a tradition, especially in the cities, of flagrant homosexuality. Dr. Magnus Hirschfeld, only four years younger than Casement, unsuccessfully petitioned the Reichstag in 1897 for repeal of Paragraph 175. The next year, with the support of major intellectuals, he petitioned again, with the same result. Germany was the home of the "scientification" of homosexuality. Here sexologists were analyzing homosexuals, taking measurements, discussing habits, classifying, devising labels. The concept of homosexuals as "decadents" was not commonly accepted by German scientists. Accusations of homosexuality in the nobility or higher echelons of society could still, however, cause scandal, much in the style of the Wilde trials.

The major scandal caused by the revelations in 1902 of Alfred Krupp's orgies with young men on the island of Capri—a notorious nest of perverts—had repercussions high and low. Kaiser Wilhelm II was a firm friend of Krupp, the richest man in Germany. The press, the public, the Social Democrats—who had ironically been in favor of the repeal of Paragraph 175—seemed bent on destroying Krupp, if not his companies, the largest armament producers in Germany. Hounded by the public, his reputation ruined, his family devastated, Krupp finally committed suicide—a popular escape of homosexuals in Germany. The Kaiser stood behind him, even in death, but other scandals were to follow. Accusations of homosexuality became a common political tactic used to destroy opponents. The inner circle of the Kaiser was even affected. In 1905 a major scandal broke, centering on several of the Kaiser's friends, especially his "special" friend Prince Phillip zu Eulenburg, a charming and accomplished man who had been intimate with Wilhelm since the mid-80s, before he became Emperor. In 1905, Friedrich von Holstein, emotionally unstable, was fired as the Kaiser's First Counselor. Since the Kaiser had happened to have been lunching with Eulenburg on the day of his dismissal, von Holstein convinced himself that Eulenburg was the person behind his dismissal. He mounted an attack of revenge, encouraging a popular journalist, Maximilian Harden, to launch a series of articles in his newspaper, *Die Zukunft*, against the "leader of a sinister and effeminate camarilla"—Eulenburg—responsible for an unhealthy influence on the Kaiser, and encouraging him to be soft on France. Harden linked Eulenburg with Kuno Count von Moltke, military commandant of Berlin, and implied they were having a homosexual affair. In 1907 Harden also named three of the Kaiser's aides-de-camp as known homosexuals. The Kaiser, horrified by the accusations and the publicity, insisted that von Moltke and several others resign their commissions; he also dismissed Eulenburg from the diplomatic service. In the ensuing libel case of *Moltke vs Harden*, it was obvious that Eulenburg was the one on trial. The newspapers—national and international—had a field day. Harden was acquitted. Von Moltke was furious. The verdict was immediately overturned. A new trial was ordered, during which Harden was found guilty. He spent four months in prison; on being freed, he went back to his old accusations against Eulenburg. By this time, Eulenburg was sickening. He collapsed several times, as witnesses—some of whom he hadn't seen for twenty-five years—came forward with "perfect memories" of seductions or near-seductions; others, hired criminals, gave disgusting false testimony. But the trial was never concluded, dragging on interminably. Twenty years later the Kaiser told Eulenburg's son that he believed that the Prince had been absolutely innocent. That was not much help. Eulenburg's life had been ruined.

In Germany, after these scandals, homosexuals went on with their lives, perhaps more discretely; Paragraph 175 remained on the books, and individuals could be charged with "unnatural sexual acts"—yet Germany continued to be the home of a very visible and active homosexual community. The most organized gay community in the world, thanks to the efforts of many devoted men like Hirschfeld.

10

Casement would never, considering his background, have "come out." People rarely did, because they couldn't. Those who did were stigmatized. To do so was to label yourself, and to become classed with a sub-culture, to name yourself a "freak," which was a depressing idea. This would mean, as Foucault once pointed out, to assume that one had a fixed sexual identity that was worth admitting in public. It was hard enough to admit it to yourself, and enjoy the risks of criminality, the flavor. Not every male who has sex—even promiscuous sex—with other males is homosexual per se. "Homosexual" or "gay" like "pervert" or "invert" are simply words. Before the politicization of sexuality, it was possible to have a gratifying sex life outside the normal, without classifying it. By naming yourself you automatically descend, as Nietzsche said, "into the depths of existence with a string of curious questions on [your] lips. Why am I alive? Why do I suffer from being what I am?" The man who asks such questions "observes that nobody tortures himself in the same way." The individual could not, and should not, Nietzsche said, "be made accountable for his nature, nor for his motives, nor for his actions, nor for the effects he produces."

Casement was not an intellectual. He did not belong to an "advanced" group of political or social thinkers. If Casement even vaguely realized the changes that had been steadily eroding social mores toward the end of the century he gave no indication. The frankness of Bloomsbury would have appalled him. He would have been grossly offended to receive a letter such as that written by Vanessa Bell to Maynard Keynes at Asheham House: "Did you have a pleasant afternoon buggering one or more of the young men we left for you? It must have been delicious out on the downs in the afternoon sun.... I imagine you, however, with your bare limbs entwined ... and all the ecstatic preliminaries of sucking.... How divine it must have been."

Casement was caught in the web of the nineteenth century, as described by Zeldin, "when homosexual activity was classified no longer just as a sin, but as either a disease, or a sign of defective upbringing, or the result of a genetic disposition. Until then, the men who had visited London's transvestite 'molly-houses', which flourished in the eighteenth century, were not considered to be homosexuals, any more than are Tahitian men who use the male prostitute to be found in every village. The word homosexual was invented only in 1869 (when Freud was thirteen years old) by the Viennese writer Benkert, in the hope of avoiding persecution, by showing that homosexuals constituted a 'third sex' independently of their will, and that they could not therefore be accused of vice or crime. [H]itherto, the names by which thy were known had been jocular, not medical classifications, and the word 'gay' revives that tradition.... This segregation created enormous anxiety...." Casement realized he was not alone, and this of course helped him—but not in view of the massive Social cliffside of Victorian morality—where the Enemy still lived.

11

The British Empire was built by, and on, individuals with unusual sexual habits.

The military was peppered with young men who "went out" to Africa, Ceylon, Burma, Australia, with lust in their hearts as well as patriotism. One miraculous surviving record is of Captain Kenneth Searight. Biographers of E.M. Forster mention an encounter on shipboard with this very frank and enthusiastic pederast. Forster and G. Lowes Dickinson, with whom he was traveling to India, had fascinating conversations with Searight, who appears to have recognized them immediately as queer. (This was 1912—when Casement was on his way home from the Putumayo.) Later, Forster and "Goldie" stayed with Searight in Peshawar, where they were treated to a wild party with the Captain, in "ripping" form, and his young colleagues. The entertaining young Captain was writing a kind of autobiography, part of which he showed Forster. Over the next five years it had expanded considerably, from a long erotic poem, to include pornographic stories of boys and illustrations (nude photographs). The manuscript contains an index with a table listing Searight's sexual partners from 1897 to 1917, including name, age, place of encounter, year, race, act(s) performed, all coded by clever pictograms. Mutual anal intercourse was his favorite, but he enjoyed fellatio, analingus and other variations. Searight traveled a lot, especially through the Punjab and Rajasthan; later he was transferred to Bangalore, where his sex life really took off. He records eleven young British soldiers as sexual partners, "Better than all eastern catamites," and his vacations in Egypt, Italy and London were full of "white" contacts which he seemed to prefer to Indians. By miracle, his manuscript survived the flames, and was later picked up in a remainder stall in Charing Cross Road. *Paidikion* is quoted by Hyam, but the manuscript is now in a private collection.

India and other far-flung colonies of the British Empire were scenes where young men with "different" sexual tastes could satisfy their cravings. The frankness with which Searight—and Forster and G. Lowes Dickinson—discussed pederasty was perhaps typical of he times among university educated men. When one "knew" them anything could be discussed—even with a notorious closet case such as Forster but also with his later friend T. E. Lawrence. The military was full of men who had joined the service with an often admitted desire for the companionship of others of the same sex, and for the erotic opportunities the military afforded. Searight's sexual experiences

abroad—even when he was the commanding officer of one of his sexual partners—speak for themselves. The British Empire was an empire of enhanced
sexuality. Casement had enjoyed at an early age—when he went out to West
Africa as purser for the Elder Dempster Line—a liberated lifestyle, "away
from home." He doubtless had been active sexually in Ireland, and England,
before sailing. Shipboard, the Congo frontier, the freedom of all-male society
would have provided heightened excitement and opportunities for sex. There
is no evidence that he used his position as British consular official, later, to
procure favors—there was no reason to, sex was so available, and so cheap.
Again, Casement's Black Diaries are an invaluable record, but quite different
from Searight's *Paidikion.*

12

Casement was not far wrong when he concluded that the Germans were treating him with contempt. Not only in the United States but also in Germany,
Government officials—among them von Wedel—ridiculed the famous Irish
"traitor." This opinion of Casement could have had deplorable consequences
in jeopardizing his authority as the representative of the Clan in Germany. To
counter any such negative assessment of Casement, Devoy—himself a none
too enthusiastic supporter of Sir Roger—issued a statement on 12 November
1915: "In the name of the Irish Nationalist leaders in America, of whom
Casement is still the accredited envoy," it began, strangely, and went on: "we
have the fullest confidence in Sir Roger Casement." If this tended to enliven
Casement's prestige it did nothing to change the view of the German military
that the Irish Brigade was a joke. When no recognition came through for his
"boys" and Casement suggested that the force (of fifty men?) be sent to Syria
and placed at the disposal of Enver Pasha, the Germans (and Devoy) were
astounded and amused. "What does Turkey have to do with the Irish?" it was
laughingly asked. In fairness to Casement, it was later suggested that he may
simply have wanted to keep the Brigade out of a hopeless fight at home.

In spite of the fumblings of the "accredited envoy" of the Clan, Monteith—a well-trained and sensible man who inspired trust—did manage to get
a training program underway, using real arms.

13

In December Casement was in Zossen with Monteith and the Brigade but
almost immediately went off for another breakdown to Munich, where his

"nerve cure" looked to last some time. St. John Gaffney was shocked by the man's state; he wanted him sent to the United States at once—but how could he go (and he was willing to), when the British were out to get him? Casement buried himself in bed. Then, on 6 March he got a note from Monteith, enclosing the following cable of 17 February from the German Ambassador in Washington:

> *The Irish leader, John Devoy, informs me that rising is to begin in Ireland on Easter Saturday. Please send arms to arrive at Limerick west coast of Ireland between Good Friday and Easter Saturday. To put off longer is impossible. Let me know if help may be expected from Germany.*

Plans were formulated at once by the General Staff. On 1 March 1916, they sent a message to the Foreign Office in Berlin, to be forwarded in code to the German Ambassador in Washington:

> *Between 20th and 23rd April in the evening, 2 or 3 trawlers will be able to deliver about 20,000 rifles and 10 machine guns, together with ammunition as well as explosives, near Fenit Pier in Tralee Bay. Irish pilot boat will have to expect vessels, before dusk sets in, north of the island of Inishtooskert, at the entrance of Tralee Bay and, at short intervals, to show two green lights close together. Delivery will have to be carried out in a few hours. Please wire whether through Devoy necessary steps can be secretly taken in Ireland. Success only possible if no effort spared.*

The message was signed by Nadolny.

Bernstorff duly consulted with Devoy and on March 12 advised the General Staff that necessary steps should be made to carry out the plan. Details were sent by courier to Ireland.

Nadolny, disregarding any involvement of Casement in all this, contacted Monteith at once. They discussed the dispatch of rifles, an experienced gun crew, German officers, machine guns, ammunition and supplies to reach Fenit, County Kerry, in time for the Irish Uprising. Lieutenant Frey mentioned the possibility of sending as many as 200,000 rifles and large supplies of ammunition. The German Admiralty then came into play. Monteith met with officials there and plans for the shipment by trawler were discussed. Three naval officers were present at this time. The problem, Monteith insisted, was getting the arms on shore. Captain von Haugwitz, a representative of the General Staff, instructed that a pilot be waiting from 10 p.m. till dawn at the north of Inishtooskert Island from the night of 20 April (Thursday) until 23 April (Sunday). He would signal with two green lights shown at intervals.

Having gone through these preliminaries, Monteith took the train for Munich. Casement was resentful at not being previously informed of the plans; but he was too ill, at any rate, to move. He was negative—a very sane reaction—about the negotiations.

"They lie always.... If they promise to give us 200,000 rifles it is not to help us, rest assured of that ... they have no feeling about Ireland at all ... only what ends of their own they are after. However, as they offer us this large armament we should be fools not to take it if we can get it. Let us get what we can."

But in Berlin the Foreign Office, the General Staff and the Admiralty differed. The General Staff believed that a large-scale operation in Ireland would be carried out and that it would change the course of the war. A small body of German troops, along with the Irish Brigade, would be sent to help the 300,000 Irish fighters, supplied with massive amounts of arms to ensure success.

Faced with such a threat, the British would be forced to send at least half a million troops to put down the revolt, troops they could hardly spare from the fighting in France. This would give Germany the edge in the war on the Continent, and bring about their victory.

This plan was dropped at once, however, considered by the General Staff as too expensive in terms of men and materiel and too risky. The Irish Revolutionary Directory in the United States appeared confused, not to say unstable, and—typically—romantic. However, a scaled down commitment could still bring about a demoralization of Britain and strengthen pro-Irish and pro-German sentiments in America.

Thus it was decided that no German officers at all would be sent to help the Irish troops and that only some 20,000 rifles (from those captured from the Russians at Tannenberg) would be offered. Perhaps a few machine guns. Two trawlers would not be necessary. A good size steamer—and one was available—could be disguised as a neutral (Norwegian) merchantman and carry the supplies to Ireland. Casement and the others could go along.

It was obvious that getting a ship through the British blockade, not to mention reaching the pier at Tralee and unloading the arms without being detected by the British Army, was highly improbable.

14

Twenty thousand rifles were certainly inadequate. Devoy estimated that he had 40,000 Irish Volunteers and only 10,000 rifles (other estimates were closer to 16,000 men and about 6,000 rifles). At any rate, the arms were badly needed.

Had the Germans been deliberately leading the Irish leaders along, with no intention of adequately supporting them? Casement thought so, and despaired. With the conviction that if he managed to arrive before Easter Sunday he might head off the rebellion, Casement wrote a letter to the Admiralty requesting to be sent by submarine with two Irishmen, O'Toole and John McGoey, to make arrangements in Dublin with the rebel leaders to receive the shipment of arms. "If I could get there, land in Ireland before this damned ship and her guns arrive, I might stop the whole dreadful thing. It is for this I still pray, but I am so sick and utterly wretched."

When one considers the condition of Europe in the course of the Great War, with hundreds of thousands of men—among them large numbers of Irish—being slaughtered regularly on the shifting battlefields of France, the suffering of a world at war and the murder of civilization, Casement's attitudes seem outlandishly egoistic. His attitudes of "sympathy" and pity for his "boys" in the Brigade, his worries about the outcome of the rising in Ireland, his continuing rage against the British Foreign Office, and his complaints of sickness and exhaustion—all this seems unrealistic, perhaps even superficial.

The Germans vetoed Casement's departure as requested. They agreed to let McGoey out on 19 March, however. Before McGoey left Casement ordered him to inform the leaders that inadequate supplies were being sent. In view of this they should cancel the uprising. He impressed on McGoey that the Germans were playing games with the Irish.

After McGoey left, Casement had an acrimonious confrontation with Admiralty officials, in which he was accused of trying to derail the uprising. He answered, roughly, that they were acting in bad faith. Both parties were correct.

Then a coded message came through via Switzerland for Sir Roger Casement, stating that the insurrection was scheduled for the evening of Easter Sunday; that a large consignment of arms to be brought into Tralee Bay must arrive there not later than the dawn of Easter Saturday; that the involvement of German officers was imperative; that a German submarine would be needed in Dublin Harbor to prohibit British forces from landing.

Desperate to stop the uprising, Casement warned the Supreme Council of the Volunteers by cable and letter (the Germans withheld the letter until the evening of his departure, when it would be too late to do any good). Then, at the last minute, the Germans decided not to send the Irish Brigade. Then they also canceled plans to send Casement, Monteith and Sergeant Bailey of the Irish Brigade on the arms ship. Instead they would be sent by submarine. This was to ensure that Casement would not try to call off the uprising. Captain Spindler, who was to have taken the Irishmen on the *Aud*, the supply ship, had already been given orders: "It is herewith brought to your attention that Headquarters believe it imperative that the Irish are put ashore at the last possible moment."

Journey into Night

1

Captain Spindler was in charge of the *Aud*. He left Berlin with his orders. His ship had been fitted out especially for the mission, with secret compartments and a crew aware only that they were to be pretending to be on a Norwegian tramp steamer. There was no wireless on board, to avoid showing an incriminating antenna, meaning that the vessel would have no way to contact German headquarters. The *Aud* left Lubeck on Sunday 9 April. They would be at Inishtooskert before the 23rd if all went well. The crew was alerted to the need for secrecy; they "conditioned" the ship to appear a sloppy tub, and learned how to act like merchant seamen. All German equipment was to be stored away in case an enemy ship was sighted. The ship was also loaded with explosives, to be detonated if they were discovered.

While they got underway, Casement and Monteith were preparing to leave Berlin. It was a depressing farewell. Monteith believed that the Germans were getting rid of Casement and himself, along with Sgt Bailey (or Beverley, his alias)—and regretted that "in Sir Roger Casement the world loses one of her best and greatest men." He suggested that Sir Roger remain in Germany but Casement insisted on going in spite of his illness and exhaustion—he was always hopelessly tired. They were given the code for sending messages to Germany and were provided with sleeping-berth tickets on the train to Wilhelmshaven. At Wilhelmshaven they were taken out to the U-20 for the voyage to Ireland. The submarine was to rendezvous with the *Aud* at Inishtooskert between 20–23 April. There would be no landing before this; the mission would be called off if they could not arrive until after the 23rd. The captain of the U-20 was Walther Schwieger, who had sunk the *Lusitania*. This model U-boat was a marked improvement on the invention by John P.

Holland who had designed the submarine with the express purpose of destroying the English fleet. The U-20 submerged and began its voyage. In London, Captain Hall was informed that Casement was on his way. The British were also aware that a ship carrying arms for the rebels would be arriving at Tralee. The arms would be used in the insurrection set for 22 April.

On the second day out a mechanical failure forced the U-20 to put into Heligoland for repairs. Casement felt certain, now, that the Germans were delaying his return. Here, however, there was another submarine waiting, the U-19, a clone of the U-20. They made the transfer to the other vessel. During the wait, Monteith sprained his wrist practicing starting the outboard motor on the small boat they might have to use to get ashore in Ireland. They left in the early afternoon on a voyage that, according to the new captain, would take them five days. Casement was worried about Monteith being incapacitated by his badly swollen hand. On the way—the submarine traveled surface for most of the voyage—they suffered from the cramped quarters, the stinking air, the grimy blankets and inedible food. Casement, horribly seasick, stayed below, prostrate with nausea and becoming weaker hourly.

On the 17th, the seas grew difficult, as the U-19 drilled steadily through the waves. Casement was retching. The smells in the choked quarters were unbelievable.

By the time they reached the west coast of Ireland, however, the worst was over. The U-19 headed south and Casement, feeling more himself, began the familiar litany. He had no idea of conditions in Dublin, or whether they even needed the arms. It was a risky business, coming ashore, and riskier still landing arms or troops. There were only three of them. Even well-manned expeditions had failed.

Then the U-19 spotted the *Aud*. The ship was only two miles away, but Lieutenant Weisbach did not make contact, having no orders to do so. Casement was now more suspicious than ever of the German intentions. The U-19 passed the Shannon estuary and sighted the Loop Head Lighthouse. They were not far from Inishtooskert Island now—and a close watch would have to be placed in case of a British patrol. It was not until after 11 p.m. that the U-19 readied itself for the culmination of its mission.

Matters were ideal for the rendezvous in Tralee Bay. The moon was out. The sea was glass. They paused one mile northwest of Inishtooskert. There they expected to meet the *Aud* and the pilot boat.

But by that time the *Aud* was no longer there.

2

On the *Aud*, Captain Spindler's main concern had been to get through the British blockade. The weather was inclement, the ship slow and clumsy. Palm Sunday was coming up; he would have to pass the blockade by then, but if visibility remained good they might be spotted. The ship headed southwest, straight into a wall of dense fog. This was lucky. Shielded by fog they might slip through. Then, as if in answer to Spindler's worst fears, a little after 7:15 an enormous gray form appeared straight ahead of them. They veered to port and then saw that they had encountered a British cruiser, which maneuvered parallel to them and, reducing speed, observed them closely. Spindler ordered emergency tactics, the crew went about its business, looking very Norwegian and very trampish. For an hour, with their attention fading, the cruiser continued alongside the *Aud*, then changed course and disappeared. Spindler was astounded at his luck, even as the seas were beginning to rise and the wind reached force 6.

Spindler made for Rockall, west of the Scottish coast, a perilous sandbank uncharted as yet, where large numbers of ships had gone aground and sunk. Here, in spite of the dangers, he could get his bearings. The gale increased, driving the ship toward the reef at one extremity of the Rockall sandbanks. As they struggled against heavy seas, suddenly they were overtaken by another British cruiser, this one on patrol without lights. It passed, oblivious, or simply ignored the *Aud*. As they reached Rockall the crew members taking depth measurements started coming up with appalling variations. Then it began to hail. All at once the ship seemed to strike. No, it was not the reef—simply masses of sea water flooding in, choking the scuppers, making the ship impossible to handle in the heavy seas. When the water flowed out they steamed ahead, on their way to Tralee. It was miraculous that they had been overlooked again by the British Navy. They had broken through the blockade.

While Spindler was wrestling with these difficulties, making for Tralee with an easy margin of days, Captain Nodolny in Berlin was giving them up for lost. Bernstorff had sent them a cable on 15 April—it would arrive the 19th—stating that the arms would have to be delivered on the evening of 23 April, Easter Sunday. Since the *Aud* was without a wireless they could not be notified of the change in plans. Devoy was informed by the German Admiralty that matters were now out of their hands.

Ignored by the British Navy, the *Aud* continued rolling toward Tralee. British cruisers sighted them, but obviously did not think it worth their while to challenge the merchantman. The crew was growing edgy. Spindler kept them busy disguising the ship. On Thursday they were nearing the Irish coast, somewhat earlier than planned. Crew members got the packing away from the cargo, in readiness for off-loading once they reached their destination. They were messing up the sea with so much waste material dumped overboard. A passing motor launch seemed intrigued by the flotsam, but did not come closer than five miles. By noon the *Aud* was a few hours from Tralee. Winches and tackle were readied. Spindler was now planning how he would get away once he had left the arms at Fenit Pier. Fenit was only seven miles from Tralee. The alarm might be sounded and the British troops be on them in less than an hour. In the event that the *Aud* would have to be scuttled, he had heavy charges of explosives placed far forward.

Then Captain Spindler realized that he had made a mistake in his calculations: he was not at Tralee Bay at all, but at the Shannon estuary, with the Loop Head Lighthouse and signaling station. Keeping an unconcerned course, he passed near Loop Head in the afternoon, still believing that for some reason he had escaped notice.

But the signaling station had already notified Queenstown of the presence of an "unusual" vessel. (Admiral Bayly had been notified by Naval Intelligence on 14 April that a German ship had left on the 12th accompanied by two submarines, to arrive the 21st in time for the rising on the 22nd.) Two destroyers were sent out at once to intercept.

A little after 4 p.m. the *Aud* was nearing Inishtooskert. Spindler had expected that his appearance would have an effect, that the waiting pilot would be out to them at once. But there was no pilot cutter, and no submarine with the green flag, no man in a green jersey, nothing.

In fact, the pilot, Mort O'Leary, had been briefed in Tralee. He was told that the arms ship would not arrive until the night of the 23rd. He would show two green lights as a signal, and pilot the ship in. When, on his way down the bay, he spotted a two-master off Inishtooskert, he thought, What a crazy place for a ship to be, exactly where the arms boat is due in a few days, and why doesn't it enter the harbor? Anyway, the two-master was a large ship. The one they had led him to expect would be much smaller.

Spotted but unrecognized, Spindler sat nervously in the harbor.

Finally, after flashing the green light, with no response from shore, he steamed back to Inishtooskert in frustration. He had left before the rising of the moon.

3

They practiced loading the Mausers—anyway, Monteith and Sgt Bailey did; Casement was incapable of functioning. The sea was calm, a sheen over darkness, as they looked for the pilot. Finally the captain of the U-19 said that he could stay no longer; the Irishmen would have to reach shore in the small boat—but without the motor, since the noise would give them away. Monteith's hand was swollen, numb, clumsy. Casement had no idea of how to handle a boat, a pistol or any kind of arm. Bailey was a marionette. They got into the boat. There were three oars. Monteith and Bailey rowed; Casement tried to steer.

The U-19 submerged.

Drifting south, they were headed for the rocks. Near the beach the sea was rough, the surf hammering. Casement called out that they were almost there—he could see the foam of the waves on the beach. Monteith looked up. He saw a massive sheet of water behind Casement's head. It broke over the boat, knocking Casement and Bailey on top of Monteith. Another wave capsized the boat. Lifejackets saved them. With difficulty they pulled the boat back over. Casement struggled clumsily into it and held it steady while Monteith and Bailey boarded. The oars were safe in the oarlocks. They got underway again, pushed and spun by the rollers. Suddenly they stuck fast. Monteith freed an oar and tried to push them off, but was knocked overboard again. Luckily, when he came to the surface he still had the oar in his fist. Another wave forced them into deep water.

When they reached the shore they waded in. With water up to his waist, almost paralyzed with cold and pain, Monteith held the boat while Bailey carried the kits to shore. Casement, totally helpless, lay somewhere on the beach, perhaps drowning. It proved impossible for Monteith to scuttle the boat with his knife. A wave rammed the bow against his foot, wrenching his ankle; he gave up. He now made for Casement, who was half-conscious and babbling, half in and half out of the water, the surf washing over him.

Monteith dragged Casement to dry ground and tried to revive him, massaging his limbs. The man seemed delirious. Bailey looked on.

Later, in his persona of Irish Martyr, writing—of course—for what he thought was "posterity," Casement gives a different, disappointingly phony, picture of his arrival: "When I landed in Ireland that morning (about 3 a.m.), swamped and swimming ashore on an unknown strand, I was happy for the first time for over a year. Although I knew that this fate was waiting on me, I was for one brief spell happy and smiling once more. I cannot tell you what I felt. The sandhills were full of skylarks, rising in the dawn.... The first sound I heard through the surf was their song as I waded in through the breakers, and they kept rising all the time up to the old rath of Currshone, where I stayed and sent the others on, and all around were primroses and wild violets and the singing of the skylarks, and I was back in Ireland again."

Monteith and Bailey buried their equipment in the sand. It was impossibly risky to carry arms with them—they would have to return later and retrieve them. The three men slowly made their way inland. They tried cleaning up their soaked and mud-splattered clothes at a stream. Reaching a farmhouse a young servant girl, Mary Gorman of Knockenagh, up early as usual, spied them. Then they came to the ruins of a fort. It was useless carrying on with Casement, who was too exhausted to move. Monteith decided to leave him out of sight in the fort, while he and Bailey went to find a car.

Back on Banna Strand, a farmer, John McCarthy—who had curiously gone to visit a "holy well" at an incredibly early hour on this Good Friday, or who was out scouting for wreckage—came across a boat awash near the shore. He wrestled it in, along with three oars. He found a dagger in a sheath inside. Nearby, in a shallow excavation, there was a black metal box. The pitiful list of buried articles was:

Three Mauser automatic pistols
1,000 rounds of ammunition
Three lifebelts
A case containing field glasses
A map of Ireland in 28 sections
One Prayer Book (Catholic Piety) with the initials of the owner on the fly-leaf
A book, "a simple confession book" by Mother Mary Loylon
A book, *The Rubayat of Omar Khayyam*
A notebook with an electric light attached
Two Perlux flashlights
Two refills for above
A cleaning rod for pistols
One pair of Kruger cufflinks
One packet of German tobacco
A green flag

A German sausage (partly eaten)

4

The Royal Irish Constabulary at Ardfert Barracks was notified. Constable Reilly and Sgt Hearn went out to Brandon Well and McKenna Fort, to check on the suspicious findings. At the fort, among the furze and blackthorn, they discovered a man in hiding. They ordered him out at gunpoint.

"If you move a hand or foot I'll shoot."

"That's a nice way to treat an English traveler."

"Have a care now."

"I'm not armed, you know."

"What are you doing here?"

"By what authority do you ask that question? Am I bound to answer you?"

"I can ask any question I like and if you don't answer I can arrest you under the Defense of the Realm Act.... What's your name?"

"Richard Morten."

"Where do you live?"

"The Savoy, Denham, Buckinghamshire."

"Your occupation?"

"I am an author."

"Give me the name of some book you have written."

"The life of St. Brendan."

"What port did you arrive at in Ireland?"

"Dublin."

"When?"

"At eight o'clock this morning."

"Have you a passport or any papers which will identify you?"

"No."

"I must ask you to come along to the barracks with me. There are some other questions I must put to you."

A search of the suspect came up with 5.6/-. There was also, it was claimed, a black knapsack, with field glasses, a flashlight, ammunition, clothes and maps. It is possible that these things were later mistakenly listed as having been in the black metal box. It was also later claimed that Sgt Hearn told the man:

"In the name of His Majesty King George the Fifth I arrest you on a charge of illegally bringing arms into the country, contrary to the Defense of the Realm Act."

In this case, they must have found the Mausers and everything else.

5

Captain Spindler sat in the *Aud*. It was dawn, and they were faced with another day of awkward and dangerous waiting. Landing the arms at Fenit Pier would be impossible unless they were guided in; and who would be there to unload the cargo, even if they avoided confrontation by the authorities?

When what was believed to be a pilot cutter sped toward them, Spindler was elated—but, instead of the expected pilot, it turned out to be a British patrol boat, the *Setter II*, armed and overtaking them. The captain went below. They were still ostensibly a Norwegian tramp steamer. The cutter tied up next to the *Aud* and the officer in charge asked for the captain. He was told in broken English that the captain was asleep and, after some talk, the first mate was sent to wake him. All of this took some time.

While the captain was supposedly getting dressed the boarding party and their officer were offered morning whiskey. Spindler explained in broken English when he appeared, that they were from Norway and taking their cargo to Genoa. He said that there had been engine trouble, forcing them to put into Tralee. The British officer off-handedly inquired about the cargo and Spindler ordered one of the hatches to be opened to show what they were carrying. "Pit-props," he said, a bunch of wooden construction materials, jumbled together. Over more whiskey, the ship's manifests (in Norwegian) were presented. Unable to read them, the British officer agreed that they were in order and had Spindler sign his record book. Taking away gifts of liquor, the crew of the *Setter II* allowed the "Norwegian" ship to continue.

They weighed anchor and headed west. But the British Navy had had word of a foreign vessel sighted in Tralee Bay and another ship, an armed trawler, the *Lord Heneage*, made for them. Spindler was prepared to run for the open sea. It was already after one in the afternoon. A shore battery had sighted them but did not fire—being warned off by the *Setter II*, still in the area. If they were attacked, Spindler had decided simply to blow the *Aud* up. The *Setter II* and the *Lord Heneage* parleyed as the *Aud* continued full steam ahead, toward the open Atlantic where Spindler might, if he was lucky, continue his farce of being a Norwegian ship headed for Genoa. But a fast British sloop, the *Bluebell*, had been sent out to intercept the *Aud*; it was now impossible to escape. Closing in, the *Bluebell* then veered away—obviously wary of U-boats accompanying the foreign ship.

Spindler saw that he was confronted by a sea full of British vessels. There were signals being exchanged. In contact by wireless with the shore, the *Bluebell* was told to proceed to Queenstown with the *Aud*. Spindler obstinately continued to signal that he was Norwegian, that he was taking his cargo to Genoa, but the British ordered him to follow them to Queenstown, where they would be examined. If they did not obey, their ship would be sunk.

Spindler saw on his charts that if he scuttled the *Aud* in the right place, he would be able to block the entrance to the Queenstown harbor.

6

Monteith and Bailey walked to Tralee. In a shop in Dominick Street, they found the *Irish Volunteer* on sale and went in. Monteith asked for the commander of the local Volunteers. George Spicer, the young son of the shop owner, was sent off to tell Austin Stack there was someone who wanted to see him. Con Collins, who had been eating breakfast with Stack, agreed with Stack that this might be a trap. They told George to return and tell the strangers they would be along in an hour. At 10 a.m. Collins arrived at the shop with Stack and was surprised to find his friend Monteith. It was, Monteith told them, urgent to pick up Casement who had been left behind. A Model T Ford was acquired, with a driver named Moss Moriarty. Stack, Collins and Bailey (now told to identify himself as David Mulcahy) got in, along with Hanna Spicer, to make it seem like an outing.

Near Banna Strand they came across a cart with a boat on it, driven by a boy, Martin Collins, followed by a constable. Then they had a flat tire. Two policemen turned up to question them. Security had intensified in the area. Collins decided they should head back. They were stopped twice on the way by other police, all armed. At one barracks they were asked about weapons and Collins gave up his revolver, a Browning.

Bailey was left near Killahen Cross. Here, Mickeen O'Connell was to take care of him. O'Connell gave him something to eat; he then took him out to the Hanlon farm at Gloundallive, near Ballyduff. It looked to Bailey like they were trying to get rid of him.

While all this was happening, Casement was at Tralee, where a priest came at his request to confess him. Father Ryan listened: Casement identified himself and asked that he warn the Irish Volunteers not to rescue him—something that at this point would have been easy to do considering the almost non-existent security. He also asked Father Ryan to tell the Volunteers that expected help was not coming from the Germans. The planned rising had to be stopped.

Later that evening, a young physician, Dr. Michael Shanahan, visited the prisoner. He had been told that "Mr. Morten" was ill. Examining the patient alone, Dr. Shanahan learned the truth, that the prisoner—whom the doctor had recognized immediately—was Sir Roger Casement. The Volunteers were to be notified that he had been arrested.

When Father Ryan met Paddy Cahill after six o'clock that evening, the news that Casement had been arrested was no surprise. Cahill said he had been told by Austin Stack that Casement was being held at Ardfert; the priest said no, he was in Tralee. Unluckily, Con Collins—who was to have set up a wireless to communicate with the *Aud* and to have organized the offloading of German arms—had been arrested and was being held at Tralee as well.

Stack went off to the Tralee Barracks, intending to find out the state of affairs. There he too was immediately arrested. They found incriminating letters in his possession, from Volunteer leaders. Casement, they said, was there indeed, and had been asking about him.

Monteith, still in hiding at Spicer's, read in the local papers about the boat being found and the mysterious stranger who had been arrested. It appeared that the authorities still did not know Casement's identity. Monteith immediately wrote out a message for the Volunteer leaders—MacNeill, Hobson, Pearse or anyone else in charge, saying that the Germans were sending only arms, and that the uprising should be called off.

Five Volunteers were being sent out from Dublin to oversee communications and help in the distribution of arms. They traveled in two cars, starting from Killarney Railway Station about 7 p.m. The second car carried Con Keating, a wireless technician, whose efforts were essential in contacting the arms ship. In the back seat rode two others, Charlie Monaghan and Donald Sheehan. The second car was supposed to closely follow the first, but it developed mechanical trouble and fell behind. When the driver, Tom McInerney, finally got the trouble fixed, they went on. At Killorglin they were stopped by a policeman, but were allowed to continue, trying to make time down the unlit road. The driver had no idea where he was; they made a wrong turn and got off the main road—and then suddenly, before he could brake, the touring car tore through the air—driving straight off the pier at Ballykissane and into the water. McInerney was the only one who wasn't drowned.

In the morning, Austin Stack and Con Collins appeared before the Magistrate and charged with conspiracy to import arms into the country. Locked up again, they learned from Father Joe Breen that Casement had been taken away by train.

<h1 style="text-align:center">7</h1>

Rebel Leaders had now received news that Sir Roger Casement had been arrested. Then they learned that the arms ship, the *Aud*, had been sunk. Pearse and MacDonagh met with MacNeill once again, on Saturday morning. They told him that it was too late to cancel the uprising. The British were planning to disarm the Irish Volunteers and to enforce conscription—thus destroying the independence movement—and to jail the leaders of the Irish Volunteers. The Professor at this seemed convinced—for the moment—that the uprising would have to go ahead.

In Dublin Castle Sir Matthew Nathan, the Under-Secretary and Lord Wimborne, the Lord Lieutenant, discussed the situation. They agreed that Casement's arrival in Ireland and the abortive shipment of arms meant that the uprising was on the way. Nathan was convinced that the Irish Volunteers should be disarmed immediately and that the leaders should be jailed. Augustine Birrell was, as usual, in London. He was, at any rate, opposed to bloodshed. He would have to be consulted. With no arms and no leaders, Nathan and Wimborne agreed, the revolt would certainly fail, or at least have to be postponed.

MacNeill, through his web of informers, learned what Nathan had in mind. He talked with Arthur Griffith. They definitely decided that they would have to call off the uprising now, and met with Pearse, Plunkett and McDonagh to convince them. Probably, MacNeill said, the British would not be able to carry out their plans immediately. This gave the Volunteers time to take evasive steps. MacNeill, who was supposedly in charge, no longer agreed to the uprising, adding that a military junta (the Supreme Council) could not control the Volunteers—and any decisions should be made by vote among the members. The Council agreed. In line with their change of heart, an announcement was placed in the *The Sunday Independent*:

*Owing to the very critical position, all orders given to Irish Volunteers for tomor-
row, Easter Sunday, are hereby rescinded, and no parades, marches or other
movements of Irish Volunteers will take place. Each individual Volunteer will
obey this order strictly in every particular.*

MacNeill sent instructions to Eamon de Valera: "As Chief of Staff I have
ordered and hereby order that no movement whatsoever of Irish Volunteers is
to be made today." Then he left for his country house in Rathfarnham.

Nathan, convinced that the revolt had been squelched, was pleased; but he
still wanted the Volunteers arrested and their leaders jailed. First, however,
there should be "military preparations sufficient to overawe armed opposition."

All was not over yet. The chief leaders of the Volunteers met in Liberty
Hall from 5 a.m. on Sunday. The session lasted until the afternoon; discussion
was, as usual, blistering. There were several important facts, agreed on by all:
1) Sir Roger Casement had been arrested; 2) the Germans had not fulfilled
their agreement; 3) no submarine would be sent to Dublin Bay; 4) the arms
ship had been sunk; 5) there was to be no German action on the east coast of
England.

The decision was unanimous: The Rebellion would go ahead as planned.

One reason for this decision, in the face of certain failure, was that the
leaders expected the United States to come in on their side. Britain, they theo-
rized, because of international outrage, would be forced to give Ireland its
independence.

Urgent messages were sent off to the Irish Volunteer units in the provinces,
informing them that the four city battalions would parade for inspection after
all and route march at 10 a.m. on Monday. Full arms and equipment would be
carried, and one day's rations.

8

Sgt Bailey (Daniel Julian Bailey, his full name) recounts the events that led up
to his arrest. "I was taken prisoner about 4 September 1914 and was sent to
Sennelager. They then took me with other Irish to Limburg, where we were
well treated for a time. I saw Sir Roger Casement about April 1915 and he
spoke to us about joining the Irish Brigade solely for the purpose of fighting
for Irish freedom. I joined to see if I could possibly get out of the country.... I
signed on as D. J. Beverley. I was made a sergeant straight away." He says he
was specially trained in explosives in Neukollen. From Zossen he was taken to

the Saxonia Hotel, Berlin, and given civilian clothing. "On Tuesday the 11th instant, a car came to the door and the three of us (Casement, Monteith and I) were driven to the War Office. They gave me a railway ticket and we got into the train for Wilhelmshaven. We were put on a submarine, the U-20, there. She steamed out and had to return, owing to an accident, to Heligoland. There we boarded the U-19 and came round the Shetlands to the west coast of Ireland. I knew now where I was going, but still got no instructions. I gathered, when near Tralee, that it was in connection with the Volunteer movement. They steamed in as near as they could, lowered the collapsible boat and put us off. When everything was ready we took the boat, the revolvers and ammunition, etc., which you have found, and I was ordered to bury them. It was about 1 a.m. or later when we were put in the boat. When in the surf, the boat was overturned and we had to wade ashore and I went back two or three times to fetch in the stuff. We buried the arms, etc., not far from where we landed. I followed them and we stopped off the road. We left our coats there and I was taken by Mr. Monteith to Tralee." (The passive voice is generously sprinkled throughout his report, as if Bailey had taken no active part in the events.)

Monteith knocked at a shop door and they went in, he says. *The Spark*, a Volunteer newspaper, caught Monteith's eye and he spoke to the shopkeeper who sent one of the girls off. Later they got food at Lavin's and then four men came to talk with Monteith. They were given new clothes to wear and were taken from the shop by a man with glasses and a girl. At the convent a car stopped. They got in, the girl went back. Mr. Stack was in the car, plus the man with the glasses and the driver, and "Mr. Stack asked if I knew where 'Mr. Rice' [the code name for Casement] was." Later they had a flat, the police stopped them many times, and took their arms. Finally Bailey was "brought to a house by itself" where he spent the night. Then Stack told him to go to the castle and knock about. "I was arrested there."

He adds more pertinent, and often erroneous, information in his declaration: "When on the submarine I overheard a conversation, from time to time, that a small Wilson liner was to be piloted into Fenit Pier. It has 20,000 rifles (with five rifles in each case) and over 1,000,000 rounds of ammunition. It was disguised as a timber ship. From what I heard there were ten machine guns ready for action and bombs and fire bombs."

9

Alerted to the developing action, not realizing that the German ship had been sunk, police reinforcements boiled toward Fenit Pier, arriving in cars, horse traps, on foot and on bicycles. But there was no sign of the *Aud*. With the British patrols in readiness, expecting the German ship, it was doubtful that the ship could escape detection, even if it got through. If it did, they would be ready.

In Tralee, with Stack and Connolly arrested, Monteith took charge of the locals, who knew nothing about the plans underway for the uprising. He found that his "forces" comprised about three hundred old men and boys with shotguns, obsolete rifles of all makes, and not much enthusiasm. They would be up against a well-armed force three times their numbers. Word from Dublin, in spite of warnings that the uprising should be cancelled, was "Everything is all right. Go ahead."

Then on Saturday evening, a man from the Limerick City Regiment turned up. He brought orders from MacNeill, the Chief of Staff, in Dublin officially calling off the uprising. Monteith's Volunteers, relieved, scattered for home and the pubs. A few weeks later, Monteith, a hunted man, would make his escape to the United States.

10

During the Admiralty Inquiry later, experts puzzled over the happenings on the Irish coast. The leaders of the Irish Volunteers also wondered what had gone wrong.

H.M.S. *Bluebell* reported firing shots across the bow of the *Aud* about ninety miles off the Southwest coast of Ireland. The ship was flying the Norwegian flag and Norwegian flags were painted on its sides; she claimed to be the *Aud* of Bergen bound for Genoa. The *Aud* was ordered to follow the *Bluebell* to Queenstown. About three and a half miles from Queenstown the *Aud* stopped engines and smoke issued from starboard. Then the German ensigns were hoisted and two boats were lowered with a flag of truce. Three German naval officers and twenty seamen were taken aboard the *Bluebell*. Explosions followed on board the *Aud* and it subsequently sank with its cargo.

The plans of the German Admiralty had been clearly stated. The U-19 was to be met separately or simultaneously by a pilot boat north of Inishtooskert Island either Thursday 20 April or any of the three following nights. Two green lights on the pilot boat were the agreed signal at night; during the day a green flag at the masthead and men with green jerseys were used as identification. The submarine and the *Aud* both arrived on the 20th but did not make contact even after two hours of cruising, so the commander of the submarine set his passengers off at night. Captain Spindler, deciding to wait until the next day, steamed back beyond Inishtooskert and moored for the night. The next morning she was stopped and boarded by the *Shatter II* but British officers suspected nothing. After an additional twenty-four hours on Tralee Bay, there was still no sign of the pilot. By this time the *Bluebell* and other ships were dispatched to intercept the *Aud*. Nothing was left for Captain Spindler but to scuttle.

The date for the rendezvous and the landing of arms had been changed by a message which reached Berlin too late (because of indirect communications) to notify the *Aud* and the U-19. Captain Hall of Naval Intelligence might easily have missed this communication. However, in Washington DC the US Secret Service raided an office of an employee in the German Embassy, Wolff von Igel, and found the message, which was relayed to London. For this reason the British Admiralty did not expect the arms shipment until Sunday.

There were other errors: 1) the German Admiralty contributed to the confusion by sending a ship with no wireless; 2) the Supreme Council of the Irish Volunteers, apprised of the changes in the dates did not send men to keep watch for the arms ship at Tralee earlier than Sunday, 3) Austin Stack, who was to be in charge of unloading, did not expect the ship before that day, nor did the pilot, Mort O'Leary.

Other accidents contributed to the mess. The Irish Volunteers sent out to destroy the British station at Cahirciveen and set up an improvised station at Tralee did not accomplish their mission. One of the cars drove off the Ballykissane Pier, drowning three men. The German Admiralty, after the raid on von Igel's office, attempted to warn the U-19 (*"Expedition betrayed. Suspend operations immediately. If possible inform steamer"*) but this message never reached the submarine.

11

Whatever Casement touched seemed to crumble. Now he was on his way to London. He reached Kingsbridge Station in the afternoon, exhausted and filthy. They took him to Arbour Hill detention center. Here he was strip-searched, a demoralizing affront to his personal integrity. He was not allowed to rest. He would be on the eight o'clock boat for England.

The newspapers that day were full of the usual propaganda, the number of men lost in France, the numbers of enemy killed, offensives, victories and defeats. There were comments on the Mesopotamian fortress of Kut-al-Amara which had fallen to the Turks after 143 days of siege. The Commander, General Townsend, had been allowed to keep his sword, a nice detail, and surrender 2,970 British soldiers and 6,000 Indian troops. At Verdun the French under Pétain were still struggling against the all-out German offensive: thousands died daily. Zeppelins were in the skies, causing fear and occasional minor destruction. Parliament was arguing about the conscription of married men and deciding to fine the conscientious objectors (the "pasty faces" as they were known) £100. The United States declared once again that it would remain neutral in the Great War. U-boats were attacking shipping.

There was nothing about Sir Roger Casement.

Casement arrived under escort at Euston Station and was taken to Brixton prison. In his cell he was sleepless, worried that the uprising in Ireland might take place in spite of his message.

The next day, Monday, Inspector Sandercock escorted Casement to Scotland Yard where at 10 a.m. he met with his interrogators: Basil Thomson, Assistant Commissioner of Police in Charge of the Criminal Investigation; Captain Reginald Hall, Director of Naval Intelligence; Major Hall of Military Intelligence (M.I.5); and Superintendent Quinn of Scotland Yard. Casement could see how insanely pleased they were to have captured him. The questioning would take three days. There was a stenographer present during part of the questions, taking down the proceedings in shorthand. Thomson was perhaps the most important interrogator. Casement began by asking for Sir William Tyrell, Private Secretary of Sir Edward Grey.

"May I ask a question? Can I see a friend?"

"No"

"I mean it would be here in your presence. It would be somebody you would approve of."

"Tell me who he is."

"Sir William Tyrell."

"I doubt very much whether he is in town. Why do you want to see him?"

"Because I am in great difficulty—not about myself. I know my own position quite well, but not so far as I am at liberty morally to answer any questions. It may involve other people."

"We know this position. Who are you?"

"Officially, I am Sir Roger Casement."

"There may be people impersonating Sir Roger Casement."

"I don't think there are many people who would care to impersonate me."

"Of course you know your own position perfectly, because you are not bound to answer any question put to you and any reply you may make will be used in evidence against you."

"May I ask what I am charged with?"

"You are not charged."

"I was charged on arrest in Kerry by the constable who arrested me."

"What did he say to you when he charged you?"

"With aiding to land arms on the coast of Kerry."

"You made no reply to that?"

"I said I should ask for legal advice."

"You are not charged at present but it is certain that you will be." (Here he shows Casement the railway ticket from Berlin to Wilhelmshaven.) "Is that your property?"

"May I look at it? ... No, it is not my property."

"Have you seen that?" (He shows Casement the code, picked up by the young boy after Casement tried to dispose of it.)

"Yes, I have seen it.... In not answering I am not endeavoring to screen myself. I am quite prepared to answer in the fullest manner when I consider it right to answer. At present it may not be."

The questioning was tedious, more of a sham, and occasionally comic (in referring to the absurd coded diary entry "Left Wicklow in Willie's yacht"). Casement made it clear that in his opinion, he had "done nothing treacherous to my country. All I ask you is to believe I have done nothing dishonorable, which you will someday learn." This was obviously lost on the little committee, who went on to elicit the facts of Casement's activities in Germany from 1914. When accused of having received money from the Germans he denied it again.

During the long examination Superintendent Quinn asked about the keys for some trunks found in Casement's Ebury Street quarters. Casement said, "Break open the locks, there is nothing in them but some old clothes and other belongings which are of no further use to me."

There is some confusion about the diaries. Another story—Thomson's—says that toward the end of the first day, Quinn brought in two large thin volumes looking like notebooks or diaries, saying:

"I found these in the trunks. They may be interesting."

"Yes, they are my private diaries."

Then Thomson thumbed through the pages and confessed that he was "horrified." Afterwards, he wrote, "It is enough to say of the diaries that they could not be printed in any age or any language." In short, he goes on, they showed Casement to be a "confirmed and habitual homosexual given to recording his practices in minute detail."

"In all probability you will be charged with high treason," Thomson said, ending the day's session.

"I hope so."

During the interrogation various accusations were made against Casement, including not only that he had been paid $50,000 by the Germans but that he had tried to "seduce the loyalty" of Irish POWs by offering them money to join the Irish Brigade. "I could have bought some of these men," Casement replied innocently, "and I could have had heaps of money from the German Government. That was what was offered to me again and again. No, I said, these men must go willingly; if they are going to commit high treason, they must do it with their eyes open."

"As long as the shorthand writer remained," Thomson later wrote in *Queer People*, "he said little beyond admitting acts of high treason, but when we were alone he became far more communicative. He rose from his armchair and sat easily on the corner of my table. The rising in Ireland, he said, was to have been on Easter Sunday; he was to have landed a week earlier. He professed to know nothing of the intrigues in America which had fixed the date for the rising. He said that he was lying ill in Munich when a 'trusted friend' asked him to go to Berlin, for the time had now come to act. When he found that the Germans intended to send only one ship with munitions and not a single German officer, he said that he charged them with criminal folly, and that the officer blushed and said, 'Well, this is all that the Government intends to do. You must go with them, because if you refuse your countrymen shall know that you betrayed them.' They wanted him to go on the *Aud* itself but he stipulated for a submarine, in order, so he said, to warn the rebels that they had no chance of success. The breaking down of the submarine prevented this. He was very insistent that the news of his capture be published as it would prevent bloodshed."

This picture (for the "historical record") does not sound like Casement at all. Sir Roger had, in fact, done little in this whole operation except lend his name and add to the chaos. "I had a lot of trouble over embarking in the manner I did," he writes. "It came upon me as a thunderclap. I came out of bed without the doctor's advice and they put it to me that I should go. I said under no circumstances will I stay. If there is going to be fighting in Ireland, I must go." What he was to do during the insurrection, since he had no idea of how to load or shoot a Mauser or handle a rifle, is difficult to say. He could hardly operate normally, he was so ill and debilitated. "They wanted me to take my Irish boys," he adds, "more than fifty, and we had a terrible fight and I won the day. I was not going to hand them over to the hangman."

A man who recorded loving kisses, Indian boys nestling between his legs, fever, heartache for innocents maimed, darkness, beautiful youths with beautiful erections, love, had facing him these inquisitors—like all such civil servants—dead inside.

There are no homosexual heroes.

Brought from Brixton again on Tuesday, he was informed that an uprising had occurred after all. He was shocked. Thomson assured him that the outbreak was minor and would soon be crushed.

Minimal Losses

1

The Royal Commission on the Irish Rebellion, is clear: "Early in the morning of the 24th April the Chief Secretary's concurrence with the proposed arrest and internment in England of the hostile leaders was asked for and obtained, but before any further steps could be taken the insurrection had broken out and by noon many portions of the City of Dublin had been simultaneously occupied by rebellious armed forces." Since Monday was a bank holiday, the populace was unprepared for such a blow. Many were at the Fairyhouse races. Thousands were at the beaches, or in the countryside, or sleeping off an Easter drunk. Because of the confusion caused by MacNeill's order calling off the uprising (precipitated by Casement's message) as well as by the holiday, only about 800 Irish Volunteers and 200 men of the Citizen Army showed up, badly armed but ready to fight.

The rebellion began with hesitation and slaughter, looting and bloodshed. Sean Connolly, assigned to Dublin Castle, took twenty men and made it through the gates, shooting one guard dead and sending the others clambering for cover. Surprise helped. Then, afraid of being caught inside the Castle, he ordered his men to withdraw. They entered the City Hall next door, which had a clear view of the entrance to the Castle. A small contingent easily took over the offices of the *Evening Mail* and the Empire Theater directly opposite. Connolly left cover to hoist the Irish flag over the newspaper and was picked off by a soldier inside the Castle. John O'Reilly took over command.

Eamon Ceannt and Cathal Brugha took fifty men and made for the South Dublin Union—near the Guinness Brewery and the City Basin. This position gave them control over Kingsbridge Station, to the north, from which Casement had left the city on his way to London. Any British troops from the

Curragh would arrive at the station. When reinforcements began streaming in they were attacked by Ceannt and his men. In spite of their losses, however, the British managed to pin down the rebels; the South Dublin Union became impossible to defend.

One of the bright tacticians of the rebels was Edward Daly, commanding the 1st Battalion. He set up headquarters at the Four Courts of Justice in the center of the city, on the north bank of the Liffey. From there he controlled a large area including Broadstone Station, the Fourth Army and Constabulary Barracks, as well as the Royal Barracks where military headquarters was established. So secure was Daly that only a few of his men were able to bottle up fifty men from the 6th Reserve Cavalry Regiment who arrived with a convoy of ammunition in Charles Street. There they sat, immobilized, for over three days. A small detail of Daly's men attacked the ammunition depot in Phoenix Park, ransacking the military stores. The British military were taken by surprise everywhere in the city.

Barricades were thrown up on the main streets from Four Courts to Blaquir Bridge and Broadstone Station. Just behind Four Courts, the Linen Hill Barracks was surrounded and effectively immobilized.

The General Post Office was chosen by James Connolly as Rebel Headquarters. It was mistakenly believed that the British would respect the building and avoid destroying such an outstanding bit of architecture, with fine broad O'Connell Street reaching from the Rotunda to the river. The GPO was easily taken. Soon the military leaders, Tom Clarke, Padraic Pearse and Sean McDermott, took charge. Fixing their Headquarters at the GPO would turn out to be one of several tactical errors on the part of the rebels, not at the moment obvious. The GPO became a command center which, if taken, would mean the end of the fighting. The telegraph system was disabled. A terse old woman in charge of the telephones, however, advised the rebels that the British troops had already taken control. Stymied, they believed her lie, which meant that the British troops were able throughout the uprising to maintain communications.

Padraic Pearse appeared on the steps of the GPO, before a crowd of jeering and incredulous Irish. He read what for the moment seemed an absurdity, a Proclamation of the Republic of Ireland. The jeering soon stopped when a British cavalry charge down O'Connell Street swept them aside. The attack was repulsed. One rebel was killed.

Only a few blocks away, Liberty Hall was occupied. The docks and the Customs House, however, on the other side of Beresford Place, proved impossible to take. On the south side of the river, Michael Mallin occupied St. Stephen's Green, from where they controlled Harcourt Street Station and some bridges over the canal. Countess Markiewicz and her boy scouts invaded the Royal College of Surgeons. To the southeast Eamon de Valera set up the headquarters of the 3rd Battalion, comprising under two hundred men, at Boland's Mills. De Valera turned out to be a wily fighter, developing highly mobile patrols of street fighters and well-placed snipers that paralyzed bumbling masses of British troops. He used the Westland Row Station's stone wall as protection.

In the early afternoon some two hundred men of the Royal Dublin Fusiliers reached the Castle by Ship Street Gate, which was protected from rebel firing. As expected, at 4:45 p.m. 1,600 British troops under General Portal arrived from the Curragh at Kingsbridge Station. They were immediately attacked by Eamon Ceannt's men. An additional thousand troops came from various stations, with a battery of 18-pounders. Four hundred troops occupied the docks and the Customs House overlooking Liberty Hall. Machine gun batteries were placed on the roof of the United Service Club and the Shelbourne Hotel, keeping the rebels in Stephen's Green under continuous fire.

In spite of the massive numbers of British troops arrayed against them, the rebels were in a good position, though not in control of the city. Another tactical mistake then occurred: the rebels decided not to storm Trinity College, which could have been taken with little cost since it was being held by stray soldiers. By not taking Trinity, the rebel forces were cut in two and a continuous line of British military posts was set up from Kingsbridge Station to Trinity via the Castle. As well, British artillery now had command of O'Connell Street.

At the end of the first day of fighting, the rebels had shown their strength, which did not necessarily lie with the central district of Dublin but included points outside. Meanwhile, in London General French called up the whole of the 59th Division at St. Albany to proceed to Ireland at once. In the Curragh and Belfast over five thousand men, with heavy weapons, including machine guns, were mobilized.

Casement, in London, learned nothing of what was occurring in Dublin. Only later, and slowly, did the news filter through to him.

The losses in Dublin during the first day of the rebellion were minimal. John O'Reilly, who had taken over command from Sean Connolly in the Castle area, had been killed; but his men maintained their positions. To the south, though, several points had had to be abandoned. There was a cordon of troops around the north of Dublin from Park Gate to the North Wall. Broadstone Station had come under massive attack, supported by artillery, but the twenty rebels guarding the Philsborough barricades held out.

2

Wednesday turned out to be sunny, after a rainy night. In the glistening air the gunboat *Helga* could be clearly seen moving up the Liffey, pausing by Beresford Place. During the night a battery of field guns had been brought into Trinity.

The *Helga* trained its guns on Liberty Hall. The bombardment was useless—the rebels had evacuated their position there hours before—but from Liberty Hall they moved on to O'Connell Street. The artillery in Trinity also began firing against the GPO, and would keep up the attack all day.

More troops moved into the city. The 178th Infantry Brigade arrived by road. The soldiers included the Sherwood Foresters with men who had seen only three months of service. Relatively untrained, they were sent to drive through de Valera's positions, and suffered disastrous losses. The battle in Lower Mount Street lasted all day. De Valera lost very few men, killing and wounding two hundred thirty-four. General Maxwell wisely decided not to push on to Trinity College that night.

The British planned their major attack against Rebel Headquarters in O'Connell Street. Troops would advance from the north, closing in on Four Courts and the area around the GPO. Dublin was being destroyed in chunks and pieces. Whole blocks were blazing out of control. Bodies of those killed, dead horses, debris and masses of rubble clogged the streets. There were frequent explosions and billowing smoke. The explosions and flames were caused by the incendiaries which the British were using. Occasional sniper fire could be heard.

The British troops included many Irish, who were shocked and demoralized by the destruction of human life and a great city. Atrocities were reported. A quartermaster sergeant went crazy at the Guinness Brewery on Tuesday night—suddenly accusing the prisoners he was guarding of being Sinn Feiners, he opened fire and killed four. (Later court-marshaled, he was found not guilty.) Then there was the odd story of poor Francis Sheehy-Skeffington, journalist, pacifist, married to a Women's Righter. Anxious during the uprising to keep people from looting, he organized a Civil Patrol. Walking home after a meeting, he was arrested near the Portobello Bridge and taken to the Barracks. Officers questioned him, he was searched and found to be carrying nothing more incriminating than a flyer announcing a meeting of the Civil Patrol against looting. The Adjutant, however, still suspecting him of being not only a pacifist but a Sinn Feiner, ordered him held. During the night, Captain Bowen-Colthurst came in and demanded the "Sinn Feiner." Bowen-Colthurst had spent sixteen years with the Royal Irish Rifles, had fought in the Boer War. He was totally ruthless in combat, had been wounded in the Battle of the Aisne, and had carried out, during the early uprising, several raiding parties. He had an insane hated of Sinn Feiners. At first hesitant, the Lieutenant in charge handed the prisoner over. Sheehy-Skeffington, hands bound behind his back, was to accompany another of the Captain's erratic "raiding" parties. The group of soldiers left the Barracks late. On the street they met two young men on their way home from a solidarity meeting. The Captain collared one for questioning. When the boy tried to get away, the Captain shot him dead. They continued to the shop of Alderman James Kelly, which Bowen-Colthurst thought belonged to a known Sinn Feiner, Tom Kelly. He blasted the inside of the shop. Two men, Dickson and MacIntyre, were found inside taking shelter. The soldiers were ordered to take Sheehy-Skeffington and the two men back to the barracks. In the early hours of Thursday they were thrown into cells. The next morning, Sheehy-Skeffington, horribly shaken, refused to eat breakfast—he was a vegetarian, he said, when accused by an officer of "causing trouble." He could not eat animal products of any kind. Captain Bowen-Colthurst was also in the Barracks. By now he had decided that Sheehy-Skeffington and the two others captured that night were Sinn Feiners. They would have to be shot. He had them brought out of their cells, and taken to the courtyard. He then ordered seven armed soldiers to form a firing squad. The Captain of the Guard, Lieutenant Dobbin, startled by the Captain's actions, sent word to the Orderly Room for Lieutenant Gibbon, who was temporarily in charge. It was too late.

The firing squad had already executed the prisoners. When it was noticed that Sheehy-Skeffington was still alive, Bowen-Colthurst commanded four soldiers to finish him off. He claimed that the prisoners had been shot trying to escape and so informed the authorities at the Castle. Major Vane, who returned to his post at the Barracks, however, was told by his officers what had really happened. He confronted the Captain, who showed no signs of remorse; he knew, he said, how to act during a state of martial law. The people in the city soon learned of the fate of Skeffington-Sheehy. The British were accused of being murderers—certainly no exaggeration, considering the number of British atrocities reported. (Captain Bowen-Colthurst was finally brought to court marshal, after Vane took the case all the way up to the Prime Minister. He was found insane. Sheehy-Skeffington's wife, the suffragette, when offered a £10,000 indemnification by the government, scornfully refused it.)

3

By Thursday almost the whole 176th Brigade was in place and troops under Colonel Portal had surrounded the O'Connell Street area. There was furious fighting all day, and reckless shelling. Dublin was beginning to look like a wasteland. Edward Daly had been forced to abandon the Linen Hill Barracks.

Arthur Griffith in the meantime had escaped from detention and had bicycled to Rathfarnham, where he met with MacNeill. They had prepared an appeal to the country for calm, which was never sent. It was much too late.

By Thursday the 177th Infantry Brigade had also arrived at Kingstown with General Sir John Maxwell in charge. He would, he announced flatly, annihilate both the rebels and the city. "Most rigorous methods will be taken by me to stop the loss of life and damage to property which certain misguided persons are causing by their armed resistance to the law. If necessary, I shall not hesitate to destroy all buildings within any area occupied by the rebels."

The whole of Dublin was imprisoned in a military ring; no one could leave or enter the city, even to bury their dead. Four Courts was surrounded and on Friday all lines of retreat had been cut.

Padraic Pearse early Friday sent his last message to the Irish—from the Provisional Government to the Citizens of Dublin, a Proclamation of the Sovereign Independent Irish State. They were shelling incessantly, trying to flush the rebels into the open.

There was no place to go but out. The GPO was ablaze, shells were coming in. At last the rebels made a break for it, dashing out of the building and down Henry Street to the heavy barricade on Moore Street. In a few yards seventeen men were killed, including O'Rahilly. James Connolly was carried on an improvised stretcher and survived the wild breakout. But they were pinned down all of Friday afternoon and Saturday morning.

At noon on Saturday, a girl advanced down Moore street, carrying a white flag and a message from Pearse to General Maxwell, asking for terms. At 2 p.m. Pearse was brought before the British general and signed an unconditional surrender.

This was not the end. The men on the periphery of the city, in units that were still in command of whole areas, were incensed. Many had not wanted a central headquarters based in a highly visible building like the GPO. They themselves remained unbeaten. They did not want to surrender. In fact it took the whole day to convince Eamon Ceannt's men, and Countess Markiewicz's boys, that the fight was over. Some of de Valera's men kept up the battle for several days. But by 30 April all of the rebel leaders had surrendered. They were beaten perhaps but they had won a victory of a different sort.

4

Critics of the uprising made excuses, chief of which was MacNeill's countermanding order. There had been other communications errors, too, which resulted in a less than complete turnout of Volunteers. The rebels had been short of ammunition. The provincial units of the Volunteers, demoralized after the sinking of the *Aud*, had offered little support—what should have been a national convulsion became a centralized rebellion. On the other hand, the provincials claimed that they had done good work. In County Wexford, six hundred men marched into Enniscorthy and refused to give up until two of their officers went to Dublin and talked with Pearse in prison. There had been a five-hour battle, led by Thomas Ashe and Richard Mulcahy, against the Royal Irish Constabulary at Ashbourne; the police had been defeated and disarmed, but later freed. In Galway the action was led by Liam Mellows who had recently escaped from custody in England; over a thousand men blew up bridges, cut telegraph lines and attacked the military barracks—then, however, the initial enthusiasm waned. Fighting died out and many Volunteers were captured. In Cork the maneuvers were disastrous: all were ready on Sunday when MacNeill's order arrived, calling off the rising, and the men dispersed. On Monday came the news of the Dublin revolt. "Come out and fight or be disarmed on Tuesday morning," the message came. Mobilization at that stage was nearly impossible. At any rate, the men were not as well supplied with rifles and ammunition as the Dubliners.

The official reckoning was: 450 killed and 2614 wounded. A hundred and sixteen British soldiers had been killed, compared with 318 rebels and civilians. Between 56 and 60 uniformed Irish Volunteers had been killed. Outside

Dublin eight civilians had been killed. The Royal Irish Constabulary and the Dublin Metropolitan Police had suffered about 15 dead.

Seventy-nine women (including Countess Markiewicz, Dr. Kathleen Lynn and Countess Plunkett) were arrested, and 3,430 men. Eoin MacNeill, late on the scene, insisted that he wanted to share the fate of the other rebel leaders.

Then came the executions. Four days after the surrender, Dublin Castle announced that the three signatories of the notice proclaiming the Irish Republic, P. H. Pearse, T. MacDonagh and T. J. Clarke, had been tried by Field Court Martial and sentenced to death. "The sentence having been duly confirmed the above three-mentioned men were shot this morning." Each day brought more, creating a wave of revulsion in the country. On 4 May it was announced that Joseph Plunkett, Michael Hanrahan, William Pearse (Padraic's younger brother) had been executed. The firing squads continued their work. On 5 May John MacBride was shot. A week later Cornelius Colbert, Michael Mallin, J. J. Heuston and Eamon Ceannt were shot. Execution by the British was not a dignified death. As Father Augustine described it, "They brought out a soap box and asked [them] to sit down, stretch out [their] legs," and they were shot.

Eoin MacNeill, Countess Markiewicz and Henry O'Hanrahan were condemned to die but General Maxwell kindly commuted their sentences to penal servitude for life.

Then, on Friday 12 May James Connolly and Sean MacDermott were shot. Connolly, in bad shape from his wounds, had to be carried to Kilmainham Jail. They had to prop him up on a chair so that he could be executed. The body was carted off to Arbour Hill Barracks where it was thrown in a ditch with the other dead and covered with quicklime.

General Maxwell described the necessity for such actions. "In view of the gravity of the rebellion and its connection with German intrigue and propaganda, and in view of the great loss of life and property resulting therefrom, the General Officer Commanding-in-Chief has found it imperative to inflict the most severe penalties on the known organizers of this detestable rising and on those commanders who took an active part in the actual fighting which occurred. It is hoped that these examples will be sufficient to act as a deterrent to intriguers and to bring home to them that the murder of His Majesty's liege subjects or other acts calculated to imperil the safety of the realm will not be tolerated."

The official tally: 160 convicted by courts-martial; 15 executed; 10 condemned to life imprisonment; 1,836 men, 5 women prisoners sent to England for internment.

There was, of course, a strong public reaction to the Easter Rebellion in England, much of it conditioned by British propaganda. A Royal Commission headed by Lord Hardinge of Penshurst was organized (and took eight weeks to issue its report). It was decided by common consent that the Chief Secretary had been responsible for allowing the situation to arise in the first place. The march of the Ulster Volunteers, the assent to arms being supplied to northern Ireland, the disregard of signs of rebellion—all these had played their part.

The *Times* of 26 April, was as usual cool and reserved: "It must be amongst the first tasks of those responsible for the suppression of the revolt to teach this class that rebellion in time of war is a crime bringing prompt and heavy punishment upon the guilty.... Nothing can be more cruel and more unwise in insurrections than half-hearted measures of suppression."

John Redmond, in the Commons, expressed "detestation and horror" at this "wicked and insane movement." Carson agreed wholeheartedly.

But in Ireland, the whole nation now seemed to be behind the uprising. It had been doomed to fail, perhaps, but it had happened. The poor had been the first to sense the disintegration of social order. They had looted when the law broke down and the rebels had taken the GPO. They broke store windows, clambered into shops and crammed their mouths with sweets, tried on elegant new duds and boots, gathered up silken garments and flounces and emerged from ruined haberdasheries to enter jewelers. In the blasted pubs and wine shops the goods were gathered up and taken away, or drunk on the premises. It was a riot of good things the people might never in their lives have touched. It revolted men like Sheehy-Skeffington and other moralists, but this was—well, revolution, and people who lived hand to mouth, working for a few shillings a week and sleeping in a single room with many others, bitten by lice and bedbugs and rats, with no toilets or running water, knee deep in filth, knew what they wanted: to break out of the spell of poverty, even for a moment.

5

John Devoy in New York had been immediately notified by coded cable that the revolt had started. He had worked for almost half a century for this moment, and had spent long days in a British prison, planning.

In a long letter to a friend he wrote, "The information about the shipload of arms by Wilson's men enabled the English to catch the vessel.... They got in the raid on von Igel's office a note of mine—the transcript of a message received in cypher from Dublin and wirelessed to Berlin the day before—17th April—a request not to land the arms before the night of Sunday 23rd.... [T]hey sent out their boats and caught the ship. Then they sent troops to Tralee and reinforced Limerick.... Casement did the rest. He landed on Friday and sent a message to MacNeill to stop it; that it was hopeless, etc. MacNeill got it on Saturday and issued his countermand." Then when he heard of the sinking of the *Aud*, he had changed his mind. "From our experience of a year of [Casement's] utter impracticability—he had been assuring us, till we were sick, that 'there was no hope for the poor old woman' until the next war—we sent with the first note from home that we transmitted to Berlin a request that *R. be asked to remain there*, 'to take care of Irish interests.' We knew he would meddle in his honest, but visionary way to such an extent as to spoil things, but we did not dream that he would ruin everything as he has done. He took no notice whatever of decisions or instructions, but without quarreling, pursued his own dreams. The last letter I got from him, written last December, said the only hope now of making a demonstration that would impress the world was to send the 'Brigade' to Egypt. *To impress the world by sending sixty men to a place where they could do nothing.*"

Devoy knew, and was worried, that Casement took no notice of the Clan. Casement was a man obsessed with the idea that he was "a wonderful leader" and that nothing could be done without him. Every letter from the "representative" in Berlin made Devoy furious and kept him awake at night. Casement said that the Germans were treating the Irish badly, that the arms they supplied were no good (but they were good enough for Russians to overrun East Prussia, Devoy remarked, and are good enough to shoot Englishmen). Even the Germans were finally exasperated by Casement's posturing. He had nothing to do with procuring the shipload of arms—it had all been done from New York.

Adler Christensen was a crook in the pay of the English, Devoy added at the end of his letter. Casement had been warned of this from Ireland. He paid no attention. (Christensen had been receiving a stipend from the Clan in the US, claiming "expenses" for himself and his "wife"—some slut, it was said, he had brought from Germany. Christensen also offered to testify against Casement—but was stopped from going.)

The figures quoted by Devoy are interesting. He says that 1500 Volunteers fought in Dublin and had held up an army of 20–25,000 British for a whole week and "our fellows had only 103 killed and wounded. The English had 2,700."

"The old Ireland is gone."

The Blackness: Diaries and Death

1

The morning of 15 May, Casement appeared in the dock at Bow Street Police Court, presided over by Sir John Dickinson. Lord Desart, Sir Charles Matthews and others were on the bench.

Another prisoner, Daniel John Bailey, was with him.

The Crown was represented by Sir F.E. Smith, K.C. (later Earl of Birkenhead), Mr. A.H. (later Sir Archibald) Bodkin, Mr. Travers Humpreys and Mr. F. J. Williamson of the Treasury.

Sir Roger Casement was represented by Mr. Artemus Jones, Mr. John Hartman Morgan (Professor of Constitutional History at University College, London), instructed by Mr. George Gavan Duffy, solicitor.

Superintendent Quinn of the Special Branch at Scotland Yard observed the case on behalf of the police.

It was charged that the defendants "unlawfully, maliciously and traitorously did commit high treason without the realm of England in contempt of Our Sovereign Lord the King and his laws."

The *Times* reported Casement as having "no fixed abode and no fixed occupation."

Neither Casement nor Bailey wishing to make a statement, they were committed for trial as "such time and place appointed."

This would be at the Bar in the High Court of Justice on 26 June 1916. Lord Chief Justice Lord Reading (Sir Rufus Isaacs) presided, with Mr. Justice Avory and Mr. Justice Horridge.

Appearing for the Crown was Attorney General Smith, the Solicitor General Sir George Cave, Archibald Bodkin, Travers Humphreys and G. A. H. Branson.

Appearing for Casement were Mr. Alexander M. Sullivan, K.C., the Second Sergeant of the Irish Bar (and also a barrister at the English Bar), assisted by Mr. Artemus Jones, Mr. Morgan and a member of the American Bar, Mr. Michael Francis Doyle.

Bailey did not appear thereafter. No evidence would be offered against him until Casement's conviction had been secured.

2

Casement had been held incommunicado in Brixton prison until at long last Gavan Duffy was permitted to see him. Casement was watched around the clock. Two soldiers were in the cell with him, "never to leave me and to look at me all the time and the sentry outside looking through the single pane—three men with eyes never off me night or day, changed every hour, and electric light full on at night, so that sleep became impossible and thought became a page of Hell."

Casement had, in spite of the surveillance, tried to kill himself with curare which he had managed to conceal in the lining of his clothes. He was unable to get enough poison into him through his veins which he had sawed open with the broken lens of his glasses, so they patched him up and continued their watch with increased attention. Then he stopped eating. They considered force-feeding him.

The guards were not all bad. One of them whispered on Saturday that the Irish rebel leaders had been executed in Dublin.

Gavan Duffy managed to get him more humane treatment. He was put for a while in the prison hospital where he fared better. He had an improved diet and was allowed magazines, books, newspapers. There were visitors. He finally got rid of his lice. He was allowed to smoke. The first letter he wrote was to a young Scotland yard officer, Inspector Sandercock, thanking him for his good heart.

The press was negative.

His cousin Gee was beside herself with anxiety. She seems about the only one working day and night to protect him from the system, his own despair, and execution.

3

Sergeant Sullivan, who had been selected to represent Casement, was a curious choice. Born in New York in 1871, Alexander Martin Sullivan was the son of a Nationalist MP. In New York, he had been a journalist before going to Dublin, where he was called to the Irish Bar in 1892. He had never practiced in English courts, was not familiar with English criminal procedures, and could not occupy the front benches with the other leading counsel. He expected to earn—If the trial ran to three days—150 guineas—not a stiff fee. Duffy was in accord; a defense fund having rapidly accumulated for the accused. Under the Treason Act of 1696 persons so charged were allowed two counsel of their own choosing (Sergeant Sullivan and Artemus Jones). Twenty-three jurors had been called—all middle-class or lower-class Londoners, a bank clerk, mechanic, tailor, coachman, baker, etc. Many were challenged; but by noon the jury was finally agreed and the opening statements could be made.

"The prisoner is not a countryman of yours," Sullivan addressed the jury in his sonorous brogue. "He is a stranger within your gates." Not a particular strong beginning for an accused traitor who said he would "most respectfully subscribe to the doctrine that no Irishman has a right to take up views or risk his life for any cause that is not in the service of Ireland." When Sullivan began to allude to the political situation in Ireland (the Easter Rebellion), the Lord Chief Justice intervened; the Attorney General reminded him that uncorroborated statements would not be tolerated. He showed himself cowed, uncertain.

The accused did not help. Casement was now convinced that he would go down in history as a martyr. He passed a note on 2 June to Sergeant Sullivan, attempting to explain the line of his defense. "I have committed Germany for all time to an Irish policy and to pronouncement in favor of Irish independence that, in all the centuries before, no other Power ever gave forth to any Irishman."

George Bernard Shaw agreed that Casement should admit all the facts, which he did, and that he should also claim to be treated as a prisoner of war, which he didn't. It would have made no difference.

In prison we lose touch with him. We hear only the scratch of his pen. He had gone from one prison—the asylum at Grünewald—to another in the Tower, but he was still alive. In Dublin there were many dead, many of his acquaintance, none of them friends: he had no friends, or had no friends who knew him intimately. He had, in the space of a couple of years, become "another" Casement: set free by circumstance from the Consular Service. He had followed a new cause but it had disintegrated in his hands. The war caught up with him.

How could you reform the dead? How many young men out there remembered him? How many were dying in the trenches in France? How many knew that he was Irish, or condemned to die, or recalled his flavor, his speech, his kindness? How many were already gone, shadows like something out of Marie Corelli, or Wilkie Collins or Rider Haggard?

4

After the statement by the King's Coroner of the Charge of High Treason (following to the Act of 1351), the facts were presented before the court: Casement had tried to enlist Irish prisoners of war in an Irish Brigade; he had published leaflets to this effect; he had persuaded and procured persons to forsake their allegiance to the King and "set forth from the Empire of Germany as a member of a warlike and hostile expedition undertaken and equipped by the said enemies of Our Lord the King, having for its object the introduction into the landing on the coast of Ireland of arms and ammunition intended for use in the prosecution of the said war by the said enemies against our Lord the King and his subjects."

Before pleading, Sergeant Sullivan raised the case of the King *versus* Lynch. Lynch had fought for six months in the Boer War against the English; a member of the Irish Brigade, he had joined the Boers and after the war, returning to England, had been sentenced to death for treason. The sentence had been commuted to life imprisonment. After three or four months he had been released and went on to stand for Parliament. This was a relatively recent case (1902) and relevant; the Lord Chief Justice ruled to consider this submission later. (F. E. Smith, a fervent Unionist, not long ago had boasted his readiness to commit treason himself, but had changed his colors since being chosen by Asquith to replace Carson on the Cabinet. He despised Casement, and had taken the case himself instead of handing it on to a subordinate.)

Another objection initially raised was that Casement was accused of intent, not deeds. The jury was asked to link two events: Casements reaching the Irish coast at approximately the same time as the arrival of the arms ship. This did not involve Casement as a responsible agent. This fact had been skillfully concealed by the Lord Chief Justice.

The trial continued in the classical English manner.

Irrelevancies swamped the jury. A host of minor witnesses were called and testified, sometimes incomprehensibly. For some reason neither Basil Thomas nor Captain Hall was called; no use was made of the stenographic report of their interviews with the accused. Casement himself abstained from any reference to these interviews, and refused to fight his adversaries on their own ground. Professor Morgan pointed out that the Act of 1351 was obsolete. It was ludicrous to try a man under such a precedent. The Lynch case, for example, was pertinent; he had actually fought against the English, unlike Casement; and he had been reprieved and pardoned.

The trial, a "monument of legal virtuosity" went ahead. It was described by Singleton-Gates as a show trial carried out "in the service of political interest, fed by personal ambition, and supported by popular prejudice." Watching from across the way, the Irish—enjoying a new national conscience—expected the worst. The long and vicious statement of the Attorney General, given before evidence was presented, reviewed Casement's official career, his retirement, the knighthood—with a reading of the "obsequious" letter of acceptance of June 1911. "What occurred," he went on, "between 1911 and 1914 to affect and corrupt the prisoner's mind I cannot tell you...." Then he presented a mass of rhetorical meandering about Britain, that "great and wealthy nation, unequaled in resources, living at peace, unassailed and almost unassailable," attacked by the forces of Darkness. "In 1914 this same nation was struggling for its possessions, for its honor, for its very existence, in the most prodigious war which has ever tested human fortitude...." He went on to say that accused had addressed the Irish prisoners at Limburg, those poor men "emotional, excitable, uninformed, the easy victims of seduction." Casement was "exposing poor men, his inferiors in education, age and knowledge of the world, to the penalties of high treason."

Casement had told the Irish POWs that the Germans were winning the war. He had offered them a bonus for joining the Brigade. He had promised them better treatment. (Those who didn't join were put on short rations, according to previous witnesses.) Treason as defined as adherence to the King's enemies in the enemy country, according to the Attorney General, was certainly applicable here.

The sinking of the *Aud* was also mentioned. Rifles had been retrieved from the sunken ship by navy divers. Then came the tedious and meticulous examining of the witness at Banna Strand, followed by the seven ex-prisoners of war in Limburg. The cross examination was minute, as was the dissection of evidence: even the half-eaten piece of sausage was brought in.

On the second day of the trial, which was being closely followed by the international press, Sergeant Sullivan again reminded the bench that the Act of the 14th century was not applicable to the present case. The Lord Chief

Justice overruled his objections. "[A]ny reason committed out of the realm may be tried ... by His Majesty's Judges in the King's Bench."

Casement begged to make a remark, which was, fortunately, shorter than usual. He corrected four misstatements which had been made in the course of the trial. He had, he said, never at any time advised Irishmen to fight with the Turks against the Russians, nor to fight with the Germans on the Western Front. He had never asked the Irish to fight for Germany, only for Ireland. He had never caused rations to be reduced for the men who refused to join the Brigade. He had never received money from the Germans, only from the Irish in the United States. "I left Germany a poorer man than I entered it," he said. He added that he had been touched by the generosity and loyalty of friends, who had supplied money during "these last dark weeks of strain and trial." The Irish Rebellion was not made in Germany and not one penny of German gold went to finance it.

Sullivan went on with his useless plea, to the wry satisfaction of the Bench. Casement, he said, had recruited the Irish Brigade in the service of their own country. He had wanted to send the Brigade not during the war, but after it, and only if Germany won; they were offered free passage to America thereafter, and £10 compensation. The fact was, even if Casement had intended to commit an act of treason, his actions resulted in no armed conflict and gave no help to Germany.

Minor theatricals on the part of the Lord Chief Justice and the Attorney General included a reference to Casement's diaries, parts of which had already been shown to journalists and individuals in Government:

Lord Chief Justice: You mentioned a passage in the diary. Is there any evidence whose diary it is?

Attorney General: It was a diary. I will give your Lordship the evidence of it. It was a diary found.

Lord Chief Justice: I know, but ...

These references were pointedly intended.

By the third day of the trial, Sullivan was thinning out and rambling. He made numerous unsubstantiated statements, began talking about the rebellion in Ireland. At last the Lord Chief Justice inquired:

Lord Chief Justice: What is the evidence of this?

Sullivan:	The evidence of the Sergeant and the evidence of Robinson.
Lord Chief Justice:	Of what you are saying now?
Attorney General:	I was most loath to intervene but I have heard a great many statements which are totally uncorroborated.
Lord Chief Justice:	You have the right to intervene.
Attorney General:	Statements as to the importation of rifles into the north of Ireland.
Lord Chief Justice:	I hesitated to intervene …
Sullivan:	I am sorry I transgressed, and regret that the rein was not applied to it.

At this point, Sullivan pressed on. He was, it was obvious, taking part in a farce in which the Lord Chief Justice and the Attorney General were the major actors. Continuing, uncertainly, he described the Irish Volunteer movement and events which had occurred since Casement's resignation from the Consular Service. He appeared unable to connect ideas. Then he stopped. He put his hand against his head.

Sullivan:	I regret, my Lords, to say that I have completely broken down.
Lord Chief Justice:	Then of course we will adjourn until tomorrow morning.

On the fourth day of the trial Artemus Jones excused Sullivan on medical grounds and begged to continue in his stead. He wound up the address to the jury on Casement's behalf.

"The ancient and valiant race from which this man springs does not produce the type of man who shrinks from death for the sake of his country. The history of Ireland contains many melancholy and sad chapters, and not the least sad is the chapter which tells and speaks eloquently of so many mistaken sons of that unfortunate country who have gone to the scaffold, as they think, for the sake of their native land." A startling, almost resigned statement. He repeated that Casement had not gone to Germany to help the Germans fight England but to protect his countrymen from the armed forces in Ireland who were not controlled by the Executive Government—a reference to the Ulster Volunteers, which again had little relevance for the jurors.

H. W. Nevinson, a war correspondent and an old friend of Casement's, was present. He said, "Lord Reading then summed up. No chance of escape was given. There was none."

The Lord Chief Justice gave a long and what now seems preposterous summing up which amused the junior counselors somewhat since it alluded in occasional hints to the 'diaries" which were, by now, notorious. The most damaging "piece of paper" was that containing the secret code that Casement had tried to dispose of.

The Lord Chief Justice, in his role of sage and kindly father, then gave instruction to a submissive and conscientious jury.

"You have to determine whether this prisoner was contriving and intending to aid and assist the enemy. If what he did was calculated to aid and assist the enemy, and he knew it was so calculated, then, although he had another or ulterior purpose in view he was contriving and intending to assist the enemy. It is necessary that you should pay particular attention to this direction, which is a direction of law to you. The questions of fact upon it, of course, you will determine for yourselves, but it is necessary that you should understand that … if he knew or believed that the Irish Brigade was to be sent to Ireland during the war with a view to securing the national freedom of Ireland, that is, to engage in a civil war which would necessarily weaken and embarrass this country, then he was contriving and intending to assist the enemy."

There was virtually no alternative: they would have to convict.

At 3:48 p.m. the jury filed back into court, having been out for less than an hour. Their verdict was unanimous. They found the defendant "Guilty of High Treason."

The King's Coroner then spoke. "Sir Roger Casement, you stand convicted of high treason. What have you to say for yourself why the court should not pass sentence and judgment upon you to die according to law?"

It was then the defendant's turn to speak. He pulled out several pages of blue prison foolscap, closely written.

The remarkable speech given by Casement is a lengthy document addressed not to the court but to the Irish, and to the world; it is typically gray, the familiar locutions drag on. He is here speaking, as he was in the Berlin Diaries, to "posterity."

There are some interesting bits:

"If true religion rests on love, it is equally true that loyalty rests on love. The law I am charged under has no parentage in love."

"I am being tried by the brutality of the 14th century."

"Loyalty is a sentiment, not a law. It rests on love, not on restraint."

"For the Attorney General of England there is only 'England'—there is no Ireland; the liberty of Ireland and Irishmen is to be judged by the power of England."

"I asked Irishmen to fight for their rights.... How then, since neither my example nor my appeal were addressed to Englishmen, can I be rightly tried by them?"

"[T]hey brought me by force and by stealth from Ireland to this country ... away from my own countrymen whose loyalty is not in doubt, and safe from the judgment of my peers whose judgment I do not shrink from."

"The English rule in Ireland exists by conquest.... It is from this law of conquest without title to the reason, judgment, and affection of my own countrymen that I appeal."

"Ireland has outlived the failure of all her hopes—and yet she still hopes."

"[The Irish have] the faculty of preserving through centuries of misery the remembrance of lost liberty."

The British Government "permitted the arming of [the Ulster Volunteers] whose leaders declared that Irish national unity was a thing that should be opposed by force of arms."

"That blessed word 'Empire' that bears so paradoxical a resemblance to charity...."

"A constitutional movement in Ireland is never very far from a breach of the constitution.... A constitution to be maintained intact must be the achievement and the pride of the people themselves."

Three small squares of black velvet were placed by their clerks on the wigs of the three judges. Then the Lord Chief Justice spoke. "And it is that you be taken hence to a lawful prison, and thence to a place of execution, and that you be there hanged by the neck until you be dead.... and may the Lord have mercy on your soul."

5

The Irish Question was not finished. Already in 1886 the country had seemed on the verge of open rebellion, with the evictions and the crisis of suffering by the poor. There had been riots in 1887, and Bloody Sunday (13 November) during which Cunninghame Graham, a close friend of Conrad, had been struck on the head and arrested, spending six weeks in Pentonville Prison. These riots, the *Times* said, were simply "lawless agitation" under cover of zeal for the unemployed and to assert the right of public assembly and free speech. The army of jobless workmen demanded the release of the Irish patriots. Cunninghame Graham wrote then, "We have as great white British slavery … as they have in any portion of Africa or the East." In his maiden speech on election to Parliament in 1886, he had said of the recent Irish evictions: "The homes destroyed in Glenbeigh were, no doubt, as dear to the poor peasant, in his lonely village on the stony mountainside in the far west, as was the shoddy mansion in South Kensington to the capitalist, as was Haddon Hall to its owner, or as was Buckingham Palace to the absent owner of that dreadful building. Who could say that the affairs of this handful of obscure tenants in a wind-swept and rain-bedewed stony corner of Ireland, might not prove to have given the first blow to that society in which one man worked and another enjoyed the fruit—that society in which capital and luxury made a Heaven for 30,000 and a Hell for 30,000,000."

Countess Markiewicz (Constance Gore-Booth) had given up her social activities to work for the Irish poor, and had organized the Irish Boy Scouts to aid in the coming rebellion. The Daughters of Erin were busy with school meals, Irish culture, and Irish Independence, against recruiting for the British Army and in favor of insurrection. Cumann na mBan (the Women's Association) was founded on 5 April 1914 to raise funds to help the Volunteers in the "coming struggle" and were pledged to assist in arming and equipping a body of Irishman for the defense of Ireland.

Of course the poor, encouraged by Redmond and Carson, joined the British Expeditionary Force, either to fight against Germany or simply for the pay and the pension after discharge (if they were not slaughtered). At home they were closely contained by the constabulary. There was one policemen for every 377 persons in Ireland, many more than in England or other civilized countries, although the crime rate was no higher than in England. The police, having little to do, were employed in keeping track of the human and animal population, of agricultural production, weather conditions and diseases.

The masses were, however, before the Easter Rebellion, both politically inert and uncommitted to independence. After surrendering, some Irish Volunteers were even attacked by the people of Dublin for the destruction they had caused, and had to be protected. At the end of the uprising the British threw hundreds of Irishmen into detention, revolutionaries along with those innocent of any participation in the uprising—a great error, since the prisons became ideal indoctrination centers.

After the crises and turmoil of the 1880s, and the failure of the Home Rule Bill, Irish Independence was alive again.

6

Sergeant Sullivan made his reputation with the Casement trial. It was a fortunate case for many involved. Later, the Black Diaries were brought forth as an excuse for Casement's conviction. Sullivan had refused to look at them. He was aware—as were all the others involved in the trial—of what they contained. "[Casement] was a megalomaniac," he later wrote, "who sincerely believed that all the world worshipped him as he deserved, and that whatever he did was right. Freddie Smith wanted me to make this defense, which he would have backed up, as the Government did not want to hang Casement in view of American feeling. Freddie made attempts to get me to use the 'Black Diaries'. It was in court that Travers Humphreys handed me the envelope. I refused to read them, as I knew all about them from Casement himself. But Casement would not accept my assurance that the Crown would not use them, and he instructed me to explain to the Jury that the filthy and disreputable practices and the rhapsodic glorification of them were inseparable from true genius; moreover, I was to cite a list of all truly great men to prove it. He was not a bit ashamed."

Casement had made attempts to have all his papers returned, since they had been obtained contrary to law. There is no record of his having discussed historical cases of homosexuality in relation with himself. He had also, before leaving the United States in 1913, left the tin trunk containing his diaries and correspondence for safekeeping with his friend, Francis J. Biggar. Biggar later opened the trunk, found extensive diaries with vivid homosexual passages, plus very explicit letters from young men and simply burned the lot.

From the time of Casement's first interrogation, Thomson and Captain Hall had intimated that the diaries were known and that they might be used against him. How they would be used was a mystery, until Captain Hall came up with a strategy. While Casement was in the Tower, Hall decided—certainly not alone—to call in a group of journalists from several newspapers (Robert Donald of the *Daily Chronicle* and Clement Shorter of *The Sphere* among them). The journalists were shown copies of parts of the diaries—typescripts, photographs. Mary Boyle Reilly was also present and wrote to Mrs. Green to inform her. Mrs. Green was dismayed. She wrote to Gavan Duffy on 8 June. This represented an "outrage of justice" but Lord Haldane could do nothing. Sullivan, refusing to see the diaries, told Rene MacColl later, "I knew it might save his life, but I finally decided that death was better than besmirching and dishonor." On 14 June, a little too late, Casement wrote to his solicitor: "Anything taken by Scotland Yard I presume can be legally recovered. They had no right to retain any papers or documents of mine—diaries, books or anything not used at the trial against me."

Before the revelations of the Black Diaries, it looked like Casement might be condemned and then pardoned, as was the case with Lynch. As time went on, his condition improved; he seemed more optimistic. When Gavan Duffy had first reached him after his arrest, he reported that Casement was "terribly changed"—his clothes were dirty, he was unshaven, his eyes red-rimmed and bloodshot, and he was unable to remember names or words. But eventually, with medical treatment and normal food, he recovered his physical and emotional stability.

On 14 June he had written to Gavan Duffy: "The English mob and vast majority of the people would like to see me hanged and want it badly. The British Government *dare not* hang me (they don't want to either—as individuals I think). They simply dare not. They would willingly bring back to life poor Sean MacDermott, Connolly, Pearse, Colbert (and the other victims of their military autocrats of Easter Week) and they are assuredly not going to add to the roll of victims, me. They know quite well what the world would say of that, and what America would say of it."

But the Black Diaries were a deadly element. And the events in the news somehow also worked against a reprieve. The upper classes, certainly, were hostile. The military humiliation at Kut in the Middle East, and the evident threat to the Suez Canal by the Turks, increased nationalistic emotions. The Germans were battering at Verdun and annihilating hundreds of thousands. There had been heavy losses at the Battle of Jutland in the North Sea. The zeppelin raids in London were infuriating. The loyal Irish had suffered massively in the war so far—so why should an Irish traitor be pardoned?

In America, the sentiments were mixed. Mostly, they favored a reprieve. William Randolph Hearst was especially concerned, putting the power of his newspapers behind the case for pardon. If Casement is guilty then so was John Adams, he wrote, along with the other signers of the American Declaration of Independence. The Negro Fellowship League sent a petition with twenty-four important signatures, including John Quinn's, asking for pardon. "There are so few heroic souls in the world," the petition read, "who dare to lift their voices in defense of the oppressed who are born with black skins, that the entire Negro race would be guilty of the blackest ingratitude did we not raise our voices on behalf of the unfortunate man who permitted himself in an evil hour to raise his hands against his own government...."

Gertrude Bannister, Casement's beloved Gee, was working frenetically to find supporters. She was, at the same time, jeopardizing her future. One of the letters she received, as she raced about seeing officials and organizing petitions, was from the governors of Queen Anne's School, Caversham, where she was employed as a teacher. The governors had earlier expressed their disapproval of her efforts on behalf of her cousin. They sent her a check for £40. This was in lieu of notice. She went to see the Shaws. Later, Charlotte Shaw wrote to T. E. Lawrence: "When Casement was arrested and brought back to England, we were, of course, much moved, but really did not pay exceptional attention to the matter, as we only knew him in a general way, our paths never having run together. But very shortly there appeared at Adelphi Terrace a Miss Gertrude Bannister, who asked for an interview. She was an Irishwoman of a fine type: sensible, shrewd, capable, responsible; at that moment teacher in a girl's school near London.... She came to us in the first place for some money, help, and in the second, to ask if we would work with her to get together a little group of people to attempt to work up some real defense for him." (In the late 1920s Lawrence contemplated writing a biography of Casement; in December 1934 he was still interested. "Casement. Yes, I still hanker after the thought of writing a short book on him," he wrote to Charlotte. "As I see it, his was a heroic nature. I should like to write upon him subtly, so that his enemies would think I was with them till they finished my book and rose from reading it to call him a hero. He had the appeal of a broken archangel. But unless the P.M. will release the 'diary' material, nobody can write of him. Do you know who the next Labor P.M. might be? In advance he might pledge himself, and I am only 46, able, probably, to wait for years: and very determined to make England ashamed of itself, if I can." After Lawrence's death, GBS wrote to Gee, now Gertrude Parry, having married Tom Parry, Casement's old friend, "As you say, [Lawrence] understood. I remember what a bound my heart gave when he said he would like to write about Roger. Perhaps he would have—who knows! But I think it was just a passing inspiration.")

Nor would the problem of the diaries go away. The ghost of Roger Casement, as Yeats said, kept beating at the door. In an acrimonious debate in the House of Common on 3 May 1956, demands by Irish Members received a less than satisfactory answer from the Government. Then on 23 July 1956 R. A. Butler, Secretary of State for the Home Department and Lord Privy Seal stated that "The Casement diaries consist of five volumes found in a trunk which the landlord of Casement's lodging in London handed to the police at their request on 25 April 1916, two days after Casement had arrived in London under arrest. The diaries were retained in Scotland Yard until 1925, since then they have been in the Home Office.... For some thirty years, successive Home Secretaries have refused to give any information about, or access to, the diaries. The position has been altered by the publication of the greater part of them abroad." He went on to say that, "Persons authorized to see the diaries will be warned that if they make any extracts from the diaries they will publish them at their own risk, having regard to the law of copyright and of obscenity." Until recently the diaries were believed by some to be forgeries. His references to "publication abroad" were to the book containing the Black Diaries published in Paris in 1954 by Olympia Press and, later the same year, by Grove Press in the United States.

Debates in the House of Commons continued through 28 July, during which interesting information was given by the Government. Emrys Hughes pointed out that the diaries were not indeed handed over by Casement's landlord to Basil Thomson on 25 April 1916. In Thomson's autobiography he mentions that "Some months earlier, when we first had evidence of Casement's treachery, his London lodgings had been visited and his locked trunks removed to Scotland Yard."

Somehow, in 1922, Peter Singleton-Gates, a journalist, had been given copies of the diaries and wanted to publish them. He was issued a stern warning, or threat, by the Government not to. It was not till some thirty years later that he found a publisher in Paris.

Gee advertised that Roger was being held in the Tower "in solitary confinement," and in a "verminous subterranean dungeon" wearing garments infested with lice and vermin—a ghastly picture, but hardly true. The room in which Casement was imprisoned is encased in the outer wall of the Tower and before and after his time there it was used as accommodation for warders, and after 1937 for resident staff. It is of brick; the original floor, still in place, is neither damp nor verminous.

It was true that Casement had tried to commit suicide, first by sawing at his finger with the broken lens of his glasses and rubbing curare into the cut, then, it was said, by swallowing bent nails. This is confirmed by medical reports.

Herbert Samuel, the Home Secretary, refused to see Gee ("Had Casement not been a man of atrocious moral character," he said, "the situation would have been even more difficult.") The Secretary of War ignored her; she was told to apply to the Home Office. Her letter to Scotland Yard elicited merely a formal acknowledgment from Thomson.

For the first few days of Casement's incarceration the authorities refused visitors, even Gavan Duffy, Casement's solicitor. Finally visits were authorized at Brixton and the trial dates were set, which gave his supporters time to act.

Casement himself wrote from Brixton, Pentonville, the Tower, a surge of prosaic and wordy letters, preparing—just in case—his martyrdom. He veers between absurd assurance of his own historical importance to dribbling senti-mentality. Sullivan considered him seriously "mental."

The fact is that he was simply a gentle, kind, loving man, confused and tired; and they were going to kill him.

Arana, for one, was pleased that he was getting his just deserts. He sent a telegram to the Tower, gloating. *You tried by all means to appear a humaniser in order to obtain titles and fortune, not caring for the consequences of your calumnies and defamation against Peru and myself, doing me enormous damage. I pardon you, but it is necessary that you should be just and declare now fully and truely all the true facts that nobody knows better than yourself.*

Would they kill him simply because of his homosexuality? Possibly, that was always the risk. They had destroyed other men for their sexual tastes, cer-tainly, if under much different circumstances; but the "upper" classes were fairly tolerant, and loyal—even to buggers. Asquith was surrounded by men whose habits were not above suspicion, and women whose habits were equally questionable. The Asquiths had, in fact, themselves been attacked during this same period. Lord Alfred Douglas carried on a campaign of slander against them because of their friendship with Oscar Wilde's literary executor, Robert Ross, who was a frequent guest at No.10 Downing Street. Douglas hurled a verbal attack against Ross accusing of "depraved homosexual practices"—and was promptly sued for criminal libel (the trial ended in a hung jury). After his discharge, Robbie was given a public testimonial, including G B. Shaw, H. G. Wells, Lady Ottoline Morrell, Bishop Gore of Birmingham. Douglas, as usual the mad fag, continued writing such doggerel as:

> Out there in Flanders all the trampled ground,
> Is red with English blood. Our children pass
> Through fire to Moloch. Who will count the loss,
> Since here "at home" sits Merry Margot, bound
> With Lesbian fillets, while with front of brass
> "Old Spiffy" hands the purse to Robert Ross.

Asquith had also been devastated by the marriage of Venetia Stanley to Edwin Montagu in 1914. For several years, Asquith had known Venetia, a friend of his daughter Violet. Venetia had been a frequent visitor to No.10 and had even accompanied the Prime Minister, Violet and Edwin Montagu on a Sicilian holiday. From then on he had sent her an increasing number of letters, many of them quite indiscreet politically. He saw her often, on weekends and long country visits, and was obviously "in love"—if this is the word for such a dangerously bizarre arrangement.

7

But there were appeals to be made. The Court of Criminal Appeal (dating only from 1907) was next. Sullivan immediately made arrangements for a 17 July hearing. There were two other possibilities, an appeal to the House of Lords or reprieve by the Home Secretary. Meanwhile, Casement went back to Pentonville by taxi, in the care of two warders.

As for the appeal to the House of Lords, this must be given approval by the Attorney General. Considering that F. E. Smith could hardly wait for Casement to be executed, the following excuse sounds slightly feeble: "This placed me in a singularly delicate position. By the Criminal Appeal Act, no such appeal can be lodged without the consent of the Attorney General. I had throughout argued that there was no substance in the point raised by the defense. I had to consider the position from a different point of view. It would have been easy to have consented, but that would have been a negation of my duty. After the most careful and anxious consideration, I came to the decided opinion that I ought not to shrink from the responsibility of refusing the application, and accordingly no further appeal took place."

The Home Secretary, Sir Herbert Samuel, had already made his views felt.

Six Petitions for Reprieve were presented, carrying signatures of noteworthy intellectuals and writers. There were some abstentions, such as Joseph Conrad. This is perhaps strange, considering his former admiration for Casement. Meanwhile he was writing Quinn, in the US, excusing himself and criticizing Casement. He was sincerely a Writer Among the Ruins, as D. H. Lawrence would say, when Conrad criticized his novels as "Filth. Nothing but obscenities." Conrad was not, however, although he despised any display of immoralilty, homophobic. His intimate friend, Normam Douglas, was a known pedophile, and his translator Vicomte Robert d'Humieres was homosexual, as were the novelists Stephen Reynolds and Hugh Walpole with whom Conrad was close. His remarks about Casement were damaging and unfair, but the Pole was not a notoriously kind man, in the way that Henry James was kind.

The Archbishop of Canterbury carried on a private appeal. He wrote to the Home Secretary, referring to the Congo and the Putumayo reports. "I find it difficult," he said, "not to think that [Casement] had been mentally afflicted, for the man now revealed to us in the evidence which has been made public, seems a different creature from the man whose actions I knew and watched." He wrote to the Lord Chancellor: "the *instinct* ... that the really *courageous* course for the Government to adopt would be the commutation of the death sentence." The Archbishop was in the House of Lords on 1 August, after the critical Cabinet meeting, and said that the Lord Chancellor had told him "that the matter had then been settled by the Cabinet. He had been impressed by my letter. He did not say whether he agreed with my conclusions or not, but he had felt the letter to be so important that he had laid it before the Cabinet that morning and they therefore had my views in full before they reached their decision."

In the United States, now that the Easter Rebellion was over and emotions had cooled, activities began to save Casement. From Washington, Cecil Spring-Rice, the British Ambassador, wrote: "All here are agreed that it will be dangerous to make Casement a martyr.... The great bulk of American public opinion, while it might excuse executions in hot blood, would very greatly regret an execution some time after the event. This is the view of impartial friends of ours here who have nothing to do with the Irish movement. It is far better to make Casement ridiculous than a martyr. The universal opinion here is that he acted as a madman. There is no doubt whatever that the Germans look forward with great interest to his execution, of which they will take full advantage. It is quite true that if he is spared, the fact that he is not executed will be used against us. But if he is executed, his execution would be an even more formidable weapon."

Casement's sister Nina, now living in Philadelphia, wrote to ask President Wilson to intervene. She was turned down. By this time, of course, American officials had been informed of the Black Diaries. Wilson had Ulster Protestant roots and was negative about the Irish Nationalist movement. Supported by Walter Hines Page, the American Ambassador in London, he decided to remain apart: "I fear that request to the British Government in this matter will produce a very disagreeable impression. Not only does Casement, a British subject, stand convicted of treason, but I am privately informed that much information about him of an unspeakably filthy character was withheld from publicity.... If all the facts about Casement ever become public, it will be well that our Government had nothing to do with him or his case, even indirectly."

On 29 July the US Senate passed a resolution favoring Casement's reprieve. This was sent to President Wilson for forwarding to the British Government. Inexplicably, the document was held up at the White House until 2 August. When, in the morning of 3 August, the First Secretary of the US Embassy in London brought the resolution to the attention of Sir Edward Grey it was with reluctance. Finally Sir Edward asked bluntly if he could look at it. After a while, he asked if the First Secretary would have any objections if it was shown to the Prime Minister.

Casement at that point had already been executed.

At the Cabinet meeting on 2 August, it had been decided that Casement would go to the scaffold. There had been talk of reprieve, but "new evidence" had come to light. Selections from the Black Diaries had been distributed, and many cabinet members considered that he was mentally deranged. However, on submitting the evidence to a psychologist, the opinion came back that he was "abnormal but not technically insane." Sir Ernley Blackwell and Sir Edward Trump of the Home Office, gave their opinion: "[Casement] had completed the full cycle of sexual degeneracy. His diaries and his ledger entries covering many pages of closely typed matter show that for years he had been addicted to the grossest sodomitical practices."

Asquith returned all the materials submitted by Gee, with a note, explaining that there were "no sufficient grounds" for reprieve.

Casement became a Catholic in prison. However, his mother had already had him secretly baptized, so this was after the fact. He was confessed, and absolved.

The execution took place a little after 9 a.m. Ellis, the executioner, fastened a strap around Casement's ankles. He placed the noose around his neck. Then he pulled the lever opening the trap door. Death was instantaneous.

On 3 August 1911, just five years before, he had been in Hyde Park. *Soldier 5/ -. 3rd Bat. G. Guards. Many types Park and H.P. Corner. Beauties.*

They buried him inside the prison, mulching his body with quicklime before covering it with earth. He was in the company of criminals.

Selected Bibliography

Asquith, Margot. *The Autobiography of Margot Asquith.* London, 1936.

Birkenhead, 1st Earl of. *Contemporary Personalities.* London, 1924.

Bullough, Vernon L. *Sexual Variance in Society and History.* New York, 1976.

Casement, Roger. "Correspondence Respecting the Subjects and Native Indians Employed in the Collection of Rubber in the Putumayo Districts." House of Commons Sessional Papers, 68 (14 February 1912–March 1913, 1–65).

Casement, Roger. "The Putumayo Indians." *The Contemporary Review* 102 (1912), 317–28.

Conrad, Joseph. *Heart of Darkness.* (Norton Critical Editions) New York, 1963.

Conrad, Joseph. *Last Essays.* London, 1976.

Crompton, L. *Byron and Greek Love. Homophobia in 19th Century England.* London, 1985.

Deacon, Richard. *A History of the British Secret Service.* London, 1982.

Gay, Peter. *The Bourgeois Experience. Vols. I and II.* London, 1984/86.

Guillaume, H. *The Amazon Provinces of Peru as a Field for European Immigration.* London, 1888.

Gwynn, Denis. *The Life and Death of Roger Casement.* London, 1931.

Hardenburg, Walter E. *The Putumayo: The Devil's Paradise*. London, 1912.

Hemming, John. *Amazon Frontier, the Defeat of the Brazilian Indians*. London,1987.

House, Colonel G. E. *Intimate Papers*. New York, 1926.

Hyam, Ronald. *Empire and Sexuality*. Manchester, 1991.

Hyde, H. Montgomery. *Roger Casement*. London, 1960.

Inglis, Brian. *Roger Casement*. Dublin, 1973.

Jenkins, Roy. *Asquith*. London, 1964.

MacColl, Rene. *Roger Casement*. London, 1956.

Monteith, Robert. *Casement's Last Adventure*. New York, 1932.

Morel, Edmund D. *King Leoopold's Rule in Africa*. London, 1904.

Sawyer, Roger. *Casement, the Flawed Hero*. London, 1984.

Singleton-Gates, Peter and Maurice Girodias. *The Black Diaries*. Paris, 1959.

Spindler, Karl. *The Mystery of the Casement Ship*. London, 1932.

Tansil, Charles Callan. *America and the Fight for Irish Freedom, 1866–1922*. London, 1957.

Tuchman, Barbara. *The Zimmerman Telegram*. New York, 1958.

Woodroffe, Joseph Froude. *The Rubber Industry of the Amazon*. London, 1915.

Woodroffe, Joseph Froude. *The Upper Reaches of the Amazon*. London, 1914.

978-0-595-44795-4
0-595-44795-3